WILSONIAN
STATECRAFT

WILSONIAN STATECRAFT

*Theory and Practice of Liberal
Internationalism during World War I*

Lloyd E. Ambrosius

A Scholarly Resources Inc. Imprint
Wilmington, Delaware

The paper used in this publication meets the minimum requirements of the American National Standard for permanence of paper for printed library materials, Z39.48, 1984.

Scholarly Resources Inc.
104 Greenhill Avenue
Wilmington, DE 19805-1897

Cover photo courtesy of the Seeley G. Mudd Manuscript Library, Princeton University, Princeton, New Jersey

Library of Congress Cataloging-in-Publication Data

Ambrosius, Lloyd E.
    Wilsonian statecraft : theory and practice of liberal internationalism during World War I / Lloyd E. Ambrosius.
        p. cm. — (America in the modern world)
    Includes bibliographical references and index.
    ISBN 0-8420-2393-3 (cloth). — ISBN 0-8420-2394-1 (pbk.)
    1. World War, 1914–1918—United States. 2. World War, 1914–1918—Diplomatic history. 3. Wilson, Woodrow, 1856–1924. 4. United States—Foreign relations—1913–1921. I. Title. II. Series: America in the modern world (Unnumbered)
D619.A6495 1991
940.3'22—dc20
                                                    91–4766
                                                        CIP

For my wife

Margery M. Ambrosius

About the Author

Lloyd E. Ambrosius is professor of history at the University of Nebraska-Lincoln. His publications include *Woodrow Wilson and the American Diplomatic Tradition: The Treaty Fight in Perspective* (Cambridge University Press, 1987), *A Crisis of Republicanism: American Politics in the Civil War Era* (University of Nebraska Press, 1990), and various articles on the history of U.S. foreign relations. He was the Mary Ball Washington Professor of American History at University College, Dublin, Ireland, in 1977-78 and was awarded a Senior Fulbright Research Grant in Germany in 1972-73.

Contents

Introduction

The purpose of this book is to analyze the theory and practice of liberal internationalism in Woodrow Wilson's statecraft during the First World War. Focusing particularly on his emerging conception of collective security within the context of the European war, this study offers a critical assessment of the president's role in world affairs. It does not attempt to provide a comprehensive history of international politics or of American participation in the war. Limited by its purpose, this book examines only certain aspects of Wilson's diplomatic and military leadership during World War I.[1]

My critique of Wilsonian statecraft has been shaped by the realist thought of Reinhold Niebuhr, Hans J. Morgenthau, George F. Kennan, and Walter Lippmann. Although they often disagreed with each other, or with their own earlier positions, these writers defined a general philosophy of realism that frequently departed from the American diplomatic tradition that President Wilson has epitomized in the twentieth century. My own interpretation differs from theirs on numerous points, but my thinking about international affairs has nevertheless benefited substantially from reading their books. I owe my greatest intellectual debt, however, to Norman A. Graebner, who was my mentor at the University of Illinois. He first introduced me to realist thought. As a student in the 1960s, and during the years of our friendship since then, I have learned much from his realist appraisal of American diplomacy.[2]

My particular perspective on Wilsonian statecraft has emerged from my own research as well as from these realists. In an earlier book, *Woodrow Wilson and the American Diplomatic Tradition* (1987), I offered my redefinition of realism. I argued that American foreign policy needed to accommodate the paradoxical reality of interdependence and pluralism in the modern world. Given the global interdependence of the international economy and the existence of worldwide empires,

the United States could no longer remain isolated from the
Old World, as it had been during the nineteenth century.
Nor, given the continuing pluralism of the modern world,
could Americans impose their ideals and practices on other
nations. This combination of interdependence and pluralism
shaped the context in which leaders in Washington needed to
define the relationship between the United States and other
countries in the twentieth century. In that book, which examined Wilson's peacemaking after World War I, I criticized
his unrealistic understanding of the modern world and, consequently, his failure to define an appropriate foreign policy
for the postwar era.[3]

Although my perspective on Wilsonian statecraft is the
same in both books, and there is inevitably some overlapping
between them, the central focus of each is different. *Woodrow
Wilson and the American Diplomatic Tradition* concentrated
on the drafting and revision of the League of Nations Covenant
during the Paris Peace Conference of 1919 and on the subsequent fight over the Versailles treaty in the United States.
Dealing primarily with the postwar era, it examined the
president's leadership during the war only to the extent
necessary to reveal the origins of his idea of collective security.
In contrast, this book focuses on the wartime years from 1914
to 1918 for the purpose of clarifying Wilson's diplomatic
style. Rather than viewing the events of this period as a
prelude to the peace settlement, it seeks to analyze his liberal
internationalism as the basis for American relations with
European belligerents during the war itself. It deals with the
postwar era in the concluding chapter only to the extent
necessary to reveal the consequences of earlier developments.

In relating Wilson's theory to his practice in the midst of
the First World War—rather than primarily as a promise for
the future—this book seeks to evaluate his emerging conception of collective security. If the league-of-nations idea
could provide a foundation for future peace, then the
president's thinking about international affairs should have
furnished realistic guidance for the United States within the
wartime context. In assessing how well it did, this book
examines the interrelationships among different aspects of
Wilson's wartime leadership. It focuses on the nexus between
ideas and diplomacy, between domestic and foreign affairs,
and between political goals and military strategy. Empha-

sizing the interaction between idealism and practicality in his statecraft, it presents a critical appraisal of his approach to war and peace.

Other historians have examined various aspects of the origins of liberal internationalism during the era of American progressivism. Notably, C. Roland Marchand, David S. Patterson, and Charles DeBenedetti scrutinized the modern American peace movement at the beginning of the twentieth century.[4] Warren F. Kuehl and Calvin DeArmond Davis explored the overall contribution of the United States to international organization during this era.[5] Ruhl J. Bartlett, Henry R. Winkler, and George W. Egerton studied the role of various groups in promoting the league-of-nations idea in the United States and Great Britain.[6] Rather than duplicating the work of these scholars, this book concentrates on Wilson's thinking about collective security and its practical implications for his diplomatic and military leadership during World War I.[7]

Wilsonian statecraft depended upon the intellectual foundations of progressive history and social science. In a changing nation and a revolutionary world, the president searched for orderly progress at home and abroad. During the war, while defining a new role for the United States in European affairs, he utilized ideas he had articulated earlier as a scholar. Wilson's understanding of the political culture of the United States thus expressed itself in his liberal internationalism, which emerged from the historical context of American progressivism.

War aims of the various belligerents have attracted considerable attention from historians in recent years. Arno J. Mayer, N. Gordon Levin, Jr., and Lloyd C. Gardner stressed the domestic origins of the American and Allied responses to war and revolution. Economic interests and class status featured prominently in their interpretations of the politics of peacemaking.[8] In his monumental study of German aims in the First World War, Fritz Fischer also emphasized these domestic factors.[9] In contrast, V. H. Rothwell and David Stevenson downplayed internal influences in the definition of war aims by Great Britain and France.[10]

Rather than positing the primacy of either domestic or foreign influences in the politics of war and peace, this book assumes that both were important. Both impacted the president and provided the context for his leadership. American foreign policy was not just a "response" to war and revolution in the Old World, nor was it merely an outward projection of domestic interests. Internal and external factors merged to form this new pattern of liberal internationalism during the First World War.

Wilson's statecraft evidenced both idealism and practicality, yet his liberal internationalism suffered from a lack of realism. He experienced serious difficulty integrating American ideals with European realities. His long-range goals aimed toward peace on the basis of his principles, while his short-term diplomatic and military actions demonstrated the prudence of a shrewd political leader. He operated on two levels. The difficulty lay in his failure to coordinate these idealistic and practical aspects of his statecraft in order to create a viable foreign policy for both the present and the future. It was in this sense that Wilson's diplomatic and military leadership was unrealistic within the context of World War I.

This thesis rejects central themes that other historians, such as Arthur S. Link, Ernest R. May, David F. Trask, John Milton Cooper, Jr., and Frederick S. Calhoun, have presented in their interpretations of Wilson's conduct of foreign relations. In one way or another, most recent scholarship has reacted against the original realist critique of American diplomacy, which Lippmann, Kennan, Morgenthau, and Robert E. Osgood offered in the 1940s and 1950s.[11] Contrary to their criticism of the president's idealism, his subsequent defenders have emphasized the practical aspects of his statecraft. They have added an important corrective to the earlier realist critique. In so doing, however, they have identified Wilson's practicality with realism, confusing his success in handling immediate problems with effective long-term leadership in world affairs.

Link argued that Wilson was "no visionary idealist." Emphasizing the realistic character of the president's statecraft, he asserted that "Wilson was never visionary, incapable of facing reality; on the contrary, he was keenly intelligent and often shrewd." Moreover, Wilson's policy toward Germany sought to preserve a balance of power in Europe: "He understood the beneficial effect of a balance of power among the great powers—to the point, in fact, that he wanted to preserve German power in Central Europe during and after the World War as a restraint on Russia and France." Link noted that "there were even *practical* advantages in idealism." He identified such practicality with his new concept of realism. In his judgment, Wilson's foreign policy evidenced "higher realism" by combining Christian idealism with a balance-of-power approach to world politics.[12]

May recognized the potential dichotomy between Wilson's idealistic and practical sides, observing that "in public life he could alternate between utterly unrealistic moral fervor and ruthless practicality." Nevertheless, in his study of American neutrality from 1914 to 1917, May concluded that "it is hard, indeed, to find fault with Wilson's statesmanship." He rejected the original realist critique, claiming that it suggested that the president should have prematurely led the United States into the European war to "prevent German victory, preserve Anglo-American control of the seas, and overturn authoritarian and militarist ideologies." These were not, in May's view, sufficient reasons for American intervention because they presupposed "a German menace that might never have materialized." Because that threat was not apparent before 1917, Wilson wisely had adhered to neutrality until then. Wilson's statecraft seemed to emulate Otto von Bismarck's realpolitik, which May inexplicably characterized as short-sighted: "Although the President's dreams could look to the eternal future, his diplomacy conformed to Bismarck's rule: it assumed any contingency more than six months away to be out of calculation. Dealing with both Britain and Germany, Wilson concerned himself with the immediate interests of his country. America's security was not threatened in the predictable future. Her economic power and her prestige were in danger. His policy fended off present threats." Praising Wilson for statecraft akin to Bismarck's, May contended that the president's combination of idealism and practicality formed "a sublime realism."[13]

In agreement with Link and May, Trask argued that Wilson effectively used force as an extension of diplomacy to achieve his aims. His statecraft was a model of successful civil-military relations. Trask concluded that "Woodrow Wilson, during 1917-1918, calculated most carefully the disposition of American military and naval power in order to achieve his larger political objects, and he also succeeded not only in preserving the vital democratic principle of civilian control over the military but also in avoiding a serious civil-military rift within the U.S. Government." Seeking to establish a new balance of power for the postwar world, the president served the interests of the United States and simultaneously those of humanity. Realism and idealism coexisted in his state-craft, Trask argued, rejecting the image of Wilson as an "impractical idealist." "On more careful investigation, how-ever," Trask asserted, "it becomes apparent that Wilson not only developed realistic and clearly articulated war goals but that he was able to coordinate his larger diplomatic purpose with the use of force perhaps better than any war President before or since."[14]

In his comparative biography of Theodore Roosevelt and Woodrow Wilson, Cooper offered an equally positive assess-ment of the latter's diplomacy. While arguing that "each man was both an idealist and a realist," Cooper emphasized that Wilson adopted a more realistic wartime policy than Roosevelt advocated. The difference between them epitomized Friedrich Nietzsche's distinction between the Warrior and the Priest. In contrast to Roosevelt's "militant idealism," Wilson showed greater concern for the material interests of the United States. "His wartime diplomacy, against considerable odds, formed another area of achievement," Cooper concluded. Contrary to such realist critics as Lippmann and Kennan, who had viewed Wilson's statecraft as "an example of the pitfalls of idealistic foreign policy," Cooper argued that "what Wilson really demonstrated was the difficulty of waging a war of limited commitments and objectives. During 1917 and 1918 he maintained a precarious balance between aid to the Allies and emphasis on separate American aims." Identifying the policy of "peace without victory" with realism in world affairs, Cooper praised the president's wartime pursuit of moderate aims and criticized Roosevelt's idealistic advocacy of total victory. He thereby reversed the stereotype of Wilson the idealist versus Roosevelt the realist.[15]

This reaction against the original realist critique culmi-nated in Calhoun's study of Wilsonian foreign policy. He, too, praised Wilson for his adroit use of power, including military force, in foreign affairs. In his interpretation, the president understood both the limits and the advantages of armed intervention in other countries. "The interventions in Mexico, Haiti, Santo Domingo, World War I, and Russia illustrated the utility of armed power as a tool of foreign policy. Although presidents before him had turned to force to implement their policies, none had used it as frequently nor as consistently as

Wilson." Noting what he regarded as "the most important lesson" that the president offered to his successors, Calhoun contended that "Wilson realized that force, as an aspect of power, must be limited in scope and invested with clear purpose and identifiable, realistic goals." The president, he further argued, effectively maintained civilian control over the military, avoiding thereby an excessive use of armed force. Calhoun concluded that "in Wilsonian foreign policy, force provided just one way to achieve international goals and Wilson confined its uses to particular, well-defined aims. . . . Each tactic complemented the others to form an overall strategy of American internationalism."[16]

In contrast to the positive assessments of Wilsonian statecraft by these historians, this book offers a critical perspective. In my judgment, the goals and methods of his foreign policy were too frequently unrelated to each other. He failed to coordinate political aims with military strategy except in general terms. His emerging vision of collective security remained essentially unconnected to the deployment of American armed forces. This dichotomy, which reflected Wilson's sharp distinction between war and peace, shaped his diplomatic style. His liberal internationalism eventually culminated in the League of Nations Covenant at the Paris Peace Conference of 1919. Yet, at the same time, the president lost control over the general staff of the American Expeditionary Forces. Without his authorization or knowledge, military intelligence officers from General John J. Pershing's headquarters engaged in negotiations with the top leaders of Germany. These secret German-American negotiations dealt with the whole range of issues relating to the armistice and the peace settlement. At stake, besides the nature of the postwar peace, was the American tradition of civilian control over the military.

Wilsonian statecraft evidenced practicality as well as idealism. Both qualities were characteristic of the president's diplomatic style. Yet his liberal internationalism, particularly his emerging idea of collective security, furnished inadequate guidance for the United States in its wartime relations with the European powers. Wilson's leadership suffered from a lack of realism in dealing with the modern world's combination of interdependence and pluralism. This weakness appeared in his approach to neutrality and mediation, in his rationale for collective security and intervention, and in his participation in war and revolution. Throughout the First World War, there was a dissonance between his American ideals and European realities.

Notes

1.   Comprehensive histories of the First World War include Bernadotte E. Schmitt and Harold C. Vedeler, *The World in the Crucible, 1914-1919* (New York: Harper & Row, 1984); and David Stevenson, *The First World War and International Politics* (New York: Oxford University Press, 1988).

2.   For summaries and critiques of realist thinking see Michael Joseph Smith, *Realist Thought from Weber to Kissinger* (Baton Rouge: Louisiana State University Press, 1986); Robert O. Keohane, "Theory of World Politics: Structural Realism and Beyond," in Ada W. Finifter, ed., *Political Science: The State of the Discipline* (Washington, DC: American Political Science Association, 1983), pp. 503-40; Jeffrey P. Kimball, "Realism, Diplomatic History, and American Foreign Relations: A Conversation with Norman A. Graebner," The Society for Historians of American Foreign Relations *Newsletter* 18 (June 1987): 11-19; and Jerald A. Combs, "Norman Graebner and the Realist View of American Diplomatic History," *Diplomatic History* 11 (Summer 1987): 251-64.

3.   Lloyd E. Ambrosius, *Woodrow Wilson and the American Diplomatic Tradition: The Treaty Fight in Perspective* (Cambridge: Cambridge University Press, 1987).

4.   C. Roland Marchand, *The American Peace Movement and Social Reform, 1898-1918* (Princeton: Princeton University Press, 1972); David S. Patterson, *Toward a Warless World: The Travail of the American Peace Movement, 1877-1914* (Bloomington: Indiana University Press, 1976); Charles DeBenedetti, *Origins of the Modern American Peace Movement, 1915-1929* (Millwood: KTO Press, 1978).

5.   Warren F. Kuehl, *Seeking World Order: The United States and International Organization to 1920* (Nashville: Vanderbilt University Press, 1969); Calvin DeArmond Davis, *The United States and the Second Hague Peace Conference: American Diplomacy and International Organization, 1899-1914* (Durham: Duke University Press, 1975).

6.   Ruhl J. Bartlett, *The League to Enforce Peace* (Chapel Hill: University of North Carolina Press, 1944); Henry R. Winkler, *The League of Nations Movement in Great Britain, 1914-1919* (New Brunswick: Rutgers University Press, 1952); George W. Egerton, *Great Britain and the Creation of the League of Nations* (Chapel Hill: University of North Carolina Press, 1978). See also Laurence W. Martin, *Peace without Victory: Woodrow Wilson and the British Liberals* (New Haven: Yale University Press, 1958).

7.   For excellent introductions to the theory and practice of international relations, including Wilson's contribution, see F. H. Hinsley, *Power and the Pursuit of Peace: Theory and Practice in the History of Relations between States* (Cambridge: Cambridge University Press, 1963); Inis L. Claude, *Power and International Relations* (New York: Random House, 1962); Geoffrey Barraclough, *An Introduction to Contemporary History*

(New York: Penguin Books, 1964); Gordon A. Craig and Alexander L. George, *Force and Statecraft: Diplomatic Problems of Our Time* (New York: Oxford University Press, 1983); and Arthur S. Link, ed., *Woodrow Wilson and a Revolutionary World, 1913-1921* (Chapel Hill: University of North Carolina Press, 1982).

8. Arno J. Mayer, *Political Origins of the New Diplomacy, 1917-1918* (New Haven: Yale University Press, 1959); idem, *Politics and Diplomacy of Peacemaking: Containment and Counterrevolution at Versailles, 1918-1919* (New York: Alfred A. Knopf, 1967); N. Gordon Levin, Jr., *Woodrow Wilson and World Politics: America's Response to War and Revolution* (New York: Oxford University Press, 1968); Lloyd C. Gardner, *Safe for Democracy: The Anglo-American Response to Revolution, 1913-1923* (New York: Oxford University Press, 1984).

9. Fritz Fischer, *Germany's Aims in the First World War* (New York: W. W. Norton, 1967); idem, *World Power or Decline: The Controversy over Germany's Aims in the First World War* (New York: W. W. Norton, 1974). See also Hans W. Gatzke, *Germany's Drive to the West: A Study of Germany's Western War Aims during the First World War* (Baltimore: Johns Hopkins Press, 1966).

10. V. H. Rothwell, *British War Aims and Peace Diplomacy, 1914-1918* (Oxford: Clarendon Press, 1971); David Stevenson, *French War Aims against Germany, 1914-1919* (Oxford: Clarendon Press, 1982). See also Sterling J. Kernek, *Distractions of Peace during War: The Lloyd George Government's Reactions to Woodrow Wilson, December, 1916-November, 1918* (Philadelphia: American Philosophical Society, 1975).

11. Walter Lippmann, *U.S. Foreign Policy: Shield of the Republic* (Boston: Little, Brown, 1943); idem, *The Cold War: A Study in U.S. Foreign Policy* (New York: Harper & Row, 1947); George F. Kennan, *American Diplomacy, 1900-1950* (Chicago: University of Chicago Press, 1951); Hans J. Morgenthau, *Scientific Man vs. Power Politics* (Chicago: University of Chicago Press, 1946); idem, *In Defense of the National Interest: A Critical Examination of American Foreign Policy* (New York: Alfred A. Knopf, 1951); Robert Endicott Osgood, *Ideals and Self-Interest in America's Foreign Relations: The Great Transformation of the Twentieth Century* (Chicago: University of Chicago Press, 1953).

12. Arthur S. Link, *Woodrow Wilson: Revolution, War, and Peace* (Arlington Heights: AHM, 1979), pp. 11-13; idem, *The Higher Realism of Woodrow Wilson and Other Essays* (Nashville: Vanderbilt University Press, 1971), pp. 127-39. Link accepted more of the realist critique in the earlier edition of his recent book, *Wilson the Diplomatist: A Look at His Major Foreign Policies* (Baltimore: Johns Hopkins Press, 1957).

13. Ernest R. May, *The World War and American Isolation, 1914-1917* (Cambridge: Harvard University Press, 1959), pp. 40, 436-37. Before Link, May, and other recent historians offered their favorable assessments, Charles Seymour, in *American Diplomacy during the World War* (Baltimore: Johns Hopkins Press, 1934), p. 255, had similarly praised Wilson's diplomacy for combining both "enlightened *Realpolitik*" and "abstract idealism."

14. David F. Trask, "Woodrow Wilson and the Reconciliation of Force and Diplomacy: 1917-1918," *Naval War College Review* 27 (January-February 1975): 23-31; idem, "Woodrow Wilson and the Coordination of Force and Diplomacy," Society for Historians of American

Foreign Relations *Newsletter* 12 (September 1981): 12-19; idem, *The United States and the Supreme War Council: American War Aims and Inter-Allied Strategy, 1917-1918* (Middletown: Wesleyan University Press, 1961); idem, *Captains & Cabinets: Anglo-American Naval Relations, 1917-1918* (Columbia: University of Missouri Press, 1972).

15. John Milton Cooper, Jr., *The Warrior and the Priest: Woodrow Wilson and Theodore Roosevelt* (Cambridge: Harvard University Press, 1983), pp. 271, 327, 337.

16. Frederick S. Calhoun, *Power and Principle: Armed Intervention in Wilsonian Foreign Policy* (Kent: Kent State University Press, 1986), p. 220.

CHAPTER 1

Intellectual Foundations

American political culture shaped the theory and practice of Wilson's liberal internationalism. As a scholar and statesman, he envisaged the United States as a special nation, whose unique experience had prepared it for new responsibilities in world affairs during the twentieth century. Both liberal idealism and shrewd practicality characterized the progressive president's response to the First World War. His statecraft combined an idealistic vision of his country's mission with a great deal of prudence in the actual conduct of diplomacy. These two traits were deeply rooted in the American heritage.

Both idealism and practicality characterized Wilson's diplomatic style. While articulating liberal principles, he was also a calculating politician. Although his vision of the future was utopian, his decisions on a daily basis usually reflected an appreciation of political limits. Adhering at first to neutrality, he later led the United States into war with the promise of making the world safe for democracy. He hoped to accomplish this goal by creating a league of nations after the war. In pursuit of this new system of collective security, the president eventually lost touch with political reality, both at home and abroad. In the final analysis, his liberal internationalism failed to provide adequate guidance for a viable postwar settlement. Meanwhile, however, Wilson's ideals served the practical purpose of justifying American participation in the European war. Despite their inadequacy as the basis for reorganizing international affairs, his general principles were useful in rallying public opinion behind the war effort.

Literary critic Van Wyck Brooks traced the dualism in the American character back to the origins of the United States. He labeled the competing impulses of idealism and practicality as "highbrow" and "lowbrow." Both had coexisted in American thought and practice since the planting of English colonies in the New World. During the contemporary emergence of the United States as a world power, this dualism persisted. In *America's Coming-of-Age,* he noted that "from the beginning we find two main currents in the American mind running side by side but rarely mingling—a current of overtones and a current of undertones—and both equally unsocial." From its origins in Puritan piety, Brooks saw the transcendental current running through Jonathan Edwards's philosophy to Ralph Waldo Emerson and then to the "chief American writers." He attributed to this current the "final unreality of most contemporary American culture." The opportunistic current, in contrast, Brooks identified with Puritan practicality, Benjamin Franklin's philosophy, and American humorists. It accounted for "the atmosphere of our contemporary business life."[1] These transcendental and opportunistic currents had shaped the political culture of American progressivism. The idealistic and practical Wilson epitomized this political culture.

In agreement with Brooks, the writer Harold Stearns emphasized the dualism in the national character. This typical combination of traits, he noted, accounted for the "mystical practicality" of the American people. "We are gifted with a peculiar dualism, which our friends might call unique versatility and our enemies hypocrisy," he observed in *Liberalism in America.* "I think it is neither, for the American impulse to idealism is no less a fact than the American impulse to practicality. We simply throw both of these human traits into a much sharper contradiction than most people." Stearns recognized that Wilson's idealistic and practical sides were authentic expressions of the American heritage. He concluded that "in President Wilson we have seen its ultimate culmination in a man who talks like a Transcendentalist and who bargains like any huckster, although even in this extreme case, probably, without conscious hypocrisy."[2] Wilsonian statecraft combined idealism and practicality in a typically American fashion.

II

Wilson's progressive philosophy of history provided one of the important intellectual foundations for his liberal internationalism. His response to the world war expressed this understanding. He viewed the United States as the vanguard of the future. Other countries, he anticipated, would eventually gain the benefits of liberty and democracy that Americans already enjoyed. Emphasizing the western frontier's contribution to the growth of these institutions in his own country, he wanted to extend it overseas. He projected American nationalism onto the Old World as the basis for his foreign policy. The idea of progress in history seemed to guarantee the universal triumph of the American way of life. He hoped to overcome any resistance from reactionary statesmen either at home or abroad. The president's understanding of progressive history embraced the Social Gospel in American Christianity. He wanted to redeem the Old World from its outmoded system of alliances that depended upon a discredited balance of power. He sought to establish a new community of nations that would rely instead on collective security. Identification of U.S. foreign policy with the progressive fulfillment of God's will on earth limited Wilson's disposition to compromise. Despite his practicality, his appeal to ideals was also an authentic part of his diplomatic style.[3]

Wilson shared a common perspective with the progressive historian Frederick Jackson Turner. As scholars, both of them had adopted similar interpretations of the American experience. The lessons of progressive history provided an intellectual framework for the president's foreign policy during the First World War. The frontier thesis offered him a persuasive argument for participation in a postwar system of collective security. Turner, too, drew upon his knowledge of the American past to advocate a new league of nations.

Long before the war, both scholars had agreed that the influence of the West, with its expanding frontier, accounted for the distinctive national character. In 1893, a few days after Turner had presented his famous paper on "The Significance of the Frontier in American History" to the American Historical Association, he read it to Wilson, who was visiting the young historian's home. A leading political scientist and historian at that time, Wilson became the first prominent scholar to endorse the frontier thesis. Later that year, in an article in *The Forum*, he emphasized the impact of the American frontier on the European heritage: "Every element of the old life that penetrated the continent at all has been digested and has become an element of new life. It is this transformation that constitutes our history." Reforming the customs of the Old World into the qualities of the New, the frontier had opened opportunities for individuals, fostered mobility within the society, and promoted free and democratic institutions. It had permitted the assimilation of immigrants while creating a sense of national identity for native-born Americans. Stressing the uniqueness of this experience, Wilson asserted: "That part of our history, therefore, which is most truly national is the history of the West."[4]

Intellectual interaction between the two scholars stimulated their thinking about American history. Although Wilson credited Turner for "all I ever wrote on the subject" of the West, the indebtedness was mutual. "I am glad that you think I helped you to some of these ideas," Turner wrote to Wilson in reference to his *Forum* article, "for I have many intellectual debts to repay to you." Four years earlier, during the spring of 1889, they had become close friends when Wilson returned to Johns Hopkins University to deliver a series of lectures. A graduate student at that time, Turner not only attended the lectures but also enjoyed long discussions with Wilson, who resided at the same boardinghouse. Wilson contributed to Turner's "general conceptions of history," expecially by interesting him in the ideas of English political theorist Walter Bagehot. These ideas helped Turner to explain the transformation of the United States from a traditional to a modern society. To Bagehot's framework, which Wilson suggested, Turner later added "the ever retreating frontier" as the agent for "breaking the bond of custom" in this country.[5]

Prior to meeting Turner, Wilson had not recognized the frontier's crucial importance in American history. Instead, he had adopted the germ theory of politics. Using a biological analogy, this theory emphasized heredity over environment in the shaping of human history. The genes of a particular race were more important than the context of that group of people in determining its destiny. Accordingly, in *The State*, he attributed the development of political institutions to racial origins. Asserting that "to the present day our institutions rest upon foundations as old as the Teutonic peoples," Wilson traced the constitutional development of the United States to its roots in England and ultimately back to "the first Teutons," who had contributed "a very fierce democratic temper." From this racial stock had come the essential character of American politics. "The history of government in England, as in Germany," he contended, "begins with the primitive politics of the Teutonic races." English settlers had carried this heritage to the New World. "The political institutions of the United States are in all their main features simply the political institutions of England, as transplanted by English colonists in the course of the two centuries which preceded our own, worked out through a fresh development to new and characteristic forms."

Despite Wilson's acceptance of the germ theory, he had recognized the uniqueness of the United States. He noted that "American politics were not long in acquiring in many respects a character peculiarly their own." Conditions in the new land had fostered constitutional liberty during the colonial era. "The settlement and development of a new country gave to the elective governing bodies of the colonies a wide and various duty of legislative regulation; the newness of the country created everywhere substantially the same new conditions of social relationship; everywhere, and more and more as the years went on, there was a very general participation in communal and colonial affairs by the mass of the people most interested: democratic institutions brought in their train equality of law and a wide-spread consciousness of community of interest." This heritage had provided the foundation for a new system of democratic government in the United States. At Philadelphia in 1787 the drafters of the Constitution had successfully incorporated this "translation of English precedent into American practice." In this way, Wilson concluded, the Founding Fathers had established the constitutional framework for liberty and democracy in the United States.[6]

In 1889, Wilson was still looking for a fully satisfactory explanation of the American character and of "the growth of the national idea and habit." In a review of James Bryce's *The American Commonwealth*, he opined that politics in the United States expressed the national character and that the "English race" had determined this character. Still, there were some unique influences at work in the American experience, particularly those "of a peculiar legal status and of unexampled physical surroundings." These American influences as well as the permanent forces of the English heritage required an explanation in order to "discover the bases of our law and our constitutions, of our constructive statesmanship and our practical politics."[7] Wilson still ignored the frontier's contribution to the national character, although Bryce had noted that "the West is the most American part of America; that is to say, the part where those features which distinguish America from Europe come out in the strongest relief."[8] Until Turner advanced the same idea during their conversations in Baltimore, Wilson did not devote his attention to the frontier's influence on American institutions.

After meeting Turner, while continuing to espouse the germ theory of politics, Wilson shifted his focus from European origins to the American West. He appealed to Turner for assistance in connection with the writing of a history of the United States from 1829 to 1889, later published as *Division and Reunion*. He requested information about the West's contribution to "the growth of the national idea, and of nationality, in our history." Turner provided only encouragement, although he had intended to comply with Wilson's request.[9] Late in 1892 he supplied a copy of his article on "Problems in American History," which first suggested the frontier thesis. By that time, however, Wilson had finished writing his book. On his own he had explored the West's role in shaping the national experience.

Wilson concluded that the frontier had produced "a new epoch," beginning with the inauguration of President Andrew Jackson in 1829: "A new nation had been born and nurtured into self-reliant strength in the West, and it was now to set out upon a characteristic career." Jackson, who was "wholly a product of frontier life," symbolized the triumph of "a distinctively American order of politics, begotten of the crude forces of a new nationality." This "masterful frontiersman" terminated "the old line of Presidents," who had been more like "old-world politicians." Breaking from the European inheritance, Jackson initiated "a rough and ready democracy." Wilson's statement of the frontier thesis in *Division and Reunion*, which appeared early in 1893, and his reaffirmation of it in the *Forum* article later that year, pleased Turner. The young historian welcomed Wilson's emphasis on the West and on "the doctrine of American *development*, in contrast to Germanic *germs*."[10]

Wilson's philosophy of history, which later would shape foreign policy during his presidency, presupposed the idea of progress. Rejecting the pessimism of Ancient and Renaissance historians, he abandoned as well their cyclical view of human events that had fostered it. Instead, he embraced the more optimistic, linear perspective of the Christian religion. His hope for the future depended ultimately on his faith in God. Wilson saw continuity from the primitive beginning of human history to the present achievements of modern civilization. "From the dim morning hours of history when the father was king and priest down to this modern time of history's high noon when nations stand forth full-grown and self-governed," he observed in *The State*, "the law of coherence and continuity in political development has suffered no serious breach." Progress was unidirectional over the long run. "Tested by history's long measurements, the lines of advance are seen to be singularly straight."

This linear view of history undergirded Wilson's early acceptance of the germ theory. Progress and race were bound together in his thinking. He traced the origins of American and European governments, which had achieved "the most notable progress in civilization," to "the Aryan and Semitic races." In a comparison between these two "progressive races," he gave considerably more credit to the Aryan or Teutonic than to the Semitic peoples. But he contrasted both of them to "the non-Aryan races" that were still living in "a savage state" of barbarism. The Semitic and Aryan races, which he identified with the Judeo-Christian heritage, were more capable than others of achieving progress.[11]

Even after he shifted his focus from the germ theory to the frontier thesis, Wilson assumed unidirectional progress from barbarism to civilization. History, as he understood it, demonstrated this pattern. Racial prejudice, typical of Social Darwinism, continued to reinforce Wilson's belief in the superiority of western civilization. Now, however, he attributed the development of liberty and democracy in the United States primarily to the American frontier rather than to Teutonic germs.

This shift in Wilson's thinking personified the transition in American historiography at the close of the nineteenth century. His institutional and administrative approach to the study of government in *The State* had reflected the conservative nationalist and evolutionary views of historian Herbert Baxter Adams, who had taught him the germ theory. Turning from that perspective, Wilson devoted more attention to social and economic issues in *Division and Reunion* and in his subsequent historical writing. Focusing on the American frontier, he also placed greater stress on the polarity between the Old and New Worlds. The new generation of progressive historians, including Carl Becker and Charles Beard as well as Turner, shared his growing interest in social and economic affairs and his belief in American uniqueness. In their philosophy of history, the idea of progress was accepted as a fundamental article of faith. As Wilson's transition exemplified, that idea represented an essential element of continuity from the conservative nationalist to the progressive historians.[12]

Wilson believed that progress toward liberty and democracy required order. "The evolutions of politics have been scarcely less orderly and coherent than those of the physical world," he proclaimed. In a lecture on "Democracy," which he delivered on numerous occasions during the 1890s, Wilson affirmed that the integral relationship between liberty and order was "the only law of political progress that Providence has yet fully unfolded." Because liberty and democracy depended upon order, he denounced radical revolution as a false method of achieving political progress. "Revolution," he asserted in *The State*, "has always been followed by reaction, by a return to even less than the normal speed of political movement." The American Revolution, which he viewed as only a "war for independence," appeared to him as an exception because it followed the natural course of history. "We look back to the great men who made our government as to a generation, not of revolutionists, but of statesmen." George Washington, whom he regarded as the greatest of these men, had clearly recognized that liberty lacked value without order. "Think of Washington's passion for order, for authority, for some righteous public force which should teach individuals their place under government, for the solidity of property, for morality and sober counsel. It was plain that he cared not a whit for liberty without these things to sustain and give it dignity." In Wilson's view, the Founding Fathers had shared Washington's understanding of political progress. "Those who framed our federal government had planned no *revolution*: they did not mean to invent an American government, but only to Americanize the English government, which they *knew*, and knew to be a government fit for free men to live under, if only narrow monarchical notions could be got out of it, and its spirit liberalized."[13]

Wilson perceived a fundamental difference between this orderly political development in the United States and the chaos of revolutionary France. He criticized the French Revolution from the same viewpoint as Edmund Burke, the Anglo-Irish conservative whose political philosophy he admired. The radicalism of that European country had produced reaction, but the moderate American Revolution—if one should even call it a revolution—had merely assisted the natural political process. In the United States, the war for independence and the founding of a new government had established liberty and democracy while preserving order.[14]

For Wilson, orderly progress in politics was organic in nature. Like other Social Darwinists, he used a biological analogy in his interpretation of history. Contrasting moderate Americans with "French philosophical radicals," he emphasized: "Democracy in America, on the other hand, and in the English colonies, has had, almost from the first, a truly organic growth. There was nothing revolutionary in its movements: it had not to overthrow other politics; it had only to organize itself. It had, not to create, but only to expand self-government." Wilson conceived of political development as an evolutionary process. "Liberty is not something that can be created by a document; neither is it something which, when created, can be laid away in a document, a completed work. It is an *organic* principle, a principle of *life*, renewing and being renewed. Democratic institutions are never done; they are like living tissue, always a-making."[15] This organic view of political development later appeared in Wilson's anxiety about radical revolution and in his vision of a league of nations.

Originally associated with the germ theory, Wilson's organic view of politics made him apprehensive of the new immigrants who were flooding into the United States at the end of the nineteenth century. Their degradation of the innate character of the American people worried him. He voiced his deep concern about "the enormous immigration which year after year pours into the country from Europe: our own temperate blood, schooled to self-possession and to the measured conduct of self-government, is receiving a constant infusion and yearly experiencing a partial corruption of foreign blood: our own equable habits have been crossed with the feverish habits of the restless old world." New immigrants threatened to replace "our Saxon habits in government" with their "radical speculative habit in politics."

Like Edward A. Ross, a prominent sociologist who later summarized his criticism of new immigrants in *The Old World in the New*, Wilson dreaded their contaminating influence. Rejecting the idea of pluralism, he emphasized instead the crucial importance of assimilation and Americanization. "The dangers attending that variety which is heterogeneity in so vast an organism as ours," he asserted as early as 1889, "are of course the dangers of *disintegration*, nothing less: and it is unwise to think these dangers remote and merely contingent because they are not as yet pressing." The prospect of chaos in the United States, like that of the French Revolution, troubled Wilson. To avoid "national paralysis," he began to call for new leadership to sustain "progressive order" in American democracy. Anticipating effective social control of new immigrants, he hoped that the United States could preserve its essential character by assimilating them into American life. This expectation of progressive leadership for the nation enabled him to maintain an abiding confidence in the melting pot.[16]

III

Wilson's belief in progress expressed his Christian faith. "Let no man suppose that progress can be divorced from religion or that there is any other platform for the ministers of reform than the platform written in the utterances of our Lord and Saviour," he affirmed in a 1911 address on "The Bible and Progress." He saw men, not women, as the agents of history. He believed that God had predestined victory for men and nations who were faithful, while those who defied God's plan would eventually suffer defeat. Over the long course of history, progress was inevitable for Christians. Wilson affirmed that "the man whose faith is rooted in the Bible knows that reform cannot be stayed." On the other hand, God's day of judgment would ensure the downfall of men who deceived the people and worked against the nation. Eventually, if not in this generation, such men who had forgotten "the image of God" and acted in "the image of the evil one" would be swept aside in "the glad day of revelation and of freedom." Despite adversity, God's chosen people could anticipate redemption in this world. This conviction, which Wilson held in common with other proponents of the Social Gospel, sustained his confidence in progressive reform at home and abroad.

In the constant struggle of life between good and evil, which would continue despite the certainty of God's ultimate triumph, Wilson looked to the Bible as the source of universal laws of morality and history. "We know that there is a standard set for us in the heavens, a standard revealed to us in this book which is the fixed and eternal standard by which we judge ourselves," he asserted. Applying this measure, Wilson concluded that the United States was the epitome of Christianity: "America was born a Christian nation. America was born to exemplify that devotion to the elements of righteousness which are derived from the revelations of Holy Scripture." In his view, there was no difference between the ideals of Christianity and of Americanism.

Wilson offered this combination of religion and patriotism as the basis for judging all nations. "We do not judge progress by material standards," he proclaimed. "America is not ahead of the other nations of the world because she is rich. Nothing makes America great except her thought, except her ideals, except her acceptance of those standards of judgment which are written large upon these pages of revelation [in the Bible]." The United States stood in the vanguard of world history, and progress seemed foreordained. This perspective provided the basis for Wilson's confidence in the country's future. Such confidence, however, could easily turn into arrogance.[17]

Wilson's Christianity undergirded his liberal internationalism. Once he decided to intervene in the European war, he justified American participation as a Christian crusade for democracy. Religion and politics were intimately connected in his statecraft. George D. Herron, an outstanding Social Gospel theologian, understood this dimension of the president's thinking more clearly than most observers. In

Woodrow Wilson and the World's Peace, a collection of articles he had published in European journals, Herron proclaimed that the ultimate goal of American foreign policy was to create the kingdom of God on earth. The theologian explained that Wilson's vision of "our common life's collective possibilities" depended upon his mystical Christianity. "The uttermost democracy, the democracy that scales the whole human octave, is to him the certain issue of the idea for which Jesus lived and died."

Furthermore, Wilson's crusade to make the world safe for democracy aimed toward the redemption of the Old World, fundamentally a religious goal. "He believes that the Sermon on the Mount is the ultimate constitution of mankind; and he intends, by hook or crook if you will, by the wisdom of the serpent and the secrecy of the priest, to get this foundation underneath the unaware American nation. He cunningly hopes, he divinely schemes, to bring it about that America, awake at last to her selfhood and calling, shall become as a colossal Christian apostle, shepherding the world into the kingdom of God." Like Wilson, Herron neglected to explain why the United States needed to carry this redemptive message back to the Old World from which it had come. Without appreciating the irony, they both regarded this Christian mission as uniquely American.

This American mission deeply influenced Wilson's evolving conception of collective security. He did not think in traditional European terms of power politics. As Herron observed, he did not regard military force as a rational method of achieving progress in civilization. Rather, the president hoped to transcend the existing international system to achieve justice for weak as well as strong nations in a new world order. Herron noted that "he stands for a universal politic so new, so revolutionary, so creative of a different world than ours, that few have begun to glimpse his vision or to apprehend his purpose. His eyes are fixed upon a goal that is far beyond the present faith of nations." Herron believed that Wilson's address to the League to Enforce Peace on May 27, 1916, best expressed this purpose. It was "perhaps the most pregnant utterance of a national chief in two thousand years."[18] In that address the president had advocated a postwar league of nations to save the world from future wars. Thus, he had expressed his desire—typical of the Social Gospel—to redeem the Old World. Moreover, he subsequently endorsed Herron's exposition of the ultimate goal of American foreign policy. On October 1, 1917, Wilson wrote to the New York publisher of the book: "I have read it with the deepest appreciation of Mr. Herron's singular insight into all the elements of a complicated situation and into my own motives and purposes."[19]

Prior to his presidency, Wilson had developed his vision of a holy war, which would help shape his diplomatic style during World War I. "No man can sit down and withhold his hands from the warfare against wrong and get peace out of acquiescence," he had proclaimed. "The most solid and satisfying peace is that which comes from this constant spiritual warfare, and there are times in the history of nations when they must take up the crude instruments of bloodshed in order to vindicate spiritual conceptions. For liberty is a spiritual conception, and when men take up arms to set other men free, there is something sacred and holy in the warfare. I will not cry 'peace' so long as there is sin and wrong in the world."[20] A holy war, he anticipated, could provide the way to peace by eradicating evil from the world.

Wilson also had suggested, in an earlier lecture, the motivation for his Christian crusade for democracy. He believed that "religion connects itself with patriotism, because religion is the energy of character which, instead of concentrating upon the man himself, concentrates upon a service which is greater than the man himself. . . . The standard is the standard of universal providence; the goal is the goal of human progress itself, and men cannot get this motive in their blood and then forget that they have fellowmen whom they are to serve." Expressing his hope for the kingdom of God on earth, he had warned that "a nation must save itself on this side of the grave; there is no other side for it."[21] When the United States later intervened in the European war, Wilson expressed this yearning for the kingdom of God on earth in his definition of American foreign policy. A redemptive war, presumably, would fulfill God's purpose by promoting human progress in world affairs.

IV

Social science provided another intellectual foundation for Wilson's statecraft. As a prominent scholar himself, he had known several leading figures in other academic disciplines besides history. During his presidency he maintained personal contact with many of them. His foreign policy during the world war emerged from an intellectual climate that he shared with social scientists and with progressive journalists at the beginning of the twentieth century. All of them devoted considerable attention to the question of control in human affairs. Like Wilson, they sensed the disintegration of existing social structures and feared the potential consequences. Stressing the necessity for orderly progress at home and abroad, they also foresaw new opportunities to achieve this goal in the modern world.

Developing a conscious awareness of "social control," Ross contributed to the emerging progressive understanding of human relations. He examined the various means that society used to subjugate individuals. Ignoring the international implications, he concentrated on the foundations of order within the United States. "The thesis of this book," Ross affirmed in *Social Control*, "is that from the interactions of individuals and generations there emerges a kind of collective mind evincing itself in living ideals, conventions, dogmas, institutions, and religious sentiments which are more or less happily adapted to the task of safeguarding the collective welfare from the ravages of egoism."[22] Social control thus provided the basis for domestic order.

As a graduate student at Johns Hopkins, Ross had attended Wilson's lectures, but the two men did not develop a close relationship. Ross identified instead with other progressives such as William Jennings Bryan, Theodore Roosevelt, and Robert M. La Follette. After his election to the presidency in 1912, Wilson briefly considered the possibility of appointing Ross as U.S. minister to China but concluded that his politics were "unsatisfactory." That he was no longer a church member was another liability. Nevertheless, the president welcomed the sociologist to the White House in 1914, and again in 1915, to discuss the problems of immigration. Placing greater confidence in the American melting pot, Wilson rejected his advice on restrictions. While Ross continued to focus on domestic affairs, Wilson applied the idea of social control to foreign relations. Calling for collective security to restrain national egoism, he developed it as a central theme in his conception of international organization.[23]

Other social scientists had influenced the future president more directly than had Ross. As a young scholar, Wilson had greatly benefited from reading *The Philosophy of Wealth* (1886) by economist John Bates Clark. He praised this book for "its moderation and its Christianity." Moreover, Wilson had incorporated its central themes into his own study of *The State*. The two men subsequently developed a close friendship.[24]

In another book, *The Control of Trusts*, Clark had offered an argument for curbing the monopolistic power of large American corporations so that these would serve the national interest. He did not oppose their size but wanted to prevent corporations from abusing their power by adopting unfair business practices. The government, he thought, should play an active role in preserving free competition. Economic rivalry among present or potential competitors would force American industry to remain efficient, thereby benefiting consumers while also enabling the United States to capture foreign markets. "There is in sight," Clark predicted, "a condition in which these corporations may serve the public. They may give us the benefit of their efficiency. They may play their part in promoting commercial expansion and put this country into a position of peaceful dominance in the world's affairs." The United States could establish its worldwide economic leadership by controlling the monopolistic tendencies of these corporations. With the "natural method" of free competition, Clark anticipated, this nation could achieve real progress on a global scale.[25] Later, Clark's guidelines for controlling the trusts appeared in the economic policies of Wilson's New Freedom.

Franklin H. Giddings, a prominent sociologist, likewise had impressed Wilson when they first met in the 1880s.[26] He, too, shared Clark's hope for American dominance over other countries. In *Democracy and Empire*, Giddings defended the new imperialism of the United States, including its acquisition of colonies during the Spanish-American War of 1898. "My studies of theoretical sociology," he asserted, "long ago led me to believe that the combination of small states into larger political aggregates must continue until all the semi-civilized, barbarian, and savage communities of the world are brought under the protection of the larger civilized nations." He viewed the United States as the prime example of a "democratic empire." Along with Great Britain, which also had reconciled democracy with empire, he wanted it to extend its rule around the world. Praising Benjamin Kidd's monograph on *The Control of the Tropics* (1898), Giddings urged "the English-speaking race" to assume the burden of governing "the inferior races of mankind" in order that "the civilized world" could continue "its economic conquest of the natural resources of the globe."

A Social Darwinist, Giddings accepted international competition as a fact of life. Especially in relations between advanced and backward peoples, he anticipated continuing conflict. Yet he also voiced the hope of the Social Gospel for a new era of peace and brotherhood among men. He presupposed that men would wield political power. He combined science and religion—or the intellectual traditions of Charles Darwin and Leo Tolstoy—in his conception of the democratic empire. "Only when the democratic empire has compassed the uttermost parts of the world," Giddings concluded, "will there be that perfect understanding among men which is necessary for the growth of moral kinship. Only in the spiritual brotherhood of that secular republic, created by blood and iron not less than by thought and love, will the kingdom of heaven be established on the earth."[27]

Like Giddings, Wilson approved the new imperial role of the United States after the Spanish-American War. He noted the political implications for this country's federal system of government, and especially the new opportunity for presidential leadership. In a new preface for the fifteenth edition of *Congressional Government* in 1900, Wilson forecast "the greatly increased power and opportunity for constructive statesmanship given the President, by the plunge into the international politics and into the administration of distant dependencies, which has been that war's most striking and momentous consequence." Wilson welcomed the growth of executive power resulting from American involvement in foreign affairs. For the United States, he affirmed, the president "must utter every initial judgment, take every first step of action, supply the information upon which it is to act, suggest and in large measure control its conduct."[28]

Giddings applied social science to international affairs. In 1912, exploring the relation of social theory to public policy with reference to war and peace, he posed the question: "After ten thousand years of so-called progress, is reason still so ineffective against instinct that only minor issues can be removed from fields of battle to arenas of intellectual conflict? Must sovereignty—the ultimate social control—forever prove and declare itself in government by slaughter, or may international relations also be brought under government by discussion?" To create the conditions for peaceful resolution of conflicts, he favored a balance of power among nations. Because of the world's interdependence, the option of isolation no longer existed. Inasmuch as the political integration of empires already had encompassed most lands and peoples, the world's current problem was to avoid war among the Great Powers.

Giddings emphasized the role of personal leadership, stating that "conspicuous or dynamic men, who become models to thousands or millions of their fellows, are true social causes, and centers of social control." These elite leaders would determine the world's future. "In the final throwing of the dice of fate, they are causes of peace and war." Their decisions, however, reflected more than personal whim. As hunger and greed were the underlying causes of war, Giddings stressed the importance of justice. "If we sincerely wish for peace, we must be willing to see a vast equalizing of industrial efficiency between the East and the West. We must also welcome every change that tends to bring about a fairer apportionment of natural resources among nations and within them, and a more equal distribution of wealth. If these conditions can be met, there will be a Parliament of Man." In other words, peace in the twentieth century would require orderly progress throughout the world.[29]

During the world war, Giddings and Clark used their social theories to advocate a new form of collective security. Although the war challenged Giddings's belief in rationality, he still accepted the analogy between nature and history. He affirmed that "the human mind that had mastered nature's way could master and control the ways of man." In an introduction for Randolph S. Bourne's collection of peace proposals, entitled *Towards an Enduring Peace*, he acknowledged that the obstacles to rational control over human affairs were greater than he had anticipated. Nevertheless, Giddings persisted in his confidence that the civilized world, and especially the English-speaking peoples, could organize its conscience and reason in order to reduce the probability of war. He advocated, as a first step, the federation of nations in a "league of peace." Clark already had reached the same conclusion. In 1915, two years before the American declaration of war, he saw the Allies as the nucleus for a postwar league of nations. He wanted neutrals such as the United States to help in forming such a league. To preserve peace, this new international organization would need to fulfill the twofold task of protecting its members from outside attacks and of settling internal disputes among them. To promote their vision of collective security, these two social scientists helped organize the League to Enforce Peace. Under the leadership of former President William Howard Taft and Harvard's President A. Lawrence Lowell, this bipartisan group became the most effective lobby for a postwar league of nations.[30]

V

Progressive journalists, as well as scholars, articulated the ideas that would culminate in Wilson's liberal internationalism.[31] Herbert Croly advocated executive leadership in both domestic and foreign affairs. In *The Promise of American Life*, a classic statement of progressive thought, he recommended subjecting individual purposes to the national interest. Only by adopting the methods of a strong national government, he argued, could the United States maintain democratic political institutions and still provide its citizens better economic and social conditions. "The Promise of American life is to be fulfilled," he predicted, "not merely by a maximum amount of economic freedom, but by a certain measure of discipline; not merely by the abundant satisfaction of individual desires, but by a large measure of individual subordination and self-denial." He wanted the nation to employ conscious social control—which he identified as the methods of Alexander

Hamilton—to achieve the egalitarian goals of Thomas Jefferson. Both Hamiltonian and Jeffersonian legacies thus would merge into Croly's new kind of American progressivism.

Linking reform at home and abroad, Croly proposed "a national foreign policy." He contended that "the United States must by every practical means encourage the spread of democratic methods and ideas. As much in foreign as in domestic affairs must the American people seek to unite national efficiency with democratic idealism." Claiming that the Monroe Doctrine already committed the United States to join Latin American nations in creating "a stable and peaceful international system," he also even anticipated the end of American isolation from the Old World. Competition from other nations increasingly required the United States to improve its domestic organization in politics and economics. Their efficiency necessitated American reform, and foreign challenges could not be ignored any longer. "The geographical isolation which affords the United States its military security against foreign attack should not blind Americans to the merely comparative nature of their isolation. The growth of modern sea power and the vast sweep of modern national political interests have at once diminished their security, and multiplied the possible sources of contact between American and European interests." Because of this growing global interdependence, Croly expected the United States eventually to join "a world system" for the preservation of international peace.

Although opposed to American involvement in "an exclusively European system," Croly foresaw the end of neutrality. Anticipating Wilson's rationale for intervention in 1917 and for the postwar League of Nations, he proclaimed that "peace will prevail in international relations, just as order prevails within a nation, because of the righteous use of superior force—because the power which makes for pacific organization is stronger than the power which makes for a warlike organization. . . . Under such conditions a policy of neutrality would be a policy of irresponsibility and unwisdom." Croly's definition of the national interest embraced this idea of collective security. He anticipated that the United States should use its power for the dual purpose of fostering democracy in Europe and promoting international peace.[32]

Walter Lippmann, a young journalist closely associated with Wilson during the world war, shared Croly's belief in the necessity for progressive American leadership at home and abroad to create unity in the chaotic modern world. The new challenge for Americans was to control their own destiny in a dynamic and pluralistic world. "The battle for us, in short, does not lie against crusted prejudice, but against the chaos of a new freedom. This chaos is our real problem," Lippmann explained in *Drift and Mastery*. The status quo was no longer an obstacle, nor was it a realistic option. Compelled to shape their own future, Americans had responded by welcoming innovation. "Our time, of course, believes in change," observed Lippmann. Progress was necessary to preserve order. "The only possible cohesion now is a loyalty that looks forward." Regarding the United States as the country best equipped to concentrate on its future instead of its past, he recommended a new purpose to replace the outmoded heritage. "We can no longer treat life as something that has trickled down to us. We have to deal with it deliberately, devise its social organization, alter its tools, formulate its method, educate and control it. In endless ways we put intention where custom has reigned. We break up routines, make decisions, choose our ends, select means." Rational control over the nation's future required both progress and order. "This is what mastery means: the substitution of conscious intention for unconscious striving. Civilization, it seems to me, is just this constant effort to introduce plan where there has been clash, and purpose into the jungles of disordered growth." In short, Lippmann recommended a pragmatic method to create progressive order out of the chaotic modern world.[33]

As editors of the *New Republic*, Croly and Lippmann strongly supported Wilson's foreign policy during the First World War. They favored intervention in 1917 and advocated a postwar league of nations. Welcoming the president's advocacy of collective security in his 1916 address to the League to Enforce Peace, they used this idea to justify U.S. participation in the European war. As secretary of the group of experts known as the Inquiry, Lippmann contributed directly to American preparations for the eventual peacemaking. He helped elaborate the principles that Wilson outlined in his famous Fourteen Points.[34]

Like the president himself, progressive journalists and social scientists lacked a clear understanding of the limitations of liberal internationalism. Despite their differences, journalists—such as Croly and Lippmann—and scholars—such as Giddings and Clark—shared the hope that the United States could achieve world peace by applying social theory to international relations. They failed to recognize the inherent weaknesses in the intellectual foundations of Wilsonian statecraft, which eventually would frustrate that hope. In practice, as the experience of World War I began to reveal, liberal internationalism provided inadequate guidance for the United States in the modern world. But that was not self-evident to Americans at the time.[35]

VI

Another intellectual foundation for Wilson's liberal internationalism came from his country's historical experience. This tradition shaped the perspective of progressive Americans at the beginning of the twentieth century. A legacy of phenomenal success during the nineteenth century encouraged them to expect a bright future. Typically, they believed that the United States could provide the impetus for reforming the world. While preserving its own unique character, this nation could assume new responsibilities overseas. In his approach to foreign affairs, Wilson epitomized American progressivism. He maintained the traditional distinction between the Old and New Worlds and accepted the myth of the United States as "a virgin continent." This national myth, which had culminated in the frontier thesis, shaped the president's view of foreign relations. As Lippmann observed, "Wilson, in spite of the complexity of his character and his mind, was moved by the old American feeling that America is a new land which must not be entangled with Europe."[36]

The myth of national innocence had helped shape the American diplomatic tradition. Prior to the First World War the United States had endeavored to stay out of the Old World's politics and wars. At the same time, it had maintained diplomatic, commercial, and cultural relations with European countries. Throughout the nineteenth century, seeking to

preserve its independence, the United States had steadfastly
avoided political and military entanglement in Europe. This
diplomatic tradition emerged from real as well as from perceived differences between the New and Old Worlds. The
Founding Fathers, having achieved independence from Great
Britain, had hoped the new nation could preserve its neutrality during future European wars. Their legacy continued to
guide the makers of foreign policy during later generations.

Throughout the nineteenth century the United States
had extended its system of government across the North
American continent. Acquisition and settlement of new
territory in the West had characterized the national experience. Beginning with the purchase of Louisiana from France
in 1803, and continuing with favorable definitions of its
boundaries in treaties with Great Britain in 1818 and with
Spain in 1819, American statesmen had doubled the size of
their nation. They had forced Spain to cede Florida, annexed
Texas in 1845, and then conquered additional territory from
Mexico. Compromise of the Anglo-American dispute over
Oregon in 1846 and victory in the Mexican War of 1846-1848
had enabled President James K. Polk to establish an empire
on the Pacific. The United States had purchased Alaska from
Russia in 1867 and then completed a century of westward
expansion with the Spanish-American War of 1898. During
this war, President William McKinley had succeeded in an-
nexing previously independent Hawaii and in capturing
Puerto Rico, Guam, and the Philippines from Spain.[37]

Relatively unchallenged by European opposition, the
westward movement of the American empire had appeared
to prove the inevitability of progress. The history of the
United States seemed to have followed a "manifest destiny."
Believing that their country stood in the vanguard of world
history, Americans had used the ideals of manifest destiny to
justify territorial and commercial expansion across the continent to the Pacific. Some also had offered unsolicited advice
to the Old World. Desiring Europeans to emulate the example of the United States, they had applauded the Greek
war for independence in the 1820s, the revolutions in western
and central Europe in 1848, and the subsequent movements
toward national unification of Germany and Italy. These
Americans had urged the Old World to implement their ideal
of national self-determination with liberty and democracy
but steadfastly refrained from direct political and military

intervention in Europe. American isolation from the Old World, which was only political and military and never cultural or commercial, had continued until the twentieth century.[38]

This diplomatic tradition contained the twin impulses to avoid and to reform the Old World. The same vision of a unique mission could justify either American imperialism or isolation from Europe. In 1900, Albert J. Beveridge, a progressive Republican senator from Indiana, defended the new imperialism by emphasizing the traditional themes of manifest destiny. Although earlier generations had restricted that concept to the North American continent, he voiced the global implications of this redeeming impulse. He claimed that "God has not been preparing the English-speaking and Teutonic peoples for a thousand years for nothing but vain and idle self-contemplation and self-admiration. No! He has made us the master organizers of the world to establish system where chaos reigns. He has given us the spirit of progress to overwhelm the forces of reaction throughout the earth."

In Beveridge's view, the peoples of the Anglo-Teutonic race possessed the unique ability to govern not only themselves but also other "savage and senile peoples." This racist argument justified imperialism, for otherwise "the world would relapse into barbarism and night." Among the civilized nations, the United States was God's chosen people. "And of all our race," Beveridge concluded, "He has marked the American people as His chosen nation to finally lead in the regeneration of the world. This is the divine mission of America, and it holds for us all the profit, all the glory, all the happiness possible to man. We are trustees of the world's progress, guardians of its righteous peace."[39] This rationale for imperialism in Latin America and Asia was consistent with traditional neutrality toward Europe. Irreconcilable conflict between the isolationist and internationalist impulses in American foreign relations arose only later in the context of World War I.

By 1913, when Wilson moved into the White House, most of his countrymen had forgotten the reasons for their isolation from Europe. They simply adhered to this tradition without question. Such ignorance had not characterized the foreign policy of the Founding Fathers. When President Washington and his cabinet had defined the policy of neutrality in 1793, they clearly recognized the rationale for this action. In the first place, they assumed the existence of the balance of power in Europe. They thought that Great Britain and France would remain as major rivals, neither defeating the other. As long as this rivalry continued, the United States could play off one western European empire against the other and gain concessions from both. If either the British or the French threatened the United States, then Americans could turn to the other side for support. The balance of power in Europe thus permitted them to adopt a policy of neutrality. The Founding Fathers appreciated as well the weakness of their new nation, realizing that even if the United States wanted to participate in Europe's wars and politics, it lacked the power to do so. It was simply impossible for the new nation to send an army or navy across the Atlantic to play a decisive role in the Old World's affairs. Fortunately, during those early years of weakness, no European empire succeeded in disrupting the balance of power. Americans therefore were able to enjoy "free security."[40]

Wilson possessed only a limited understanding of the European balance of power, regarding it as a problem rather than a blessing in foreign affairs. The domestic American experience of the nineteenth century shaped his view of the world. He largely ignored the fact that the balance of power in Europe had contributed to stability among competing powers and that the United States had benefited from the resulting peace for most of the century. He did not comprehend American affairs within this global context. Instead, he employed his own nation's domestic history as a guide to international relations. In his response to the world war, the president relied upon his conception of American nationalism. For him, the closing of the frontier in 1890 marked the turning point toward greater involvement by the United States in world affairs. Because free land was no longer available in the West, the "complex civilization" of the East, which was "more like the Old World than the New," would set the nation's future pattern.[41]

In contrast to its previous concentration on developing the West, Wilson predicted, the United States would assume new responsibilities as a world power in the future. He anticipated that "the twentieth century will show another face. The stage of America grows crowded like the stage of Europe. The life of the new world grows as complex as the life of the old. A nation hitherto wholly devoted to domestic development now finds its first task roughly finished and turns about to look curiously into the tasks of the great world at large, seeking its special part and place of power. A new age has come which no man may forecast. But the past is the key to it; and the past of America lies at the centre of modern history." Because the United States stood in the vanguard, its heritage would provide the model for the world in the new century.[42]

In Wilson's view, the closing of the frontier required the United States to project its influence abroad. Thus, internal affairs shaped foreign policy. Accordingly, the American people were forced after 1890 to search for "new frontiers for ourselves beyond the seas." The Spanish-American War of 1898 appeared as the natural consequence. This transition from domestic to foreign expansion, he believed, would require Americans to become "apostles of liberty and of self-government." The lack of progress toward democracy in Cuba and the Philippines, while they remained within the Spanish empire, would necessitate an American contribution to their political education, like England's to that of the American colonies. The Philippine revolt against American—as well as Spanish—rule appeared to confirm Wilson's presupposition that these people failed to understand the importance of order in a democracy. Before they could enjoy the benefits of freedom, they needed instruction from the United States, by force if necessary.

He believed that "they must first take the discipline of law, must first love order and instinctively yield to it. . . . We are old in this learning and must be their tutors." Philippine independence was inconceivable until the United States had first established its control over the islands. This form of American imperialism was paternalistic, although it was not essentially directed toward the creation of a colonial empire. It would later provide a model for the system of mandates under the League of Nations. Although Wilson failed to appreciate the irony, he encouraged Americans to "seek to serve, not to subdue, the world."[43] The idea of pluralism for other countries, such as Cuba and the Philippines, was not acceptable to him. It seemed no more appropriate abroad than at home.

During the First World War, President Wilson understood the events in Europe within the context of the American historical experience. All of history, he thought, eventually would conform to a progressive pattern. The modern world seemed to be moving toward democracy.[44] To explain his country's involvement in world affairs, Wilson combined his belief in unidirectional progress toward democracy with his version of the frontier thesis. Applying this historical interpretation, he outlined the intellectual parameters for a new foreign policy. The president announced on October 5, 1916, that it was no coincidence that the United States had intervened against Spain in Cuba only eight years after the closing of the frontier. As a consequence of the Spanish-American War, this nation established its guardianship over Cuba and possessed both Puerto Rico and the Philippines. The closing of the frontier at home had led to the opening of a new frontier abroad. "Ever since then," he concluded, "we have been caught inevitably in the net of the politics of the world."

Even this projection of the American frontier overseas, according to Wilson, did not require the United States to abandon its unique character. It could remain faithful to its own diplomatic tradition. He emphasized this point by reaffirming the wisdom of Washington's Farewell Address: "You know that we have always remembered and revered the advice of the great Washington, who advised us to avoid foreign entanglements. By that I understand him to mean to avoid being entangled in the ambitions and the national purposes of other nations." Preservation of its own character, rather than strict adherence to traditional neutrality, seemed to be the appropriate course for the United States.

The Old World-New World polarity thus continued to influence Wilson's thinking as he urged the American people to anticipate a league of nations. On May 27, 1916, in his address to the League to Enforce Peace, the president had announced his support for postwar collective security. Now, he reaffirmed this commitment, promising that at "the end of this war, we want all the world to know that we are ready to lend our force without stint to the preservation of peace in the interest of mankind." The closing of the frontier in the West had led to this new role for the United States in foreign affairs. "What disturbs the life of the whole world is the concern of the whole world, and it is our duty to lend the full force of this nation, moral and physical, to a league of nations which shall see to it that nobody disturbs the peace of the world without submitting his case first to the opinion of mankind." The internal experience of the United States thus required a new foreign policy for the future.[45]

Wilson's response to the European war alternated between his twin impulses to avoid and to redeem the Old World. His liberal internationalism embraced traditional American aloofness along with a missionary zeal to transform the world. As Lippmann later noted, "the instinctive American isolationist view of Woodrow Wilson" appeared even in his plans for a league of nations. The president was, paradoxically, at once isolationist and internationalist.[46]

Turner, like Wilson, used the same interpretation of American history to justify apparently opposite foreign policies. In 1916 he expressed his belief that the United States should adhere to its traditional policy of neutrality. He asserted that "in spite of tendencies to break down American isolation and to sweep the United States into the world conflict, it does not follow that we should be carried into that maelstrom, and particularly not on European terms. Washington's warnings against entangling alliances still have validity and they gain new force from the awful tragedy which meets our gaze whenever we look across the Atlantic." Yet Turner soon shifted his position and favored participation in the European war and in a postwar league. Subsequently, he appealed to the memory of Washington to suggest the projection of the American heritage onto Europe: "It is a great name! The nation which he founded has become a great nation—so great that the question turns upon whether its economic and moral force is not strong enough to impress an American system and American ways upon Europe rather than to submit to fear from the influence of Europe upon itself."[47]

At the end of the world war, Turner drew upon his knowledge of American history to offer his ideas for a league of nations. In his study of sectionalism in the United States, he had noted the major contribution of national political parties in maintaining the Pax Americana. He suggested to Wilson that international political parties likewise could serve as a check on nationalism. He also wanted to counter the threat of radical parties, which already were organized on an international basis. In particular, Turner hoped to "keep the

Bolsheviki serpent out of the American Eden." By forming
international parties in the future league, he thought that
the United States also could thwart the Bolshevik menace to
"the existence of Edens anywhere."[48] Although Wilson did not
adopt Turner's particular suggestion, he, too, advocated collective security as a protection against chaos and radicalism.
Both men wanted orderly progress instead of radical
revolution.

Progressive history and social science, buttressed by the
American experience in the nineteenth century, thus provided intellectual foundations for Wilson's liberal internationalism. Scholars and journalists reinforced this
understanding by emphasizing conscious social control as
the means to achieve orderly progress in the modern world.
Wilson articulated this new intellectual perspective. Emphasizing the polarity between the Old and New Worlds, he
hoped during the world war either to preserve American
innocence by remaining neutral or to redeem Europe by
participating in a Christian crusade for democracy. Convinced
that the United States stood in the vanguard of world history,
he projected this image overseas. Internationalizing the
political culture of his own country, the president used it as
the basis for a new foreign policy. Progressive history, which
incorporated the Social Gospel and Social Darwinism, helped
shape his vision of a postwar league of nations. The idea of
progress seemed to guarantee the universal triumph of
American ideals and practices in foreign affairs.

Notes

1. Van Wyck Brooks, *America's Coming-of-Age* (1915), in idem, *Three
Essays on America* (New York: E. P. Dutton, 1970), pp. 19-20.

2. Harold Stearns, *Liberalism in America: Its Origins, Its Temporary
Collapse, Its Future* (New York: Boni & Liveright, 1919), pp. 36-37, 53.
From a less critical perspective, Cooper, *The Warrior and the Priest*, pp.
123-24, notes Wilson's combination of expediency and principle.

3. Knud Krakau, "American Foreign Relations: A National Style?"
Diplomatic History 8 (Summer 1984): 253-72, correctly emphasizes
the close connection between style and substance in American foreign
relations.

4. Woodrow Wilson, "Mr. Goldwin Smith's 'Views' on Our Political History," *The Forum* 16 (December 1893): 489-99, in Arthur S. Link, ed., *The Papers of Woodrow Wilson*, 63 vols. (Princeton: Princeton University Press, 1966-1990), 8:346-57; Woodrow Wilson, *A History of the American People*, 10 vols. (1901, 1902; reprint ed., New York: Harper & Brothers, 1918), 10:84-90.

5. William E. Dodd (historian) to Frederick Jackson Turner, October 3, 1919, Turner to Dodd, October 7, 1919, in Wendall H. Stephenson, "The Influence of Woodrow Wilson on Frederick Jackson Turner," *Agricultural History* 19 (October 1945): 250-53; Turner to Wilson, December 20, 1893, in Link, *Papers* 6:335-54; Frederick Jackson Turner, "The Significance of the Frontier in American History," in idem, *The Frontier in American History* (New York: Henry Holt, 1920), p. 38; Turner to Skinner, March 15, 1922, in Constance Lindsay Skinner, ed., "Turner's Autobiographical Letter," *Wisconsin Magazine of History* 19 (September 1935): 91-103; William E. Dodd, *Woodrow Wilson and His Work* (Garden City: Doubleday, Page, 1920), pp. 20, 27-28; Geroge C. Osborn, "Woodrow Wilson and Frederick Jackson Turner," *Proceedings of the New Jersey Historical Society* 74 (July 1956): 208-29; idem, *Woodrow Wilson: The Early Years* (Baton Rouge: Louisiana State University Press, 1968), pp. 165, 189-91, 235, 260, 277-80, 305-6; Henry Wilkinson Bragdon, *Woodrow Wilson: The Academic Years* (Cambridge: Harvard University Press, 1967), pp. 178, 188-94, 233-43; Ray Allen Billington, *Frederick Jackson Turner: Historian, Scholar, Teacher* (New York: Oxford University Press, 1973), pp. 59, 70-71, 75-76, 187-90, 213.

6. Woodrow Wilson, *The State: Elements of Historical and Practical Politics* (Boston: D. C. Heath, 1889), pp. 366-67, 449, 464, 469, 473.

7. Woodrow Wilson, "Bryce's American Commonwealth," *Political Science Quarterly* 4 (March 1889): 153-69, in Link, *Papers* 6:61-76.

8. James Bryce, *The American Commonwealth*, 2 vols. (London: Macmillan, 1889), 2:681.

9. Wilson to Turner, August 23, 1889, Turner to Wilson, August 31, 1889, January 23, 1890, in Link, *Papers* 6:368-71, 381-84, 478-79.

10. Fulmer Mood, "Turner's Formative Period," in Louise P. Kellogg, ed., *The Early Writings of Frederick Jackson Turner* (Madison: University of Wisconsin Press, 1938), pp. 36-38; Woodrow Wilson, *Division and Reunion: 1829-1889* (New York: Longmans, Green, 1893), pp. 2-3, 10-11, 23, 118; Turner to Wilson, July 16, December 20, 1893, in Link, *Papers* 6:278-79, 417.

11. Wilson, *The State*, pp. 2-7, 17-21, 575-76.

12. John Higham, *History: The Development of Historical Studies in the United States* (Englewood Cliffs: Prentice-Hall, 1965), pp. 150-82; Richard Hofstadter, *The Progressive Historians: Turner, Beard, Parrington* (New York: Vintage Books, 1970); Cushing Strout, *The Pragmatic Revolt in American History: Carl Becker and Charles Beard* (New Haven: Yale University Press, 1958).

13. Wilson, *The State*, p. 575; idem, "Democracy," in Link, *Papers* 7:350, 363; idem, "The Ideals of America," *Atlantic Monthly* 90 (December 1902): 728; idem, *History of the American People* 4:51-158. On the linkage between progress and order in Wilson's political thought see Lloyd Ambrosius, "Woodrow Wilson and the Quest for Orderly Progress," in Norman A. Graebner, ed., *Traditions and Values: American Diplomacy, 1865-1945* (Lanham: University Press of America, 1985), pp. 73-100; and Niels Aage Thorsen, *The Political Thought of Woodrow Wilson, 1875-1910* (Princeton: Princeton University Press, 1988), pp. 15-16, 162-74.

14. Wilson, "Ideals of America," 727; idem, "Edmund Burke: The Man and His Times," in Link, *Papers* 8:318-43.

15. "Nature of Democracy in the United States," in Link, *Papers* 6:228-29.

16. Edward Alsworth Ross, *The Old World in the New: The Significance of Past and Present Immigration to the American People* (New York: Century, 1914); "Nature of Democracy," in Link, *Papers* 6:233-39; Wilson, *History of the American People* 10:98-100; Edward N. Saveth, *American Historians and European Immigrants: 1875-1925* (New York: Columbia University Press, 1948), pp. 122-49.

17. "The Bible and Progress," in Ray Stannard Baker and William E. Dodd, eds., *The Public Papers of Woodrow Wilson*, 6 vols. (New York: Harper & Brothers, 1925-1927), 2:291-302; "Religion and Patriotism," in Link, *Papers* 12:474-78.

18. George D. Herron, *Woodrow Wilson and the World's Peace* (New York: Mitchell Kennerley, 1917), pp. 68-69, 76-77. For a brilliant summary of the religious dimension in Wilson's foreign policy see Robert M. Crunden, *Ministers of Reform: The Progressives' Achievement in American Civilization* (Urbana: University of Illinois Press, 1984), pp. 225-73.

19. Mitchell Pirie Briggs, *George D. Herron and the European Settlement* (Stanford: Stanford University Press, 1932), p. 249; Charles Howard Hopkins, *The Rise of the Social Gospel in American Protestantism, 1865-1915* (New Haven: Yale University Press, 1940), pp. 184-200.

20. Baker and Dodd, *Public Papers* 2:294.

21. "Religion and Patriotism," in Link, *Papers* 12:475-76. See also Ernest Lee Tuveson, *Redeemer Nation: The Idea of America's Millennial Role* (Chicago: University of Chicago Press, 1968), pp. 91-214; and John M. Mulder, *Woodrow Wilson: The Years of Preparation* (Princeton: Princeton University Press, 1978), pp. 229-77. In contrast, Cooper, *The Warrior and the Priest*, p. 171, deemphasizes this linkage between religion and politics, arguing that "Wilson drew a sharp distinction between . . . religion and politics. . . . Despite a shared idealism in style and to some extent in content, Wilson did not adopt Roosevelt's brand of political evangelism."

22. Edward Alsworth Ross, *Social Control: A Survey of the Foundations of Order* (New York: Macmillan, 1901), p. 293. For the importance of the idea of social control in sociology see Morris Janowitz, *The Last Half-Century* (Chicago: University of Chicago Press, 1978), pp. 3-52.

23. On the Ross-Wilson relationship see Edward Alsworth Ross, *Seventy Years of It: An Autobiography* (New York: D. Appleton-Century, 1936), pp. 40, 87-89, 97-100, 106-7, 110-11, 245-47, 293-94; William Jennings Bryan to Wilson, June 2, 1913, in Link, *Papers* 27:492; Wilson to Bryan, June 25, 1913, and John R. Mott (YMCA general secretary) to

Wilson, July 3, 1913, in Link, *Papers* 28:4, 22-23; Henry P. Fairchild (sociologist) to Wilson, March 17, 1914, in Link, *Papers* 29:352; and Joseph P. Tumulty (president's secretary) to Wilson, January 21, 1915, in Link, *Papers* 32:95-98.

24. Wilson to John Bates Clark, August 26, 1887, in Link, *Papers* 5:564-65; Bragdon, *Woodrow Wilson*, pp. 178, 222-23; Osborn, *Woodrow Wilson*, pp. 313-14.

25. John Bates Clark, *The Control of Trusts: An Argument in Favor of Curbing the Power of Monopoly by a Natural Method* (New York: Macmillan, 1901), p. 55.

26. Wilson to Ellen Axson Wilson (his wife), February 11, 1889, in Link, *Papers* 6:82-83.

27. Franklin Henry Giddings, *Democracy and Empire: Their Psychological, Economic and Moral Foundations* (New York: Macmillan, 1900), pp. v, 284-85, 357.

28. Woodrow Wilson, *Congressional Government: A Study in American Politics* (1885; reprint ed., Boston: Houghton Mifflin, 1900), pp. xi-xii. See also idem, *Constitutional Government in the United States* (New York: Columbia University Press, 1908), pp. 77-78.

29. Franklin H. Giddings, "The Relation of Social Theory to Public Policy," *International Conciliation*, 58 (September 1912): 3-13; idem, *Studies in the Theory of Human Society* (New York: Macmillan, 1922), pp. 209-23.

30. Randolph S. Bourne, ed., *Towards an Enduring Peace: A Symposium of Peace Proposals and Programs, 1914-1916* (New York: American Association for International Conciliation, [1916]), pp. vii-xi, 135-42; Bartlett, *The League to Enforce Peace*, pp. 30-38; Sondra R. Herman, *Eleven against War: Studies in American Internationalist Thought, 1898-1921* (Stanford: Hoover Institution Press, 1969), pp. 55-85.

31. John A. Thompson, *Reformers and War: American Progressive Publicists and the First World War* (Cambridge: Cambridge University Press, 1987).

32. Herbert Croly, *The Promise of American Life* (1909; reprint ed., New York: Capricorn Books, 1964), pp. 22, 289-314. See also William E. Leuchtenburg, "Progressivism and Imperialism: The Progressive Movement and American Foreign Policy, 1898-1916," *Mississippi Valley Historical Review* 39 (December 1952): 483-504.

33. Walter Lippmann, *Drift and Mastery: An Attempt to Diagnose the Current Unrest* (1914; reprint ed., Englewood Cliffs: Prentice-Hall, 1961), pp. 16-17, 147-48.

34. Charles Forcey, *The Crossroads of Liberalism: Croly, Weyl, Lippmann, and the Progressive Era, 1900-1925* (New York: Oxford University Press, 1961), pp. 221-315; David W. Noble, *The Progressive Mind, 1890-1917* (Chicago: Rand McNally, 1970), pp. 53-64, 165-79; Arthur S. Link, *Wilson*, 5 vols. (Princeton: Princeton University Press, 1947-1965), 5:18-19, 23-26, 304, 390-91; Edward M. House to Wilson, October 29, 1918, U.S. Department of State, *Papers Relating to the Foreign Relations of the United States, 1918*, Supplement 1: *The World War* (Washington, DC: Government Printing Office, 1933), 1:405-13.

35. On the idea of collective security in the twentieth century see Roland N. Stromberg, *Collective Security and American Foreign Policy: From the League of Nations to NATO* (New York: Frederick A. Praeger,

1963); and George W. Egerton, "Collective Security as Political Myth: Liberal Internationalism and the League of Nations in Politics and History," *International History Review* 5 (November 1983): 496-524.

36. Woodrow Wilson, "The Proper Perspective of American History," *The Forum* 19 (June 1895): 553; idem, "The Significance of American History," *Harper's Encyclopaedia of United States History* (New York, 1902), 1:xxvii, in Link, *Papers* 12:179; Walter Lippmann, *Men of Destiny* (New York: Macmillan, 1927), p. 122; Henry Nash Smith, *Virgin Land: The American West as Symbol and Myth* (Cambridge: Harvard University Press, 1950); David W. Noble, *Historians against History: The Frontier Thesis and the National Covenant in American Historical Writing since 1830* (Minneapolis: University of Minnesota Press, 1965).

37. R. W. Van Alstyne, *The Rising American Empire* (Oxford: Basil Blackwell, 1960); Alexander DeConde, *This Affair of Louisiana* (New York: Charles Scribner's Sons, 1976); Norman A. Graebner, *Empire on the Pacific: A Study in American Continental Expansion* (New York: Ronald Press, 1955); Frederick Merk, *The Oregon Question: Essays in Anglo-American Diplomacy & Politics* (Cambridge: Harvard University Press, 1967); idem, *The Monroe Doctrine and American Expansionism, 1843-1849* (New York: Vintage Books, 1966); David M. Pletcher, *The Diplomacy of Annexation: Texas, Oregon, and the Mexican War* (Columbia: University of Missouri Press, 1973); Alan Dowty, *The Limits of American Isolation: The United States and the Crimean War* (New York: New York University Press, 1971); Ernest R. May, *Imperial Democracy: The Emergence of America as a Great Power* (New York: Harcourt, Brace & World, 1961); Walter LaFeber, *The New Empire: An Interpretation of American Expansion, 1860-1898* (Ithaca: Cornell University Press, 1963); William Appleman Williams, *The Roots of the Modern American Empire: A Study of the Growth and Shaping of Social Consciousness in a Marketplace Society* (New York: Vintage Books, 1969); David Healy, *U.S. Expansionism: The Imperialist Urge in the 1890s* (Madison: University of Wisconsin Press, 1970); Hans-Ulrich Wehler, *Der Aufstieg des amerikanischen Imperialismus* (Göttingen: Vandenhoeck & Ruprecht, 1974); Göran Rystad, *Ambiguous Imperialism: American Foreign Policy and Domestic Politics at the Turn of the Century* (Lund: Esselte Studium, 1975).

38. Albert K. Weinberg, *Manifest Destiny: A Study of Nationalist Expansion in American History* (Baltimore: Johns Hopkins Press, 1935); Frederick Merk, *Manifest Destiny and Mission in American History: A Reinterpretation* (New York: Vintage Books, 1963); James A. Field, Jr., *America and the Mediterranean World, 1776-1882* (Princeton: Princeton University Press, 1969); Myrtle A. Cline, *American Attitude toward the Greek War of Independence, 1821-1828* (Atlanta: Higgins-McArthur, 1930); Henry Blumenthal, *A Reappraisal of Franco-American Relations, 1830-1871* (Chapel Hill: University of North Carolina Press, 1959); Merle Eugene Curti, "Austria and the United States," *Smith College Studies in History* 11, no. 3 (April 1926): 141-206; Henry M. Adams, *Prussian-American Relations, 1775-1871* (Cleveland: Press of Western Reserve University, 1960); John Gerlow Gazley, *American Opinion of German Unification, 1848-1871* (New York: Columbia University Press, 1926); Howard R. Marraro, *American Opinion on the Unification of Italy, 1846-1861* (New York: Columbia University Press, 1932).

39. U.S. Senate, 56th Cong., 1st sess., *Congressional Record*, vol. 33, pt. 1, p. 711 (January 9, 1900).

40. C. Vann Woodward, "The Age of Reinterpretation," *American Historical Review* 66 (October 1960): 1-19.

41. Woodrow Wilson, "The Making of the Nation," *Atlantic Monthly* 80 (July 1897): 2.

42. Wilson, "Significance of American History," in Link, *Papers* 12:184.

43. Wilson, "Ideals of America," 726-34.

44. Wilson, *The State*, p. 603.

45. Baker and Dodd, *Public Papers* 4:344-48.

46. Lippmann, *Men of Destiny*, p. 123.

47. Frederick Jackson Turner, "Why Did Not the United States Become Another Europe?" and "Washington the Nationalist," in Wilbur R. Jacobs, ed., *Frederick Jackson Turner's Legacy: Unpublished Writings in American History* (San Marino: Henry E. Huntington Library, 1965), pp. 124-25, 148; Billington, *Frederick Jackson Turner*, pp. 345-56; Wilbur R. Jacobs, *The Historical World of Frederick Jackson Turner: With Selections from His Correspondence* (New Haven: Yale University Press, 1968), pp. 143-49.

48. Frederick Jackson Turner, International Political Parties in a Durable League of Nations, [November 1918], Woodrow Wilson Papers, Ser. 5A, Box 3, Library of Congress, Washington, DC.

CHAPTER 2

Neutrality and Mediation

Wilson's liberal internationalism began to develop before the
United States intervened in the First World War. His idea of
collective security slowly emerged during the initial period of
American neutrality. Before the European war in 1914, the
president had stated two themes that would characterize his
foreign policy. In reference to the Mexican Revolution, he
announced the two elements of the "only one possible standard" that should guide the United States in controversies
with other nations: "our own honor and our obligations to the
peace of the world."[1] While attempting to protect the nation's
honor and independence, he sought to end the war through
mediation. Edward M. House, his close friend and informal
adviser, traveled to Europe in search of peace.

Adhering to the American diplomatic tradition, the president quickly responded when the European crisis of July
1914 erupted into war. On August 4 he issued a proclamation
of neutrality. Two weeks later, Wilson elaborated his views
on the war in an appeal to the nation, explaining that "the
effect of the war upon the United States will depend upon
what American citizens say and do. Every man who really
loves America will act and speak in the true spirit of neutrality, which is the spirit of impartiality and fairness and
friendliness to all concerned." Recognizing the difficulty of
adhering to this advice, the president nevertheless urged the
American people to remain absolutely neutral.[2]

On the eve of the war, Wilson had sent House to Europe
for the purpose of evaluating the current status of international relations. Impressed by the Anglo-German naval rivalry
and the "militarism" in the Old World, House had discovered
no easy remedy for the tensions among the Great Powers.

"The situation is extraordinary," he reported from Berlin in late May. "It is jingoism run stark mad. Unless some one acting for you can bring about an understanding, there is some day to be an awful cataclysm. No one in Europe can do it." He sensed a future opportunity for the United States to play a leading role in resolving European conflicts but proposed no particular action at this time. After further visits to Paris and London, he prepared to depart for the United States. Two days before the assassination of Austrian Archduke Franz Ferdinand and his wife at Sarajevo on June 28, 1914, House concluded that he had accomplished his mission. He naively informed the president that "a long stride has been made in the direction of international amity." Even after the assassination, he evidenced no sense of urgency for direct American participation in European diplomacy. House returned to the United States in July during the midst of the prewar crisis.[3]

The American ambassadors in London and Paris, Walter Hines Page and Myron T. Herrick, recognized the gravity of the situation more clearly than did House. On his own initiative Page offered to the British foreign secretary, Sir Edward Grey, the good offices of the United States. He hoped to avert the danger of a general war. Approving this action, Wilson himself extended this offer to all the European powers. None of them, however, welcomed American mediation. He experienced the limits of his influence over European affairs as the Central Powers and the Allies resorted to war. Although House initially had not favored Wilson's modest diplomatic overture, he soon embraced the idea and thereafter collaborated with him in seeking to end the war.[4]

Throughout the remainder of 1914, House attempted in vain to convince the European belligerents to accept American mediation. With the president's approval, he established contacts with the European representatives in Washington. Concentrating on the British and German ambassadors, Sir Cecil Spring-Rice and Count Johann von Bernstorff, House proposed "a durable peace" on the basis of ending militarism and restoring Belgium. He sought to stop the war before either the Central Powers or the Allies achieved victory. "If the war continues," Spring-Rice conveyed House's message to Grey, "either Germany or Russia becomes supreme in

Europe. Both alternatives are fatal to balance of power. It would be better to begin negotiations before the balance is upset." Without making any formal commitment the British foreign secretary personally endorsed the general goals of House's proposal. He refused, however, to enter into peace negotiations until Imperial Germany agreed to evacuate Belgium and pay it an indemnity. Beyond the restoration of Belgian independence, he advocated "a durable peace" that would protect the Allies from future German aggression. Although he, too, wanted to avoid Germany's total defeat, Grey intended to guarantee western Europe against German hegemony.

Beginning to consider American involvement in some form of collective security, Grey instructed Spring-Rice on December 22 that "an agreement between the Great Powers at the end of this war with the object of mutual security and preservation of peace in future might have stability if the United States would become a party to it and were prepared to join in repressing by force whoever broke the Treaty." When Spring-Rice broached this idea, House immediately rejected it, asserting that the American government would approve no such agreement. Neither he nor Wilson intended to entangle the United States in European affairs to that extent. Given this attitude, the British resisted House's initiative. From Germany came more rejection of American mediation. Undersecretary of State Arthur Zimmermann politely declined to negotiate with the Allies as House had proposed.[5]

Wilson hoped for a quick conclusion to the war on the basis of the current stalemate. In an off-the-record interview with a *New York Times* correspondent in mid-December 1914, he expressed his desire for a deadlock in the European war. Fearing that victory by either side would promote revenge and result in a future war, he believed that a stalemate was the precondition for permanent peace. Yet Wilson viewed the prospect of an Allied victory with less apprehension than a peace imposed by the Central Powers. He did not, however, intend to intervene with U.S. armed forces to determine the outcome. Regardless of what happened to the balance of power in Europe, he wanted to preserve American neutrality.[6]

II

Unable to end the European war, the president began to
develop the idea of collective security in the Western Hemisphere. House encouraged him to take this circuitous route to
peace in Europe. During his earlier trip to Europe, House
had suggested the extension of Wilson's Latin American
policy to the Old World as a way to reduce its tensions. This
policy, as outlined in a major presidential address at Mobile,
Alabama, on October 27, 1913, had called for "the development
of constitutional liberty in the world." Wilson had pledged
the United States not to conquer any additional territory
from its neighbors but to work with them for their mutual
advantage. The opening of the Panama Canal, he anticipated,
would produce closer ties between North and South America.
In December 1914 he discussed with House the idea of an
agreement among the nations of the New World "that would
weld the Western Hemisphere together." House hoped that it
"would serve as a model for the European Nations when
peace is at last brought about."

Wilson now prepared his own plan to join the United
States and Latin American nations in a mutual guarantee of
territorial integrity and political independence under republican governments. He also wanted to establish governmental
control over the manufacture and sale of munitions. After
further consultation with Secretary of State William Jennings
Bryan about this proposal for a Pan-American treaty, the
president added provisions for the peaceful settlement of
international disputes through diplomacy or arbitration. In
January 1915, preparatory to Bryan's formal presentation of
the proposed treaty, House shared this plan for Pan-American
collective security with the ambassadors of Argentina, Brazil,
and Chile. With the anticipated approval of these ABC
countries, Wilson expected the smaller nations of Latin
America to accept the treaty. This hemispheric solidarity
would then provide an example for peacemaking in the Old
World.[7]

Despite the persistent refusal of the belligerents to welcome American mediation, Wilson decided to send House on
another mission to Europe. Going first to London in February
1915, he attempted to formulate some plan to initiate peace
negotiations. House shared Grey's conviction that the war

could not end without the restoration of Belgium and the establishment of an as-yet-undefined "permanent settlement." The British foreign secretary attempted to convince House that the United States should participate in "some general guaranty" of the eventual peace settlement. Evading this suggestion, House proposed a second convention, at which the neutrals and belligerents could determine "the principles upon which civilized warfare should in the future be conducted." At the first convention, or peace conference, the belligerents themselves would settle the issues of the current war. As the two conventions might be held jointly, House hoped that his idea would contribute to the opening of peace negotiations. This proposal, which Wilson approved, reflected House's knowledge that neither the Allies nor the Central Powers welcomed American mediation. It also expressed the interest of the United States in protecting "the rights of neutrals" without entangling itself in the Old World.

Proceeding to Paris and Berlin, House continued to promote his idea of a second convention. In Germany, he emphasized its potential contribution to freedom of the seas. He reported to Wilson in late March "that our thought went far beyond the Declaration of Paris, or the proposed Declaration of London, and that we have in mind the absolute freedom of commerce in future warfare, and that navies should be used almost wholly for protection against invasion." As Germany was suffering from the British blockade, this explanation sounded appealing, but House failed to obtain any specific commitment in Berlin. Returning to Paris and London in April, House endeavored to convince the Allies to adopt his idea as a way to open peace negotiations. Here, too, he failed. Irreconcilable differences between the two sides doomed House's mission.[8]

Relations with the European belligerents changed substantially with the sinking of the *Lusitania* on May 7, 1915. Along with many Americans, Wilson abandoned his attitude of neutrality. When a German submarine sank this British passenger liner, resulting in the death of 124 Americans out of a total loss of 1,198 persons, many politicians and editors who had heeded his earlier advice about impartiality now joined in condemning this act as a barbaric threat to civilization. From London, House advised that "America has come to the parting of the ways when she must determine whether

she stands for civilized or uncivilized warfare." He urged the
president to take a strong stand against Germany over this
attack on American citizens as well as on foreign civilians.[9]

The United States officially protested against the sinking
of the *Lusitania* and the wanton destruction of life. In its
second protest note, which Wilson had drafted, the government
asserted that "the sinking of passenger ships involves principles of humanity which throw into the background any
special circumstances of detail that may be thought to affect
the cases, principles which lift it . . . out of the class of
ordinary subjects of diplomatic discussion or of international
controversy." Especially because the German submarine had
not warned the *Lusitania* of the attack and had not attempted
to rescue the victims, which international law required under
the rules of cruiser warfare, the president condemned the
torpedoing of this ship. "The Government of the United States
is contending for something much greater than mere rights
of property or privileges of commerce. It is contending for
nothing less high and sacred than the rights of humanity,"
the note proclaimed. Prior to the *Lusitania* affair, Wilson had
not asserted the right of Americans to travel on passenger
ships of belligerent nations. Yet he now regarded the German
violation of this right as a breach of universal moral law.
"The rights of neutrals in time of war," he affirmed in the
third note, "are based upon principle, not upon expediency,
and the principles are immutable."[10]

Secretary Bryan resigned during the midst of the *Lusitania*
crisis. Refusing to sign the second protest note, he preferred
to sacrifice the dubious neutral right of Americans to travel
on belligerent ships through the war zone. Adhering to the
policy of impartial neutrality, he also wanted to protest against
British violations of American commercial rights. Wilson
rejected this policy, explaining that "England's violation of
neutral rights is different from Germany's violation of the
rights of humanity."[11]

Wilson abandoned impartial neutrality and accepted
Bryan's resignation. Yet he still anticipated a peaceful conclusion to the present crisis. He expected to remain neutral
in fact if not in thought. In this context, attempting to reconcile
moral indignation with neutrality, he proclaimed that the
United States was "too proud to fight."[12] By sending strong
protests and taking no further action, he also sought to
satisfy the contradictory desires of the American public.

Wilson hoped, as he explained to Bryan, to "carry out the double wish of our people, to maintain a firm front in respect of what we demand of Germany and yet do nothing that might by any possibility involve us in the war."[13]

As Wilson recognized, the American people wanted not only to stay out of the European war but also to contribute to the redemption of the Old World. "Our one desire," noted Herbert Hoover, chairman of the Commission for Relief in Belgium, "is to help to find some solution which would prevent our own country from being joined in this holocaust . . . and at the same time contribute something towards the ultimate redemption of Europe from the barbarism into which it is slowly but surely drifting from all sides." Like Hoover, the president felt the tension between the twin impulses in American attitudes toward Europe. They both hoped somehow to reconcile the conflicting tendencies to isolate the United States and to redeem the Old World.[14]

Wilson's chief foreign-policy advisers recognized the difficulty of his position. House informed the British foreign secretary that "the vast majority of our people desire the President to be very firm in his attitude towards Germany and yet avoid war." Robert Lansing, who had succeeded Bryan as secretary of state, described the difficulty of protecting neutral rights without involving the United States in the war. "It is a difficult policy," he noted, "a policy of patience, of extreme forbearance, a policy of endurance, which under normal conditions would be humiliating and contrary to the dignity of the United States."[15]

The *Lusitania* affair convinced Lansing that Imperial Germany threatened civilization. In his diary he recorded that "the German Government is utterly hostile to all nations with democratic institutions because those who compose it see in democracy a menace to absolutism and the defeat of the German ambition for world dominion." Viewing the world war as a struggle between absolutism and democracy, he thought that the United States should intervene to help the Allies if they ever faced a real threat of defeat. Combining elements of a balance-of-power conception with a more traditional understanding of the American mission, the new secretary of state viewed Germany as a threat both to the nation's security and to its principles. Anticipating American intervention in the war, Lansing favored a policy that the president had not yet adopted. Wilson refrained from accepting

Lansing's interpretation of the war as a struggle between democracy and absolutism until 1917, when he affirmed it in his war message to Congress.[16]

During his first wartime mission to Europe in the spring of 1915, House had concluded that Imperial Germany desired peace only on the basis of victory. Discussions in Berlin with Chancellor Theobald von Bethmann-Hollweg and at the Foreign Office had convinced him that Germany would not accept conditions of peace that would satisfy the minimal Allied demands. Even if the political leaders desired peace, he believed that the German people and military leaders would reject a moderate settlement. Only the idea of freedom of the seas, which the German leaders interpreted as a restriction on the British navy, had evoked a positive response during these discussions. The sinking of the *Lusitania* two months later confirmed House's impression about Germany's aggressive ambitions. This convinced him of the virtual inevitability of war between the United States and Germany. Although with greater flexibility and less ideological consistency, House now shared Lansing's conviction that German victory in Europe would imperil the United States.[17]

III

During the summer of 1915, in correspondence with House, Grey fostered the idea of a league of nations. He developed the suggestion of a postwar system of collective security that he had made during House's visit to London in February. At that time he had intimated that the British government might consider a peace settlement short of victory if it could count on the United States to help prevent future aggression. House had rejected the idea as a violation of the American diplomatic tradition. During April, upon House's return to London from the continent, Grey had reverted to the league idea. It offered the obvious advantage of focusing attention on postwar plans rather than on the controversies over British violations of American neutral rights. The foreign secretary evidenced no interest in peace on the basis of freedom of the seas, a proposal that House had suggested after his discussions in Berlin. Only in connection with a postwar league of nations, not in relation to the present war, would he consider the issue of freedom of the seas.[18]

Grey continued to nurture House's conception of collective security after his return to the United States. Looking back on the crisis of July 1914, the foreign secretary concluded that the prewar negotiations had failed when the Germans refused to attend a conference to discuss the issues. "If neutral nations and the opinion of the world generally had been sufficiently alert to say that they would side against the party that refused a Conference," Grey speculated, "war might have been avoided." He hoped to prevent this difficulty in the future by creating "some League of Nations that could be relied on to insist that disputes between any two nations must be settled by the arbitration, mediation, or conference of others." The "lesson" that he derived from the war was that the Great Powers should organize together to enforce international law through a sanction. Yet Grey showed little interest in American mediation of the present war. Although avoiding an outright rejection of such a prospect, he favored an Allied victory, postponing a league of nations for the future. "If the end of this war is arrived at through mediation," he informed House, "I believe it must be through that of the United States. All our efforts are of course concentrated on saving ourselves and our Allies by securing victory in the war. But it is in my mind continually that the awful sufferings of this war will, to a great extent, have been in vain unless at the end of it nations are set and determined together that future generations shall not fall into such a catastrophe."[19]

By the autumn of 1915, House began to respond to Grey's suggestions. Early in September, on his own initiative, he asked the British foreign secretary if he thought that "the President could make proposals to the belligerents at this time upon the broad basis of the elimination of militarism and navalism and a return, as nearly as possible, to the status quo?" Grey answered by offering his conception of a league of nations and poignantly raising the question of American participation. He explained on September 22 that for him "the great object of securing the elimination of militarism and navalism is to get security for the future against aggressive war. How much are the United States prepared to do in this direction?" Besides contemplating the elimination of militarism and navalism only as a future possibility, the foreign secretary rejected House's suggestion of peace on the basis of status quo ante bellum. He asserted that "England is bound to fight on with her Allies, as long as they will fight, to secure victory, and I do long to see the bullied provinces of

Alsace and Lorraine restored to the freer Government of France, and Russia ought to get her outlet to the sea. But the minimum to avoid disaster is the restoration of Belgium and the preservation of France in terms of peace." Justifying British determination to achieve an Allied victory, Grey de-•scribed the German threat to western civilization. He explained that the democracies of France, Belgium, and Great Britain faced the perils of German absolutism. Although evading American mediation, Grey encouraged the United States to play a larger role in Europe.[20]

German submarine warfare threatened to draw the United States more deeply into European affairs. The sinking on August 19 of the *Arabic*, a British freighter carrying 423 passengers and crew, confirmed House's suspicions about Germany. Although only two of the forty-four casualties were Americans, he thought that the United States should sever diplomatic relations with Germany and warn it that a subsequent incident would result in a declaration of war. Secretary Lansing likewise recommended a diplomatic break, believing that the United States could exert more influence over the future peace settlement as a belligerent. Wilson, however, avoided such provocative action. House was disappointed at his reluctance. The *Arabic* crisis ended on September 1 when the German government promised that its submarines would abide by the rules of cruiser warfare under international law. Ambassador Bernstorff assured Lansing that German submarines would not attack passenger liners without first giving a warning and afterward rescuing the passengers and crew.[21]

Despite these assurances, which Bernstorff repeated to House later that month, Wilson's friend deeply distrusted Imperial Germany. Within this context he developed another plan for American mediation. House wanted the president, after gaining the Allies' approval, to call for peace negotiations on "the broad basis of both military and naval disarmament." If the Central Powers accepted this proposal, Wilson would contribute to peace in Europe, thus achieving "a master stroke in diplomacy." On the other hand, if the Central Powers rejected the proposal, the United States could increase the pressure on Germany for concessions by breaking diplomatic relations and perhaps ultimately declaring war.[22]

Wilson as well as Lansing showed some interest in House's plan. As they began to consider it, Grey's letter of September 22 arrived in Washington. For some inexplicable reason, it encouraged Wilson in the belief that Great Britain would welcome American mediation. Consequently, he approved House's offer to write a letter to Grey proposing mediation. Before extending this offer, House submitted his letter dated October 17 for Wilson's endorsement. Nevertheless, he presented the plan informally to Grey as his own. "It has occurred to me," stated House, "that the time may soon come when this Government should intervene between the belligerents and demand that peace parleys begin upon the broad basis of the elimination of militarism and navalism." He requested the Allies to approve the plan before he suggested it to Wilson. If the president then authorized the plan, House offered to travel to Europe on a peace mission. He explained to Grey that "after conferring with your Government I should proceed to Berlin and tell them that it was the President's purpose to intervene and stop this destructive war, provided the weight of the United States thrown on the side that accepted our proposal could do it." While endorsing House's plan, Wilson kept his options open, explaining that he did not want to commit his administration to "take part to force terms on Germany, because the exact circumstances of such a crisis are impossible to determine." If the Allies welcomed American mediation, if he then decided to implement the plan, and if the Central Powers rejected peace negotiations, Wilson still wanted to retain the freedom to decide unilaterally whether the United States would join the Allies in the war. This significant reservation appeared to House as "quite important."[23]

Despite his caution, Wilson apparently shared some apprehensions about a German victory. "Much to my surprise," House recorded after one of their conversations in September, "he said he had never been sure that we ought not to take part in the conflict and if it seemed evident that Germany and her militaristic ideas were to win, the obligation upon us was greater than ever." Moreover, as a consequence of the *Lusitania* affair, the president had turned his attention to military and naval preparedness. House encouraged him in this direction, contending that greater American capability for war might both deter Germany and enable the United States to impose peace. Two months earlier, on July 21, Wilson had instructed Secretary of War Lindley M. Garrison and Secretary of the Navy Josephus Daniels to prepare plans for expanding the armed forces, to be submitted to Congress in December. This shift toward greater preparedness revealed a new presidential attitude. During the previous session, two Massachusetts Republicans, Senator Henry Cabot Lodge and his son-in-law Representative Augustus P. Gardner, had proposed a review of the nation's defenses. Strong resistance from the White House had contributed to the failure of their measure. Wilson's indifference toward military and naval affairs had distressed not only Republicans but also some Democrats at that time.[24]

Even in October, when he finally began to speak publicly in favor of military preparedness, Wilson emphasized security without suggesting possible involvement in European affairs. "No matter what military or naval force the United States might develop," he announced, "statesmen throughout the whole world might rest assured that we were gathering that force, not for attack in any quarter, not for aggression of any kind, not for the satisfaction of any political or international ambition, but merely to make sure of our own security." The president never suggested that the United States might need to enter the European war to prevent an Allied defeat or preserve the balance of power. He did not clarify the danger of a German victory. Rather than suggesting the possibility of a new American military role in the Old World, he advocated preparedness solely for the defense of the United States and the Western Hemisphere.[25]

Wilson revealed no inclination toward involvement of American armed forces in Europe when he presented his plans to Congress. In his annual message on December 7, 1915, he justified military preparedness for the exclusive purpose of national security, adding that the United States faced no immediate threat. Throughout his message ran a single theme: "preparation of the nation to care for its own security and to make sure of entire freedom to play the impartial role in this hemisphere and in the world which we all believe to have been providentially assigned to it." This rationale for enlarging the army and navy left the American people uninformed about possible participation, whether military or diplomatic, in European affairs. Not even suggesting the possibility of mediation under House's plan, Wilson reaffirmed the policy of neutrality. "We have stood apart, studiously neutral," he asserted. "It was our manifest duty to do so." If he ever seriously intended to implement House's plan, leading possibly to a diplomatic break and war with Germany, Wilson's public statements during the autumn of

1915 failed either to educate the American people about this action or to instill confidence among the Allies in his leadership.[26]

Further evidence, if the Allies needed it, that the president was not yet ready to abandon the policy of neutrality appeared in the form of the first major U.S. protest against the British maritime system. On October 21, 1915, just three days after approving House's plan for American mediation, Wilson endorsed the note that Lansing had submitted for his consideration earlier that month. With his approval, the secretary of state instructed Ambassador Page to deliver to Grey this protest against the off-shore blockade and the definition of contraband that Great Britain had adopted. The Wilson administration thus affirmed its determination to continue "championing the integrity of neutral rights" in the spirit of "impartiality which from the outbreak of the war it has sought to exercise in its relations with the warring nations." This reaffirmation of impartial neutrality revealed Wilson's genuine reluctance to entangle the United States in the Old World.[27]

In view of this protest, which Page delivered in London on November 5, Grey understandably wondered what House meant by freedom of the seas. He gave House and Wilson an opportunity to clarify their definition of navalism and militarism, but they refrained from explaining their conditions for peace. Lacking a clear definition of "the elimination of militarism and navalism," the foreign secretary decided to reject House's plan for American mediation without even submitting it to the British cabinet or to the other Allies. He suggested that the president should wait until the belligerents requested such mediation, or commit himself firmly, before expecting a favorable answer. "I do not see," Grey informed House, "how [the Allies] could commit themselves in advance to any proposition without knowing exactly what it was, and knowing that the United States of America were prepared to intervene and make it good if they accepted it." Although avoiding an official response, he suggested that if Great Britain accepted the American position regarding the blockade and contraband, "it would be tantamount to admitting that, under modern conditions, we could not prevent Germany from trading, at any rate through neutral ports, as freely in time of war as in time of peace and that we must either continue the difference of opinion with your Government, or give up definitely and openly any attempt to stop goods going to and from Germany through neutral ports." He clearly intended to accept no such definition of neutral rights or freedom of the seas, for this would "strike the weapon of sea power out of our hands, and thereby ensure a German victory."[28]

Grey's negative response disappointed House but did not discourage him. He thought that "the offer which I made in my letter, which was practically to insure [sic] victory to the Allies, should have met a warmer reception." He explained its rejection by claiming that "the British are in many ways dull." To overcome their apparent stupidity, House suggested to Wilson that he undertake another mission to Europe. By mid-December the president accepted this proposal. In discussions of the mission's purpose, he displayed even less interest than earlier in House's plan for American mediation. Rather than anticipating U.S. intervention in the war to prevent a German victory, Wilson, as House noted, "seemed to think we would be able to keep out of the war. His general idea is that if the Allies were not able to defeat Germany alone, they could scarcely do so with the help of the United States because it would take too long for us to get in a state of preparedness. It would therefore be a useless sacrifice on our part to go in." Even House, doubtless responding in part to Wilson's mood, anticipated no American participation in the war in the foreseeable future.[29]

IV

By the end of 1915, Wilson showed more interest in plans for the world's future peace than in conflicts of the present war. House shared his reluctance to involve the United States in the Old World to settle territorial disputes and fix indemnities. Since the sinking of the *Lusitania*, Bernstorff had encouraged House to focus on freedom of the seas. Seeking to improve German-American relations, the ambassador urged the United States to require Great Britain to abide by international law. The Germans wanted the British to lift their illegal blockade. House expanded this idea of freedom to include both land and sea. He hoped to end German militarism as well as British navalism. After Bernstorff indicated his government's interest in discussing peace on this basis, House advised Wilson that the goal of his mission to Europe should be to achieve general disarmament. He counseled the president to demand an end to the war. House emphasized that "we were not concerned regarding territorial questions or indemnity, but we were concerned regarding the larger questions which involved not only the belligerents, but the neutrals also." From the perspective of a neutral nation, he thought that the United States should avoid entangling itself in the controversies over territory and indemnity, leaving those issues for the Allies to settle with Germany.[30]

In his instructions for House's new mission to Europe, Wilson combined the goal of general disarmament with his emerging vision of collective security. Drawing upon Grey's earlier suggestions, he outlined his idea of a postwar league of nations for the first time. By eliminating militarism and navalism and establishing a league, he hoped to guarantee peace in the future. This long-range purpose seemed more important to him than the specific European conflicts over territories or indemnities. He agreed with House that the United States should not concern itself with "local settlements" such as "territorial questions, indemnities, and the like." Instead, it should concentrate on "the future peace of the world." He thought that this goal could be achieved with a limited set of mutual guarantees among nations. "The only possible guarantees, that is, the only guarantees that any rational man could accept, are (a) military and naval disarmament and (b) a league of nations to secure each nation against aggression and maintain the absolute freedom of the seas." The president approved the use of only "our utmost moral force" to encourage either the Allies or the Central Powers to end the war if the other side agreed to negotiate on his terms. Thus, he reconciled his idea of a postwar league of nations with American neutrality during the present war.[31] His statecraft pursued the idealistic goal of preserving future peace and the practical goal of avoiding current entanglement, but it ignored the realities of Europe at war over the distribution of territory and economic resources.

Arriving in London early in January 1916, House spent two weeks with Grey and other British leaders, trying to convince them of the relevance of the American proposals. He linked the new idea of a league with his earlier plan for mediation. He attempted, but without much success, to overcome British fears regarding the American definition of freedom of the seas. Before his departure from the United

States on this peace mission, he had written to Grey: "You are quite wrong in thinking that we have any desire to lessen the effectiveness of England's sea power at this time. It is the one reassuring potential element in the war." House reiterated this assurance in London. Yet, under Wilson's instructions, he also urged the British to modify their maritime system. The vagueness of the president's conception of a league of nations caused further doubts about the American role in Europe. Various British officials made futile attempts to obtain information about his attitude toward the specific issues of the present war. "They wanted to know," House reported to Wilson, "how far you would be willing to enter into an agreement concerning European affairs. I thought you would not be willing to do this at all, but you would be willing to come to an agreement with the civilized world upon the broad questions touching the interests and future of every nation." He included in that category "the general elimination, so far as practicable, of militarism and navalism."[32] Defined in these terms, the goals of U.S. foreign policy soared beyond the realities of wartime Europe.

Throughout these discussions, House emphasized American neutrality as the essential prerequisite for his plan's success. He feared that Germany's refusal to offer a satisfactory apology for sinking the *Lusitania* might produce a diplomatic break because "the whole plan rests upon our being able to deal with all the belligerents." As he explained to Grey, House thought that it would be "far better for the democracies of the world to unite upon some plan which would enable the United States to intervene than for us to drift into the war by breaking diplomatic relations with the Central Powers." Emphasizing to Grey, and also to Arthur J. Balfour—who would later replace Grey as foreign secretary—the importance of maintaining U.S. diplomatic relations with Germany, House said that otherwise "the plan I proposed now would be impossible of success."[33]

House exemplified the typical dualism in American attitudes toward the Old World. At once unilateralist and universalist, he endeavored to avoid entanglement in European affairs even while defining a new U.S. role in international relations. Rather than confronting the specific issues of the war, he fluctuated between the twin impulses to isolate the United States and to redeem the Old World. Summarizing his position during the discussions, House reported to Wilson:

"The general line of my argument was that you had arranged a closer union of the Americas so if it was thought best not to enter a worldwide sphere, we could safely lead an isolated life of our own. If this were decided upon, I told them, we would increase our army and navy and remain within our own hemisphere." The president's proposal for a Pan-American treaty as well as his plans for military preparedness, both of which House had vigorously supported, were designed to enhance this alternative. "On the other hand," he further reported, "I explained, you believed that in order to fully justify our existence as a great nation, it might be necessary to bring to bear all our power in behalf of peace and the maintenance of it." The president's vision of collective security to preserve "permanent peace among civilized nations" anticipated this other alternative. For both House and Wilson, the American mission in the world could express itself in both the policy of neutrality and the idea of a league of nations.[34]

Proceeding to Berlin in late January, House explored the possibility of peace with Chancellor Bethmann-Hollweg and with officials at the Foreign Office. More than ever before, he recognized that the Imperial German government would settle for nothing short of victory. Based on his observations, he also concluded that it would soon resort to "an aggressive undersea policy." Extravagant German war aims and prospects of another submarine crisis confirmed House's suspicion that Germany directly threatened the United States.[35]

Convinced of this danger, House decided to exceed Wilson's instructions by preparing for decisive action to support the Allies. He urged the French and British governments to accept his own plan for American mediation. This initiative would culminate in the House-Grey memorandum on February 22, 1916. In Paris he attempted to convince French leaders that the war's continuation held many perils. House used an argument that he had employed earlier in his discussions with British and German officials. He warned the French that the Allies might break apart in the future rather than defeat the Central Powers. He had presented the opposite specter to the Germans. Advocating the opening of peace negotiations before such an eventuality, he outlined his plan for mediation at a critical meeting with Premier Aristide Briand and Jules Cambon of the Foreign Ministry on February 7. House reached what he thought was "a complete understanding" with these French leaders. He summarized this agreement in his diary: *"In the event the Allies are successful during the next few months I promised that the President would not intervene. In the event they were losing ground, I promised the President would intervene."* House's promise expressed his belief that the United States should not permit a German victory. For the present, however, French leaders expressed no immediate desire for American mediation.[36]

Reporting this understanding to Wilson, House offered further information about the potential schedule for implementing his plan. He explained that "in the event the Allies had some notable victories during the spring and summer, you would not intervene, and in the event that the tide of war went against them, or remained stationary you would intervene." He also summarized the rationale for reviving his plan for mediation. If the United States entered the war, House wanted to do so for some larger purpose than countering Germany's submarine warfare. Wilson faced "a great opportunity" to restore peace, accomplishing what the "incompetent statesmanship" of the Old World had failed to achieve. In House's opinion, this humanitarian purpose would justify American intervention better than the protection of neutral rights from Germany's submarines ever could.[37]

Returning to London, House urged British leaders to approve his plan. Concentrating on Grey and Prime Minister Herbert Asquith, and also Balfour and David Lloyd George, he sought to persuade them to accept American mediation before the United States entered the war over the submarine issue. But they viewed such a possibility without alarm. Grey and Lloyd George frankly told him that they would welcome the United States as a belligerent. Trying to overcome British reluctance, House emphasized the prospect that Russia, Italy, and even France might conclude a separate peace with the Central Powers. "In these circumstances," he cautioned, "we would probably create a large army and navy, and retire entirely from European affairs and depend upon ourselves." Despite these attempts to frighten them, none of the British leaders appeared anxious to accept House's plan. Asquith thought that House's assessment of the Allies was excessively pessimistic, while Lloyd George and Balfour wanted to postpone any decision. All of them, however, continued to negotiate with House. They appreciated Anglo-American interdependence, although they rejected the extreme alternatives that he depicted. They desired neither American mediation of European disputes nor total American indifference toward the Old World.[38]

Once the Allies indicated their willingness to implement his plan, House expected the president to convene a peace conference. Anticipating that the Central Powers would refuse to attend such a conference, he thought that the United States then could join the Allies on the humanitarian issue of world peace. "If my plan was adopted," he noted, "I believed it would inevitably lead to an alliance between the United States and Great Britain, France, and Italy, the democracies of the world." If, on the other hand, Germany accepted Wilson's invitation, House assumed that he personally would convene a conference at The Hague to discuss the conditions of peace. Prime Minister Asquith wanted especially to know what role the president would play during such a conference. House's explanation convinced the British leaders that his plan at least would not jeopardize Allied interests. The next day Grey offered to draft a memorandum summarizing the plan. From the French ambassador in London as well as from House himself, he had learned of House's earlier understanding with Briand and Cambon. Grey prepared the memorandum in the form of a report to the French government. House's search for peace now culminated in an agreement with Great Britain along the lines of his previous understanding with France.[39]

The House-Grey memorandum of February 22, 1916, outlined the plan for American mediation. The British foreign secretary reported to the French that "Colonel House told me that President Wilson was ready, on hearing from France and England that the moment was opportune, to propose that a Conference should be summoned to put an end to the war." The memorandum also included House's warning that the Allies should agree to implement the plan before defeat was imminent. During the discussions with the Allied leaders, House had gone into greater detail than ever before regarding specific peace terms. To Briand and Cambon he had indicated that France might regain Alsace and Lorraine, and that Russia and Germany might obtain concessions in Asia Minor at the expense of Turkey. On his way from Paris to London, House had suggested during a brief visit with King Albert of Belgium that his country should consent to sell the Belgian Congo to Germany as compensation for its loss of other

African colonies to the British Empire. House definitely favored the restoration of Belgium itself. Although avoiding
firm commitments, he continued these discussions with
British leaders. Lloyd George attempted in vain to gain an
explicit agreement from him on the terms that the United
States would support at the proposed peace conference. House
expressed only his own views.[40]

Immediately returning to the United States, House solic-
ited Wilson's endorsement of his plan for American mediation.
On March 6 he explained the project and gained the president's
approval of the House-Grey memorandum. The circumstances
surrounding this decision suggested a substantial difference
between House and Wilson in their interpretations of the
document. Although welcoming the prospect of a peace conference, the president refused to give any commitment that
might involve the United States in the war. He carefully
inserted the word "probably" into the document, thereby
avoiding a definite promise regarding American action following an unsuccessful peace conference. He declined to
promise that the United States would leave the conference as
a belligerent on the Allies' side even if Germany were to
make extravagant demands. House reported this significant
change when notifying Grey about Wilson's endorsement of
the memorandum.[41]

V

Wilson's public and private statements during the early
months of 1916 revealed the significance of adding the word
"probably" to the House-Grey memorandum. At the beginning
of the year, Joseph P. Tumulty, his personal secretary, had
urged him to take "vigorous action" in the submarine controversy, informing him that the American people were beginning
to think that "there was a lack of leadership" in Washington.
Wilson welcomed no such advice. He earnestly strove to
prevent a rupture in diplomatic relations with Germany.
"You must know," the president explained, "that when I
consider this matter, I can only consider it as the forerunner
of war. I believe that the sober-minded people of this country
will applaud any efforts I may make without the loss of honor
to keep this country out of war."[42]

Seeking to insulate the Western Hemisphere from the Old World's problems, Wilson continued to promote Pan-Americanism. Along with first Bryan and then Lansing at the State Department, he and House had endeavored throughout 1915 to convince the ABC countries to accept the proposed treaty. They attempted to persuade the Latin Americans to join the United States in a partnership to uphold the Monroe Doctrine. After a year of failure, the president decided to publicize his proposal for a Pan-American treaty. He appealed to the Latin American nations to unite with the United States "in guaranteeing to each other absolutely political independence and territorial integrity." Addressing the Pan-American Scientific Congress in Washington on January 6, 1916, he advocated "the ordered progress of society" in South as well as North America. The purpose of the treaty, he explained, was to achieve "not only the international peace of America but the domestic peace of America." It would provide, in effect, a guarantee against internal revolution as well as external aggression. Wilson claimed that "it is just as much to our interest to assist each other to the orderly processes within our own borders as it is to orderly processes in our controversies with one another." This form of international social control offered "the hope of the world."[43]

Charles W. Eliot, president emeritus of Harvard University, seized upon Wilson's advocacy of Pan-Americanism to encourage him to expand the U.S. role in world affairs. From the beginning of the European war, Eliot had identified with the Allies. If necessary to prevent Germany and Austria-Hungary from achieving victory, he thought that the United States should end its strict neutrality. The American people, he told the president, would approve the use of force to protect western civilization despite the advice of George Washington in his Farewell Address to keep out of European affairs. By early 1915, Eliot had hoped that the ABC countries would join the United States in "an American League" to restore order in Mexico, believing that this would provide "a suggestive precedent for a European League to keep the peace of Europe." After Wilson's Pan-American address, therefore, Eliot urged him to express the same sympathy for France as he did for Latin America, emphasizing the American stake in "the portentous struggle between democracy and autocracy." The president rejected this advice because it conflicted with "the policy of detachment from the European struggle which I have hitherto so sedulously sought to maintain." Wanting him to abandon this traditional policy, Eliot advised Wilson to identify the United States with the French republic. He did not think that the American government should remain aloof as "an umpire or conciliator" between the opposing coalitions. Eliot implored Wilson to expand his Pan-Americanism into a humanitarian proclamation of American ideals for the benefit of the Old World as well.[44]

Wilson's reluctance to entangle the United States in Europe appeared in his justification for preparedness as well as his answer to Eliot. As Congress began to consider his program for military and naval preparedness in mid-January 1916, Tumulty advised Wilson to take his case to the country. He wanted the president to defend it against the pacifists on one side and the militarists on the other. Both extremes, from Bryan to Theodore Roosevelt, appeared to jeopardize its chances in Congress.[45]

Wilson accepted Tumulty's advice to explain his preparedness program to the country. Traveling in late January and early February from New York to Milwaukee, on to Kansas City, and back to Washington, he delivered most of his addresses in the Midwest. As in his annual message to Congress, he advocated a larger army and navy for the sole purpose of defending the United States and the Western Hemisphere. He promised to adhere to the nation's diplomatic tradition, reiterating his determination to remain neutral in thought as well as deed. "There is no precedent in American history for any action of aggression on the part of the United States or for any action which might mean that America is seeking to connect herself with the controversies on the other side of the water," the president proclaimed. "Men who seek to provoke us to such action have forgotten the traditions of the United States, but it behooves those with whom you have entrusted office to remember the traditions of the United States and to see to it that the actions of the Government are made to square with those traditions." Wilson defended his military and naval program with the two themes of peace and honor, using the standard that he had first stated in reference to the Mexican Revolution. He now applied these themes to the European war. He reiterated his commitment to peace but warned that at some time in the future the United States might not be able to avoid war without sacrificing national honor. To prevent this possible sacrifice, the president exhorted the American people to support military and naval preparedness.[46]

Wilson defended his foreign policy against critics who advocated American intervention into the European war and also those who opposed his preparedness program. He explained that "there are actually men in America who are preaching war, who are preaching the duty of the United States to do what it never would before—seek entanglement in the controversies which have arisen on the other side of the water—abandon its habitual and traditional policy and deliberately engage in the conflict which is now engulfing the rest of the world. . . . I believe that I more truly speak the spirit of America when I say that that spirit is a spirit of peace." At the same time, the president refused to pay the price of national honor to preserve peace. In reference to the second group he observed: "Yet there are some men amongst us preaching peace who go much further than I can go. . . . There is a price which is too great to pay for peace, and that price can be put in one word. One can not pay the price of self-respect." Although hoping to maintain neutrality, Wilson signaled his willingness to enter the war if that became necessary to preserve the national honor.[47]

Given Wilson's categories of thought, the question of war or peace would depend upon his definition of American rights. He articulated his views on this subject during the preparedness campaign: "We are more indispensable now to the nations at war by the maintenance of our peace than we could possibly be to either side if we engaged in the war, and therefore there is a moral obligation laid upon us to keep out of this war if possible." Yet peace was not obligatory under all circumstances. He also argued that "there is a moral obligation laid upon us to keep free the courses of our commerce and of our finance, and I believe that America stands ready to vindicate those rights. But there are rights higher than either of those, higher than the rights of individual Americans outside of America, I mean the rights of mankind. We have made ourselves the guarantors of the rights of national sovereignty and of popular sovereignty on this side of the water in both the continents of the Western Hemisphere." Whether or not the Latin American nations joined the United States in the proposed Pan-American treaty, Wilson intended to uphold the Monroe Doctrine. In the New World he resolved to establish control by the United States through either multi-lateral or unilateral methods. Besides the defense of the Western Hemisphere and the protection of U.S. commerce and finance, he identified the national honor with the right of Americans to travel on belligerent passenger ships.[48]

In February 1916, encouraged by Bryan, Congress began to consider various resolutions to prohibit American citizens from traveling on passenger liners of belligerent countries. Despite overwhelming support for this measure in both the Senate and the House of Representatives, including that of the Democratic leadership, the president refused to modify the position that he had taken during the *Lusitania* crisis. He explained in a public letter to Senator William J. Stone that he would "not consent to any abridgement of the rights of American citizens in any respect. The honor and self-respect of the nation is involved. We covet peace, and shall preserve it at any cost but the loss of honor. To forbid our people to exercise their rights for fear we might be called upon to vindicate them would be a deep humiliation indeed." Wilson fully identified the protection of neutral rights with the preservation of American independence. He continued, lifting a statement from one of Tumulty's letters, to assert that "what we are contending for in this matter is of the very essence of the things that have made America a sovereign nation. She cannot yield them without conceding her own impotency as a nation and making virtual surrender of her independent position among the nations of the world." Investing his own ego on this issue and making it a matter of national prestige, Wilson intended to dominate Congress. Because most supporters of resolutions to limit the right of Americans to travel on the belligerents' passenger ships were Democrats, Wilson's strong letter succeeded in thwarting congressional action. They decided not to challenge their own party's leader in the White House.[49]

Democrats in Congress, however, again with Bryan's encouragement, challenged the president's plans for expanding and reorganizing the army and navy. When his preparedness campaign failed to have an appreciable effect on senators and representatives, Wilson decided to compromise. His flexibility exceeded that of Secretary of War Garrison, who resigned from the cabinet. Eventually, the president obtained most of his program as Congress enacted legislation for the army in

June and for the navy in August 1916. Two years after the beginning of the European war, the United States was just starting to improve its armed forces.[50]

Despite fears of Bryan Democrats to the contrary, Wilson sincerely attempted to follow a policy of neutrality. His endorsement of Lansing's proposal for a modus vivendi clearly revealed this attempt. On January 18, 1916, the secretary of state had proposed that the Allies disarm their merchant ships in return for a pledge from the Central Powers to abide by the rules of cruiser warfare under international law. Lansing and Wilson hoped to avert another submarine crisis in German-American relations. Because armed British merchant ships attacked German submarines when they came to the surface to give a warning, the Germans had argued that adherence to cruiser rules virtually prohibited the use of submarines against Allied commerce. The difficulty for the United States arose from the fact that many ships, such as the *Lusitania*, carried cargoes of contraband as well as passengers. In effect, American insistence that German submarines abide by the rules of cruiser warfare to avoid the loss of American lives had protected Allied shipping from this new weapon. Both Lansing and Wilson wanted to extricate the United States from this unneutral position. They hoped to gain Allied approval of the modus vivendi in order to remove any reason—or even pretext—for Germany to resort to indiscriminate submarine attacks that would involve the United States in the war. They sought thereby to avoid forcing Berlin into a choice between abandoning submarine warfare and ignoring traditional international law.[51]

Lansing's modus vivendi had seriously antagonized the Allies and jeopardized House's peace mission. The British saw no reason to make any concession in return for a German pledge to abide by international law as they understood it. An American conflict with Germany over submarines would not appear as bad news to them. This negative response in London prevented the United States from reaching an agreement that was mutually acceptable to the Allies and the Central Powers. Aware of intense British and also French reaction against the modus vivendi, House had urged Wilson to drop the secretary's proposal before it resulted in the failure of his mission. Acting on this advice, the president reluctantly decided on February 13 to suspend the negotiations. He immediately notified House. Two days later Lansing announced this decision to the press. It cleared the way in London for the conclusion of the House-Grey memorandum. British leaders had indicated their general approval of House's plan for American mediation, and now Grey offered to summarize this agreement in a memorandum.[52]

Despite the significance of Wilson's decision to drop the modus vivendi proposal, he retained his basic commitment to the policy it represented. He still hoped to avoid conflict with Germany over submarines. In contrast to House, he lamented the negative British reaction to this attempt to preserve American neutrality. As in mid-January when he had first approved Lansing's proposal, the president still believed that the modus vivendi would sacrifice neither British nor German interests, while it would enhance American neutrality by averting a submarine crisis.[53]

All of these circumstances early in 1916 indicated the significance of Wilson's insertion of "probably" into the House-Grey memorandum. Both his private statements to Tumulty and Eliot and his public addresses during the preparedness campaign emphasized his determination to maintain neutrality. The proposed modus vivendi represented a sincere attempt to adjust this policy to the new forms of warfare. He hoped thereby to avoid conflict with Imperial Germany over submarine warfare, a goal shared by Congress and especially by its Democratic members. The lack of military and naval preparedness, as the president emphasized, precluded American participation in the European war in the near future. Because Congress had not yet enacted his program to expand U.S. armed forces, he realized that the country was not prepared for war. Under these circumstances it would have been irresponsible for Wilson to approve the House-Grey memorandum without the significant qualification that he inserted. He acted with prudence. This was a prime example of practicality in his diplomatic style, for neither he nor the country was ready to implement a new foreign policy that would involve the United States in the European war. The president still offered no realistic assessment of the balance of power, ignoring the potential necessity for American military involvement in Europe to preserve it. Traditional aloofness continued to characterize the nation's stance toward the Old World.

Notes

1. Baker and Dodd, *Public Papers* 3:71.
2. Ibid. 3:151-59; Proclamation, August 4, 1914, Wilson Papers, Ser. 4, File 1645.
3. Diary of Colonel House, May 11, 1914, House to Wilson, May 29, June 3, 26, July 3, 9, 9, 1914, House to Arthur Zimmermann, July 8, 1914, House to William II (German kaiser), July 8, 1914, in Link, *Papers* 30:22-23, 108-9, 139-40, 214-15, 247-48, 265-67; House to Wilson, May 28, June 3, 17, 26, July 1, 3, 9, 1914, Edward M. House Papers, Drawer 49, File 3, Yale University Library, New Haven, Connecticut; Wilson to House, May 15, June 16, July 9, 1914, House Papers, Drawer 49, File 15. See also John Milton Cooper, Jr., " 'An Irony of Fate': Woodrow Wilson's Pre-World War I Diplomacy," *Diplomatic History* 3 (Fall 1979): 425-37.
4. Myron T. Herrick to Bryan, July 28, 1914, Walter Hines Page to Wilson, July 29, August 2, 9, 1914, Page to Bryan, July 29, 31, 1914, Remarks at a Press Conference, July 30, 1914, House to Wilson, July 31, August 1, 22, 1914, Diary of Colonel House, August 30, 1914, in Link, *Papers* 30:313-17, 323-25, 327, 329-31, 366-71, 432-33, 461-65; House to Wilson, July 31, August 1, 3, 5, 5, 22, 1914, House Papers, Drawer 49, File 3; Wilson to House, August 3, 4, 5, 6, 25, 1914, House Papers, Drawer 49, File 15; Bryan to Wilson, August 28, 1914, U.S. Department of State, *Papers Relating to the Foreign Relations of the United States: The Lansing Papers, 1914-1920*, 2 vols. (Washington, DC: Government Printing Office, 1939-40), 1:7.
5. House to Wilson, September 5, 1914, House to Zimmermann, September 5, 1914, in Link, *Papers* 30:488-89; Cecil Spring-Rice to Edward Grey, September 8, 20, October 10, December 24, 1914, James W. Gerard (U.S. ambassador to Germany) to German Foreign Office, September 8, 1914, Jean Jules Jusserand (French ambassador to the United States) to French Foreign Ministry, September 8, 1914, Page to Bryan, September 10, 1914, Bryan to Wilson, September 16, 1914, House to Wilson, September 18, 22, October 8, December 26, 27, 1914, Remarks at a Press Conference, September 21, 1914, Diary of Colonel House, September 28, December 3, 19, 23, 1914, Gerard to Wilson, December 8, 1914, Grey to Spring-Rice, December 22, 1914, Zimmermann to House, December 3, 1914, in Link, *Papers* 31:13-15, 21-22, 37, 45, 62-63, 76-77, 94-95, 137, 140-41, 384-87, 426-27, 490, 517-20, 522-23, 535, 540-41; House to Wilson, September 5, 6, 16, 18, 19, 20, 22, October 6, 8, 24, November 11, December 26, 27, 31, 1914, House Papers, Drawer 49, File 3; Wilson to House, September 8, 19, October 10, 16, 23, 29, 1914, House Papers, Drawer 49, File 15.
6. H. B. Brougham, "Memorandum of Interview with the President," December 14, 1914, in F. Fraser Bond, *Mr. Miller of "The Times"* (New York: Charles Scribner's Sons, 1931), pp. 142-43; Wilson to Otto J. Krampikowsky (Chicago resident), December 14, 1914, Wilson Papers, Ser. 4, File 1645G.

John W. Coogan, *The End of Neutrality: The United States, Britain, and Maritime Rights, 1899-1915* (Ithaca: Cornell University Press, 1981), argues persuasively that Wilson abandoned impartial neutrality under

international law early in the war. However, the president's sacrifice of
traditional neutral rights, resulting in a pro-British or anti-German bias
in American policy on maritime issues, did not indicate a desire to
intervene in the European war. He still hoped to keep the United States
out of the war, despite his reluctance to insist upon British compliance
with traditional maritime law. Coogan asks the right question and gives
the correct answer (p. 217): "Did Wilson then deliberately mislead an
isolationist public with promises of neutrality, all the while pursuing a
'realistic' policy of nonbelligerent aid to the Allies under the justification
of national security and in hope of creating a better world? The evidence
indicates that such was his effect but not his intent. The president saw no
contradiction between his public promises of neutrality and his unneutral
actions on maritime rights because he never admitted, in public, in
private, or to himself, that those actions were in any way unneutral."
Coogan criticizes Ross Gregory, *Walter Hines Page: Ambassador to the
Court of St. James's* (Lexington: University Press of Kentucky, 1970),
and John Milton Cooper, Jr., *Walter Hines Page: The Southerner as
American, 1855-1918* (Chapel Hill: University of North Carolina Press,
1977), for exaggerating the differences between Page and Wilson on the
war. This criticism is appropriate with regard to maritime rights, but not
on all questions throughout the war.

7. House to Wilson, July 4, 9, November 30, 1914, House Papers,
Drawer 49, File 3; Wilson to House, December 2, 1914, House Papers,
Drawer 49, File 15; Baker and Dodd, *Public Papers* 3:64-69; Diary of
Colonel House, December 16, 1914, Draft of a Pan-American Treaty,
[December 16, 1914], in Link, *Papers* 31:468-73; Diary of Colonel House,
January 13, 1915, in Link, *Papers* 32:63-66; Wilson to Bryan, January 28,
29, 1915, Bryan to Argentine, Brazilian, and Chilean Ambassadors,
February 1, 1915, *Foreign Relations: Lansing Papers* 2:471-73.

8. Wilson to House, January 5, 16, February 15, 22, 1915, House to
Wilson, January 8, 15, 22, February 9, 11, 15, 17, 18, 20, 20, 22, 23,
March 8, 9, 9, 14, 20, 22, 26, [29], April 11, 11, 12, 1915, Diary of
Chandler P. Anderson (lawyer), January 9, 1915, Diary of Colonel House,
January 13, 25, 1915, Page to Wilson, February 10, 1915, Zimmermann
to House, February 4, March 2, 1915, Gerard to House, February 15,
March 6, 1915, House to Gerard, February 17, 1915, House to
Zimmermann, February 17, 1915, Gerard to Bryan, February 19, 1915,
Johann von Bernstorff to German Foreign Office, February 19, 1915, in
Link, *Papers* 32:17-18, 41-42, 44-50, 63-67, 75, 81-82, 107, 119-22, 204-7,
211-15, 220-21, 234, 237-38, 242, 252-56, 262, 264-65, 266-68, 276-78,
340-41, 349-52, 372-75, 402-3, 411, 438-39, 455-56, 504-7, 513-14; House
to Wilson, April 17, 18, 30, 1915, Grey to House, [c. April 15, 1915], April 30,
1915, in Link, *Papers* 33:10-14; House to Wilson, January 3, 8, 15, 18, 20,
21, 21, 22, 22, 29, February 8, 9, 11, 11, 12, 13, 15, 17, 18, 20, 20; 21, 22,
23, 24, 27, 27, 28, March 1, 2, 5, 5, 7, 8, 9, 9, 13, 14, 15, 15, 16, 16, 20, 21,
23, 24, 26, 27, 27, April 5, 11, 11, 12, 13, 14, 16, 17, 18, 20, 22, 22, 26, 30,
30, 1915, House Papers, Drawer 49, File 4; House to Wilson, May 3, 1915,
House Papers, Drawer 49, File 5; Wilson to House, January 5, 16, 17, 17,
18, 28, 29, February 13, 15, 20, [22], 25, March 1, 8, 13, [18], 23, April [2],
15, 19, May 4, 1915, Gerard to Bryan, January 24, 1915, Page to Bryan,
January 15, 1915, House Papers, Drawer 49, File 16.

9. House to Wilson, May 9, 11, 13, 13, 1915, House Papers, Drawer 49, File 5; Link, *Wilson* 3:373.

10. Lansing to Gerard, June 9, July 21, 1915, U.S. Department of State, *Papers Relating to the Foreign Relations of the United States, 1915*, Supplement: *The World War* (Washington, DC: Government Printing Office, 1928), 437, 481; Lansing to Bryan, June 7, 1915, Lansing to Wilson, July 21, 1915, *Foreign Relations: Lansing Papers* 1:440-45, 463-64.

11. Wilson to Bryan, June 2, 1915, *Foreign Relations: Lansing Papers* 1:421; Link, *Wilson* 3:358-425. For an outstanding analysis of Bryan's thinking and of differences between him and Wilson see Kendrick A. Clements, *William Jennings Bryan: Missionary Isolationist* (Knoxville: University of Tennessee Press, 1982). See also idem, *Woodrow Wilson: World Statesman* (Boston: Twayne, 1987), for a generally favorable assessment of Wilson's presidency.

12. Baker and Dodd, *Public Papers* 3:321.

13. Wilson to Bryan, June 7, 1915, *Foreign Relations: Lansing Papers* 1:439.

14. Herbert Hoover to Wilson, May 13, 1915, Wilson to Hoover, May 26, 1915, Wilson Papers, Ser. 4, File 1645J.

15. House to Grey, June 17, July 8, 1915, House Papers, Drawer 9, File 8; Diary of Robert Lansing, I, May 3, 1915, Library of Congress.

16. Lansing Diary, I, July 11, 1915, January 9, 1916. See also Daniel M. Smith, *Robert Lansing and American Neutrality, 1914-1917* (Berkeley and Los Angeles: University of California Press, 1958); and Edward H. Buehrig, *Woodrow Wilson and the Balance of Power* (Bloomington: Indiana University Press, 1955), pp. 131-50. Both Smith and Buehrig exaggerate the realistic aspects of Lansing's thinking. While concerned with preserving a balance of power against Germany's bid for hegemony, he also hoped to protect American maritime rights from British as well as German violations. These conflicting priorities produced contradictions in Lansing's advice. He never clearly resolved whether Great Britain's sea power protected or threatened American interests.

17. Link, *Wilson* 3:223-27; House to Grey, April 12, June 1, 17, August 12, 1915, House Papers, Drawer 9, File 8; House to Wilson, June 16, 1915, House Papers, Drawer 49, File 5; Diary of Edward M. House, June 22, 1915, Yale University Library, New Haven, Connecticut.

18. Link, *Wilson* 3:218-19, 229-31; Grey to House, April 16, 24, 1915, House Papers, Drawer 9, File 8; House to Wilson, May 7, 1915, House Papers, Drawer 49, File 5.

19. Grey to House, July 14, August 10, 26, 1915, House Papers, Drawer 9, File 8; House to Wilson, August 9, 13, 1915, House Papers, Drawer 49, File 5; House to Wilson, August 9, 13, 1915, Grey to House, July 14, August 10, 1915, in Link, *Papers* 34:144-46, 186, 370-72.

20. House to Grey, September 3, 14, 1915, Grey to House, September 22, 1915, House Papers, Drawer 9, File 8. For Grey's overall views on war aims and mediation see Rothwell, *British War Aims*, pp. 18-38; and C. M. Mason, "Anglo-American Relations: Mediation and 'Permanent Peace,' " in F. H. Hinsley, ed., *British Foreign Policy under Sir Edward Grey* (Cambridge: Cambridge University Press, 1977), pp. 466-87.

21. House Diary, August 21-22, 1915; Wilson to House, August 21, 31, 1915, House Papers, Drawer 49, File 16; House to Wilson, August 22, 22, 23, 30, 31, 1915, House Papers, Drawer 49, File 5; Bernstorff to House, August 21, 1915, House to Bernstorff, August 23, 1915, Bernstorff to House, August 28, 1915, House Papers, Drawer 2, File 44; Wilson to Edith Bolling Galt (his future second wife), c. August 23, 23, 25, 1915, House to Wilson, August 22, 22, 30, 31, 1915, Bernstorff to House, August 21, 28, 1915, Lansing to Wilson, August 24, 1915, Wilson to Lansing, August 26, 1915, Wilson to House, August 31, 1915, Bernstorff to Lansing, September 1, 1915, in Link, *Papers* 34:296-99, 318-19, 329, 368-69, 372-73, 381-82, 388, 400-401; Link, *Wilson* 3:564-87.

22. House Diary, September 22, October 8, 1915; House to Wilson, September 10, 13, 17, 26, 28, October 1, 1915, House Papers, Drawer 49, File 5; Bernstorff to House, September 8, 11, 15, 1915, House Papers, Drawer 2, File 44.

23. House Diary, October 8, 12, 14-15, 17, 19, 1915; House to Grey, October 17, 1915, House Papers, Drawer 9, File 8; House to Wilson, October 17, 1915, House Papers, Drawer 49, File 5; Wilson to House, October 18, 1915, [House to Grey], October 17, 1915, House Papers, Drawer 49, File 16; Wilson to House, October 18, 1915, [House to Grey], October 17, 1915, in Link, *Papers* 35:80-82.

24. House Diary, July 10, August 22, September 22, 1915; House to Wilson, July 12, 14, 15, August 8, 1915, House Papers, Drawer 49, File 5; Wilson to House, July 14, 1915, House Papers, Drawer 49, File 16; Wilson to Garrison, July 21, 1915, Wilson to Daniels, July 21, 1915, Joseph P. Tumulty Papers, Box 4, Library of Congress, Washington, DC; Link, *Wilson* 3:137-43, 588-93.

25. Baker and Dodd, *Public Papers* 3:386.

26. Ibid. 3:406-28.

27. Lansing to Wilson, October 9, 1915, Wilson to Lansing, October 21, 1915, *Foreign Relations: Lansing Papers* 1:303-5; Lansing to Page, October 21, 1915, *Foreign Relations, 1915*, Sup., pp. 578-89; Wilson to House, October 18, 1915, Page to Lansing, October 15, 1915, House Papers, Drawer 49, File 16; House to Wilson, October 19, 1915, House Papers, Drawer 49, File 5; Horace Plunkett (Irish politician) to House, October 1, 1915, in Link, *Papers* 35:8-11; Link, *Wilson* 3:682-91.

28. Grey to House, November 9, 1915, House to Grey, November 10, 1915, Grey to House, November 11, 1915, House Papers, Drawer 9, File 8; House to Wilson, November 25, 1915, House Papers, Drawer 49, File 5; House Diary, November 10-11, 1915.

29. House Diary, November 25, 28, December 15, 1915; Diary of Colonel House, December 15, 1915, in Link, *Papers* 35:355-61.

30. Bernstorff to House, July 10, July 27, September 4, November 25, 1915, House to Bernstorff, July 12, 28, 30, November 26, 1915, Memorandum, October 30, 1915, Lansing to Bernstorff, November 24, 1915, Bernstorff to Lansing, November 25, 1915, House Papers, Drawer 2, File 44; House to Wilson, November 10, 11, 19, December 1, 7, 16, 21, 22,

1915, House Papers, Drawer 49, File 5; Bernstorff to Theobold von Bethmann-Hollweg, November 23, 1915, House to Wilson, December 22, 1915, in Link, *Papers* 35:240-43, 381-82.

31. Wilson to House, December 17, 24, 1915, House Papers, Drawer 49, File 16; House to Wilson, December 26, 1915, House Papers, Drawer 49, File 5; House Diary, December 24, 1915.

32. House to Grey, December 7, 1915, House Papers, Drawer 9, File 8; House to Wilson, January 11, 1916, House Papers, Drawer 49, File 6; House to Grey, December 7, 1915, in Link, *Papers* 35:383.

33. House to Wilson, January 15, 16, 1916, House Papers, Drawer 49, File 6; House Diary, January 6, 10, 1916.

34. House Diary, January 6, 8, 10, 14-15, 1916; House to Wilson, January 7, 7, 10, 11, 13, 15, 16, 1916, House Papers, Drawer 49, File 6; Wilson to House, January 9, 12, 1916, House Papers, Drawer 49, File 17.

35. House to Wilson, January 30, February 3, 1916, House Papers, Drawer 49, File 6; House Diary, January 28, 1916; House to Wilson, [January 30, February 1], February 3, 1916, in Link, *Papers* 36:52, 85, 122-23.

36. House Diary, February 2, 7, 1916; House to Wilson, February 3, 7, 1916, House Papers, Drawer 49, File 6; House to Wilson, February 3, 7, 1916, in Link, *Papers* 36:125-26, 138.

37. House to Wilson, February 9, 1916, House Papers, Drawer 49, File 6; House to Wilson, February 9, 1916, in Link, *Papers* 36:147-50.

38. House Diary, February 10-11, 1916; House to Wilson, February 10, 10, 11, 13, 1915, House Papers, Drawer 49, File 6; House to Wilson, February 10, 10, 11, 11, [13], 1915, in Link, *Papers* 36:166-68, 170, 173.

39. House Diary, February 10-11, 14-15, 17, 21-23, 1916; House to Wilson, February 15, 1916, House Papers, Drawer 49, File 6; Wilson to House, February 13, 1916, House Papers, Drawer 49, File 17; Wilson to House, February 12, [15], 1916, House to Wilson, February 25, 1916, in Link, *Papers* 36:173, 180, 217.

40. Memorandum, February 22, 1916, House Papers, Drawer 9, File 8; House Diary, February 7-8, 14, 1916; House to Wilson, February 9, 1916, House Papers, Drawer 49, File 6; House to Wilson, February 9, 1916, in Link, *Papers* 36:150-51. See also Buehrig, *Woodrow Wilson and the Balance of Power*, pp. 211-28.

41. House Diary, March 6-7, 1916; Note by E. M. H., [March] 7, 1916, House to Grey, March 8, 19, 1916, House Papers, Drawer 9, File 8; Diary of Colonel House, March 6-7, 1916, House to Grey, [March 7, 1916], in Link, *Papers* 36:262-63, 266-67. For the relationship between House and Wilson see especially Alexander L. George and Juliette L. George, *Woodrow Wilson and Colonel House: A Personality Study* (New York: Dover, 1964). Although their Freudian analysis is not persuasive, the Georges offer shrewd insights into the personalities of Wilson and House. But see also the critique of this book in Inga Floto, *Colonel House in Paris: A Study of American Policy at the Paris Peace Conference, 1919* (Princeton: Princeton University Press, 1973).

42. [Conversation with the president], January 4, 1916, Tumulty Papers, Box 4. For Tumulty's career as the president's secretary see John M. Blum, *Joe Tumulty and the Wilson Era* (Boston: Houghton Mifflin, 1951), pp. 55-259.

43. Baker and Dodd, *Public Papers* 3:439-45; Bryan to Eduardo Suarez-Mujica (Chilean ambassador to the United States), April 29, 1915, Bryan to Wilson, May 19, 1915, House to Lansing, October 12, 1915, Lansing to Wilson, November 11, 1915, January 6, 1916, *Foreign Relations: Lansing Papers* 2:482-88, 491-93; House to Wilson, July 19, 25, 1915, House Papers, Drawer 49, File 5. For Wilson's attempt and failure to promote Pan-Americanism see Mark T. Gilderhus, "Pan-American Initiatives: The Wilson Presidency and 'Regional Integration,' 1914-17," *Diplomatic History* 4 (Fall 1980): 409-23; idem, "Wilson, Carranza, and the Monroe Doctrine: A Question in Regional Organization," ibid. 7 (Spring 1983): 103-15; and idem, *Pan American Visions: Woodrow Wilson in the Western Hemisphere, 1913-1921* (Tucson: University of Arizona Press, 1986), pp. 45-56, 65-68, 74-77.

44. Charles W. Eliot to Wilson, August 6, 20, 22, 1914, in Link, *Papers* 30:353-55, 418-20, 434-35; Eliot to Wilson, February 19, 1915, in Link, *Papers* 32:263-64; Eliot to Wilson, January 15, 21, 1916, Wilson to Eliot, January 18, 1916, in Link, *Papers* 35:486, 500-501, 506-8.

45. Tumulty to Wilson, January 17, 1916, Tumulty Papers, Box 4.

46. Baker and Dodd, *Public Papers* 4:49.

47. Ibid. 4:71-72.

48. Ibid. 4:91.

49. Wilson to William J. Stone, February 24, 1916, ibid. 4:122-24; Tumulty to Wilson, February 24, 1916, Tumulty Papers, Box 4; Link, *Wilson* 4:167-68.

50. Link, *Wilson* 4:15-54, 327-41. For the politics of preparedness see John Milton Cooper, Jr., *The Vanity of Power: American Isolationism and World War I, 1914-1917* (Westport: Greenwood, 1969), pp. 87-105.

51. Lansing to Wilson, January 7, 1916, in Link, *Papers* 35:448-49; Lansing to Wilson, January 17, 1916, Wilson to Lansing, January 17, 1916, *Foreign Relations: Lansing Papers* 1:336; Lansing to Spring-Rice, January 18, 1916, U.S. Department of State, *Papers Relating to the Foreign Relations of the United States, 1916*, Supplement: *The World War* (Washington, DC: Government Printing Office, 1929), pp. 146-48.

52. Lansing to Wilson, January 27, 1916, Lansing to House, February 2, 1916, House to Lansing, February 14, 1916, *Foreign Relations: Lansing Papers* 1:338-39, 342; Lansing to Wilson, January 27, 1916, in Link, *Papers* 35:531-34; Spring-Rice to Grey, February 17, 1916, in Link, *Papers* 36:192-93; House to Wilson, February 7, 10, 10, 13, 1916, House Papers, Drawer 49, File 6; Wilson to House, February 13, 1916, House Papers, Drawer 49, File 17; Link, *Wilson* 4:142-66.

53. Wilson to House, February 16, 1916, House Papers, Drawer 49, File 17; House to Wilson, February 15, 1916, House Papers, Drawer 49, File 6; Wilson to House, [February 16, 1916], House to Wilson, February 21, 1916, in Link, *Papers* 36:185, 203.

CHAPTER 3

Collective Security and Intervention

Woodrow Wilson eventually led the United States into World War I, justifying intervention with his emerging idea of collective security. When Imperial Germany's submarine warfare finally forced him to abandon neutrality, the president called for the redemption of the Old World. His understanding of progressive history and social science furnished the intellectual foundations for a new foreign policy. He promised to create a postwar league of nations, applying American ideals to international relations. Yet, as Wilson's diplomacy also demonstrated a genuine prudence, practicality as well as idealism characterized his liberal internationalism.

The Allies, painfully aware of Wilson's reluctance to entangle the United States in European affairs, fought to achieve their goals without counting on American assistance. Although they would welcome the United States as a belligerent on their side, they did not want interference from Washington with their pursuit of victory over the Central Powers. They steadfastly resisted American mediation even after the conclusion of the House-Grey memorandum. Instead of peace based on deadlock in the war, the British foreign secretary anticipated Germany's eventual defeat. In a memorandum for the cabinet, Sir Edward Grey asserted: "Nothing but the defeat of Germany can make a satisfactory end to this war and secure future peace." He believed that Great Britain, which was less exposed than the continental Allies, should not seriously contemplate peace negotiations until they were ready. Grey took into account the situation in the United States. In his judgment, American mediation on the basis of eliminating militarism and navalism posed a danger to British interests. Any conception of freedom of the seas that reflected Secretary of State Robert Lansing's modus vivendi would hardly satisfy Great Britain. Even Edward House, during his recent mission, had refused to obligate the United States regarding the postwar territorial settlement. The president's general attitude toward Europe, as reiterated during his preparedness campaign, had demonstrated that his conception of a just peace did not coincide with Allied aims.[1]

II

Distrustful of Wilson's perspective, Grey resisted House's attempts to initiate American mediation. He appreciated the significance of the president's addition of the word "probably" to the House-Grey memorandum, despite House's effort to denigrate it. The British, he explained, would refuse such mediation until the French first requested it, and they were still unwilling to entrust their future to a peace conference under American auspices. Grey declined even to recommend this course to the French.[2]

Despite Allied disinterest, the United States persisted in promoting mediation to end the war before German submarines destroyed that option. The prospect of war with Berlin over the submarine issue continued to motivate the Wilson administration to seek peace in Europe. A new crisis erupted after a German submarine torpedoed the *Sussex* on March 24, 1916. This British-owned channel steamer, flying the French flag and carrying 325 passengers on that day, managed to reach port without sinking. Although none of the twenty-five Americans on board was killed, the president, and especially House and Lansing, believed that the incident required a decisive response. By firing at the *Sussex* without warning, the submarine commander violated the pledge that Germany had given after the *Arabic* sinking. House and Lansing favored an immediate break in diplomatic relations with Germany. Wilson hesitated, however, to take such drastic action because he believed it would preclude American mediation. To overcome the president's reluctance, House argued that a diplomatic break would not necessarily prevent Germany from accepting this mediation. On the other hand, the failure of the United States to protest against the German violation of international law would sacrifice the Allies' respect and render mediation impossible. "Our becoming a belligerent," House insisted, "would not be without its advantages in as much as it would strengthen your position at home and with the Allies."[3]

Wilson decided to seek peace among the European belligerents before protesting against the attack on the *Sussex*. On April 6 he drafted a cable, which House would send to Grey, urging the Allies to accept American mediation. In a separate letter House explained that "the President and I both think if we are once in the war it will lengthen it indefinitely for the reason that there will be no one left to lead the way out." Opposition in Congress to war with Germany over the right of Americans to travel on ships of belligerent countries also concerned House. Attributing his own belief to Wilson, he further explained that "we are not so sure of the support of the American people upon the submarine issue, while we are confident that they would respond to the higher and nobler issue of stopping the war."[4]

Promptly responding, Grey again refused to suggest American mediation to the Allies. He obviously preferred an American break with Germany. "I cannot think that the entry of the United States into the war would prolong it," he observed, "whether it came about over the Sussex or over a conference and conditions of peace—indeed I feel it must shorten it." Grey's answer expressed a feeling of "profound disappointment" in the United States. As Ambassador Walter Hines Page informed Wilson, the British expected the United States to sever diplomatic relations with Germany before attempting to use its moral influence to end the war.[5]

Wilson finally decided to deliver a strong protest to Germany over the *Sussex* after receiving additional information about the attack. Now he also recognized that this action would not jeopardize the illusory prospects for mediation. Displaying the moral indignation that had characterized the *Lusitania* notes, he condemned German submarine warfare against Allied merchant ships as well as passenger liners. Rather than breaking diplomatic relations, as House and Lansing had advised, Wilson demanded an unequivocal pledge from Germany that its submarines would follow the rules of cruiser warfare under international law. The United States would sever diplomatic relations if the Imperial German government refused this pledge. Fortunately for the Wilson administration, Chancellor Theobald von Bethmann-Hollweg prevailed upon the kaiser to meet the president's condition. The Germans promised that their submarines, whether in the war zone or elsewhere on the high seas, would not attack either merchant ships or passenger liners without first giving a warning and afterward rescuing the victims. This *Sussex* pledge of May 4, 1916, ended the immediate crisis, thus allowing the United States to preserve both its national honor and its neutrality.[6]

Public opinion favoring some kind of peace initiative seemed to increase after the *Sussex* incident. Hamilton Holt, editor of *The Independent* and a founder of the League to Enforce Peace, urged the president to combine mediation with the idea of collective security. Unaware that Wilson already had made this linkage in preparing for House's mission earlier in the year, Holt asked him "whether it would be practicable to offer mediation now on the basis of a League to Enforce Peace? Perhaps if the future peace of the world can be guaranteed, the immediate problems will become relatively insignificant and can be easily arranged." Wilson and House had privately reached the same conclusion. They realized, moreover, that the Allied rejection of American mediation and the German concession in the *Sussex* pledge would increase tensions between the United States and the Allies. The American people would criticize British violations of neutral rights. In view of British and French reluctance to implement the House-Grey memorandum, Wilson decided to publicize his views in a major foreign-policy address. He had earlier declined William Howard Taft's invitation to speak at the annual convention of the League to Enforce Peace. Now, however, he welcomed this opportunity to proclaim his new vision of collective security.[7]

Wilson conceived of a future partnership among all peace-loving states to prevent aggression. Such a league of nations would extend Pan-Americanism throughout the world. He anticipated that the United States would exercise the controlling influence. Typical of American liberal culture, House advised the president to emphasize the similarity between private and public morality in the international conduct of the Great Powers. He presupposed the universality of

American values. Secretary Lansing favored a future league to promote international conciliation and arbitration but opposed any guarantee involving force. "I do not believe," he warned Wilson, "that it is wise to limit our independence of action, a sovereign right, to the will of other powers beyond this hemisphere." He feared that the extension of Pan-Americanism throughout the world would permit the European powers to violate the Monroe Doctrine. A league of that sort might enable them to interfere in American affairs and entangle the United States in the Old World.[8]

At the League to Enforce Peace convention on May 27, 1916, Wilson announced his commitment to postwar collective security. Proclaiming the views that he had expressed privately to House in December 1915, he reconciled a future league of nations with American neutrality during the current war. The twin impulses to isolate the United States and to reform the Old World characterized his new policy. Indifferent toward the aims of the opposing coalitions and the origins of the European war, he stated that "with its causes and its objects we are not concerned." Yet he emphasized global interdependence, claiming that the war had brought progress toward international unity and acceptance of universal rights.

Wilson explained his hope to promote peace in the present war and in the future. He called upon the belligerents to resolve their own conflicts and then to join the United States in a new system of collective security. He advocated "such a settlement with regard to their own immediate interests as the belligerents may agree upon. We have nothing material of any kind to ask for ourselves, and are quite aware that we are in no sense or degree parties to the present quarrel. Our interest is only in peace and its future guarantees." Wilson thus expressed the traditional American aloofness from the Old World while he anticipated a global role for the United States. His liberal internationalism combined unilateralism and universalism. He wanted the future "universal association" of nations to protect freedom of the seas. He also expected it to prevent wars that violated "treaty covenants" or started "without warning and full submission of the causes to the opinion of the world." Such a system of collective security would offer "a virtual guarantee of territorial integrity and political independence."[9]

Advocates of a league of nations applauded Wilson's address. Holt thought that it ranked next to the Declaration of Independence and the Monroe Doctrine as a classic American proclamation. Walter Lippmann agreed, claiming that "in historic significance it is easily the most important diplomatic event that our generation has known." Previously, he had called for the use of pragmatic methods—"mastery" instead of "drift"—to deal with the problems of American life. Then, contemplating the origins of the world war, he applied pragmatism to international relations. Weak states and chaotic conditions in the Middle East, Africa, Asia, and Latin America had created arenas of friction among the Great Powers, he argued in *The Stakes of Diplomacy*. Until the world found a better form of organization to replace modern imperialism, Lippmann expected this rivalry to continue. The war itself would not resolve the underlying difficulties that were destroying Europe. "The problems which drove it to the war will still require constructive solutions. Those problems arose out of the chaos and backwardness of weak states."

Advocating peace through organization, but dubious about the prospect of preserving liberalism in a centralized world state, Lippmann recommended permanent international commissions to deal with the world's "weak spots." He wanted to give these commissions extensive legislative and administrative power, although he refused to endorse a coercive League of Peace. The commissions could exercise "international control" as an alternative to imperialism and, if successful, might eventually serve as the embryo of a liberal world state. Aware of the world's diversity and the potential advantages of a balance of power among "civilized" nations, he still hesitated to call for such an ambitious form of internationalism to replace traditional American isolation from the Old World. But after Wilson endorsed the idea of collective security, Lippmann's initial skepticism about a universal league of nations gave way to greater enthusiasm.[10]

The president hoped that the Allies would welcome the promise of collective security, seeing in it the opportunity to end the war short of victory. This would enable the United States to promote peace without abandoning neutrality. "We are much more able to influence a just settlement now than we would be if the war continued very much longer, or if we should be drawn into it," House explained to Grey.[11]

Wilson's address generally failed to instill confidence in his leadership among the Allies, although it invigorated the League of Nations Society in Great Britain. His indifference toward the causes and objects of the war confirmed doubts in London and Paris about American mediation. Determined to achieve victory over the Central Powers, the Allies wanted no premature peace conference to end the war in a stalemate. The president's promise that the United States would help guarantee the political independence and territorial integrity of future members of a league of nations lacked credibility in view of his aloofness toward the current plight of Belgium and France. Seeking to counter this negative Allied reaction, House protested in vain that "if we are to take part in maintaining the peace of the world we could hardly be indifferent to the war and its causes and the President never intended to leave such an impression." Despite numerous exchanges with Grey and French Ambassador Jean Jules Jusserand, House failed to satisfy the Allies, who placed little confidence in American mediation or a league of nations because the United States developed these plans as adjuncts of its policy of neutrality.[12]

In view of the failure of his peace initiative, Wilson believed that he had no alternative but to insist that Great Britain as well as Germany should respect the neutral rights of the United States. His determination increased in mid-July after the British government, which already had disregarded the previous U.S. protest against its blockade and its definition of contraband, published a list of American firms trading with the Central Powers for the purpose of discriminating against them. The president was now, as he told House, "about at the end of my patience with Great Britain and the Allies." He decided to send "a very sharp note" to defend his country's rights against these British violations. This action clearly reaffirmed American neutrality as the election of 1916 approached.[13]

In his campaign for reelection Wilson defended his policy of neutrality and proclaimed his emerging idea of collective security. Both of these facets of his foreign policy expressed his Americanism. When he formally accepted the Democratic nomination on September 2, the president emphasized the importance of keeping out of the war for the purpose of restoring peace. He believed that the United States was uniquely qualified to undertake this task because it was the only disinterested nation in the world. As he privately stated, it had "nothing to gain and nothing to lose" and "certainly . . . nothing to fear" from the war. While other neutral nations pursued their own special interests, the United States championed apparently universal ideals. Although European statesmen failed to appreciate this unique characteristic, Wilson's belief in his country's innocence undergirded his twin impulses to isolate the United States and to redeem the Old World.[14]

Promising to keep the United States at peace without sacrificing national honor, the president warned that the election of the Republican candidate, Charles Evans Hughes, would result in war. Identifying him with prominent Republican advocates of greater military preparedness and closer ties with the Allies, such as Theodore Roosevelt, Henry Cabot Lodge, and elder statesman Elihu Root, Wilson defined the voters' choice as peace or war. His own reelection, he claimed, would enable the United States to stay out of the European war.[15]

Wilson also reaffirmed his commitment to a postwar league of nations. He announced that the era of "splendid isolation," or neutrality in that traditional sense, was over. He reconciled his idea of collective security with George Washington's advice, claiming that the United States still would avoid entanglement in the Old World while championing the rights of humankind. At Omaha on October 5, he explained his liberal internationalism. The acceptance of new global responsibilities by the United States, he asserted, represented the natural culmination of this nation's own experience. Its progressive history provided the foundation for a new foreign policy. Because of the frontier's closing in 1890, Americans had turned their attention to the outside world. The European war demonstrated that the United States no longer could escape the impact of foreign affairs. As a consequence, it needed to participate in a postwar league of nations. Wilson thereby harmonized his emerging vision of collective security with his continuing advocacy of neutral rights. From this perspective the rights of Americans were identical with those of all humanity. Adherence to neutrality during the present war and advocacy of a future league of nations therefore represented complementary, rather than contradictory, goals for the United States. The president's diplomatic style, combining both isolationist and internationalist features, expressed his fundamental belief in American exceptionalism.[16]

III

After winning the November 1916 election, Wilson turned his attention to a new peace overture. This action offered the best hope for keeping the United States out of the European war. Unlike Ambassador Page or some prominent Republicans, he refused to identify the interests of the United States with the Allies. British violations of American rights as well as Germany's potential resumption of submarine warfare made the international conditions increasingly intolerable. If he could end the war, then this would remove American difficulties with both the Allies and the Central Powers without sacrificing either national honor or neutrality.

House's conversations with Johann von Bernstorff encouraged the president to believe that Berlin might respond favorably to an initiative from Washington. The German ambassador had fostered this belief to gain American assistance in forcing the Allies to open peace negotiations with the Central Powers. He hoped thereby to forestall another German-American confrontation over submarine warfare. In this context Wilson began to prepare a peace note for submission to the belligerents later in the year.[17]

House, in contrast to his earlier optimistic attitude, now believed that prospects for successful peace negotiations were quite meager. He doubted that Imperial Germany would approve any terms acceptable to the Allies. He feared that the German government, however, might approve an American invitation to attend a peace conference, while still pursuing its aim of defeating the Allies. If the Allies, as he expected, then refused to attend the conference, the United States would find itself in an embarrassing position. He remembered Grey's earlier objections to American mediation, although he had not fully shared these with Wilson. In view of the general Allied unwillingness to implement the House-Grey memorandum, and especially of British violations of American neutral rights, House had concluded that the "reactionary forces in England" were gaining control of the cabinet. Despite his growing distrust of internal British politics, he still hoped to prevent the United States from aligning with the Central Powers. He discounted Bernstorff's assurances that Germany would welcome the opportunity to participate in a future league to enforce peace of the kind envisaged by Wilson. Consequently, House cautioned the president against any hasty action that might alienate the Allies and play into the hands of the Germans.[18]

Political considerations overruled the negative advice of Colonel House. During the campaign, by stressing his determination to avoid war, Wilson had regained William Jennings Bryan's support. He feared that, unless he made some dramatic gesture for world peace, Bryan again might become an active critic. Adopting an idea that the Nebraskan had proposed in *The Commoner*, the president decided to ask the belligerents to specify their war aims. In making this decision he consciously scrapped "those old plans" for American mediation that were outlined in the House-Grey memorandum. Instead, relying more on Lansing and less on House for advice, he prepared a peace note for delivery to both sets of belligerents.[19]

Wilson's peace note, transmitted by the State Department on December 18, 1916, stated explicitly that the United States was not proposing mediation but was merely requesting the Allies and the Central Powers to reveal the precise objectives for which they were fighting. The president minimized the differences between the opposing coalitions. He affirmed what he deemed to be "the fact that the objects which the statesmen of the belligerents on both sides have in mind in this war are virtually the same, as stated in general terms to their own people and to the world. Each side desires to make the rights and privileges of weak peoples and small states as secure against aggression or denial in the future as the rights and privileges of the great and powerful states now at war. Each wishes itself to be made secure in the future, along with all other nations and peoples, against the recurrence of wars like this and against aggression or selfish interference of any kind." To achieve these common goals and to prevent future wars, Wilson suggested a universal system of collective security to replace the old alliances and balance of power. His conception of a new international order depended upon a peace settlement reflecting the current deadlock in the war. For the first time, the president showed an interest in the specific terms of a European settlement. Yet by minimizing the differences between the Allies and the Central Powers, he revealed that he was still far more interested in peace per se than in the war aims of either side.[20]

Six days before Wilson sent his peace note the German government had made an overture of its own. On December 12, Chancellor Bethmann-Hollweg told the Reichstag of the Central Powers' willingness to begin peace negotiations with the Allies. That same day he formalized the proposal by dispatching a note to the Allied governments through the United States. Wilson feared that Germany's initiative might jeopardize prospects for Allied acceptance of his own proposal. To prevent this result, he hastened to send his note and instructed Lansing to dissociate the United States completely from the German initiative.[21]

House then attempted to persuade the British to postpone their response to Germany, fearing that a negative answer would harden Allied attitudes against any peace discussions. David Lloyd George, who had succeeded Asquith as prime minister earlier that month, informed the House of Commons on December 19 that his new cabinet shared the determination of the other Allied governments to continue the war until their objectives were achieved. He refused to consider peace on the basis of the present military situation as Germany desired. On December 30 the Allies formally rejected the Central Powers' invitation to start peace negotiations.[22]

The Allies had accurately assessed Germany's war aims in their refusal to negotiate. Berlin's military and political leaders wanted peace but without surrendering control over the Allied territory that they had occupied early in the war. Unwilling to express this desire candidly, Bethmann-Hollweg decided to reject Wilson's request for a statement of objectives. Foreign Secretary Arthur Zimmermann informed the American ambassador in Berlin, James W. Gerard, of this decision on December 26. Declining to state their specific aims, the Germans instead wanted the United States to press the Allies into accepting their own proposal. As Zimmermann's answer revealed, they desired direct negotiations with the Allies without any American participation

except to arrange the peace conference. The Germans hoped
in this manner to consolidate their previous military gains
without facing the risk that the United States might demand
concessions for the Allies' benefit.[23]

Despite Germany's negative response, Wilson continued
his search for peace. He quickly endorsed the initiative that
House undertook in discussions with Bernstorff on December 27. Although previously critical of the president for minimizing differences between the war aims of the Allies and the
Central Powers, House adopted the same tactic to encourage
the Germans to reconsider their answer. American willingness
to focus on the "permanent peace" of the world rather than on
the belligerents' war aims greatly encouraged the German
ambassador.[24]

After Wilson approved House's initiative, Bernstorff reported the December 27 conversation to Berlin, emphasizing
the opportunity that this new American approach offered to
Germany. Since May 27, 1916, when the president had first
publicly advocated a postwar league of nations, the Germans
had recognized the advantage of encouraging the United
States to concentrate on the future peace rather than on the
present war. In mid-August, Chancellor Bethmann-Hollweg
instructed Bernstorff to welcome any American peace proposal
as long as it permitted the belligerents to determine the
conditions for ending the current war. Acting under these
instructions during discussions with House in October and
November, Bernstorff had encouraged the belief that Germany
would respond favorably to a new peace overture by the
United States.

Wilson's peace note, by calling for specific statements of
war aims, temporarily thwarted the Berlin plan. The situation
quickly reversed when House suggested that Germany should
indicate a willingness to join in preparations for permanent
peace. In his report to the Foreign Office the ambassador
suggested an affirmative statement on the questions of a
league of nations, arbitration, and military and naval disarmament. He reminded his superiors in Berlin that "Wilson
lays comparatively little importance on the territorial side of
the peace conditions. I am still of the opinion that the chief
emphasis should be laid on what are here called the guarantees for the future." Noting the divergence between present
and future conditions of peace, Bernstorff urged his government to exploit this fundamental weakness in the emerging
American policy toward Europe.[25]

Zimmermann seized the opportunity that House's initiative opened to Berlin to achieve its war aims. Although absolutely opposed to American participation in peace negotiations, he hoped to convince the Wilson administration of Germany's desire to end the war. In accordance with Bethmann-Hollweg's policy of keeping "two irons in the fire," the foreign secretary wanted either to use American influence to bring the Allies into direct negotiations with Germany or to neutralize American reaction to its anticipated use of unrestricted submarine warfare. To convince the president that Germany genuinely desired peace, he authorized Bernstorff to inform House that the German government would join the United States in creating a league of nations and reducing military and naval armaments after the war. Zimmermann even offered to conclude an arbitration treaty. At best, if this response satisfied Wilson, the United States might force the Allies to begin negotiations with the Central Powers on the basis of the German peace note. If, as expected, the Allies still refused to negotiate, the president might blame them for continuing the war and then acquiesce in Germany's unrestricted submarine warfare.

By achieving its war aims in negotiations with the Allies or by preventing the United States from entering the war, the German government hoped to profit from the discussions concerning permanent peace. On January 15, 1917, Bernstorff conveyed Zimmermann's answer to House, temporarily convincing him that Germany earnestly desired peace. House, who initially had been pessimistic about Wilson's peace overture, now became positively ecstatic. Wilson, more cautious than his friend, wanted further information from the German ambassador. He wanted to know, for example, whether Germany would interpret an arbitration or "Bryan" treaty with the United States as a prohibition against submarine warfare during any future investigation of a dispute over the use of submarines. Yet he, too, was hopeful that the United States had finally discovered the road to peace.[26]

Despite his reservations, Wilson thought that Germany now posed less of an obstacle to peace than did the Allies. He regarded Allied war aims, which were outlined on January 10 in response to his peace note, as an unjustifiable demand for victory. Disheartened by the Allies and encouraged by Germany, he decided to state his own views to the Senate. Earlier that month, after House's initiative had evoked a positive response from Bernstorff, the president had begun to draft his "peace without victory" address. He completed this major statement of his European policy after receiving the Allies' answer.[27]

Thus, addressing the Senate on January 22, 1917, Wilson outlined the conditions under which the United States would join a postwar league of nations for the preservation of permanent peace. Calling on the belligerents to accept the American vision of a "peace without victory," he affirmed that "the right state of mind, the right feeling between nations, is as necessary for a lasting peace as is the just settlement of vexed questions of territory or of racial and national allegiance." Blaming the balance of power for the rivalries in the Old World, Wilson wanted to convert Europe to a new system of collective security. "Is the present war a struggle for a just and secure peace," he asked, "or only for a new balance of power? If it be only a struggle for a new balance of power, who will guarantee, who can guarantee the stable equilibrium of the new arrangement? Only a tranquil Europe can be a stable Europe. There must be, not a balance of power, but a community of power; not organized rivalries, but an organized common peace."

Wilson projected the ideals of his nationalism onto the Old World. Demanding the transformation of Europe, he called for its acceptance of "American principles, American policies." He assumed the universal applicability of his own country's heritage. His conception of a league of nations reflected its traditional aversion to entangling alliances. "I am proposing," Wilson announced, "that all nations henceforth avoid entangling alliances which would draw them into competitions of power, catch them in a net of intrigue and selfish rivalry, and disturb their own affairs with influences intruded from without. There is no entangling alliance in a concert of power. When all unite to act in the same sense and with the same purpose all act in the common interest and are free to live their own lives under a common protection." His ideals transcended the realities of the war between the Allies and the Central Powers. Once the Old World accepted these American principles, then the problem of reconciling international conflicts would, presumably, cease to exist. All nations would unite in pursuit of their common interest. What he neglected to explain, however, was how to move from the present wartime conditions to this postwar utopia.

Wilson envisaged the league of nations as the worldwide expansion of the Monroe Doctrine. He proposed "that the nations should with one accord adopt the doctrine of President Monroe as the doctrine of the world: that no nation should seek to extend its polity over any other nation or people, but that every people should be left free to determine its own polity, its own way of development, unhindered, unthreatened, unafraid, the little along with the great and powerful." Although Latin American nations had refused to accept his proposed Pan-American treaty, Wilson projected the same idea beyond the Western Hemisphere to the entire world. This would allow the United States to exercise its influence overseas but without entangling itself in the Old World. By focusing on conditions of permanent peace, he adopted the very approach that Bernstorff had encouraged. He explicitly left the settlement of the specific issues in the war to the European belligerents. "We shall have no voice in determining what those terms shall be," he announced. If the settlement failed to satisfy his sense of justice, he would not oppose it, but in that case he wanted no part in guaranteeing it.[28]

Characteristic of liberal internationalism, Wilson's diplomatic style combined unilateral and universal qualities. His foreign policy took American principles and applied them worldwide. At once idealistic and practical, he sought both to protect traditional American interests and to promote peace in the Old World. Calling for "peace without victory," he reaffirmed his country's neutrality while anticipating a postwar league of nations. He believed that strict adherence to neutrality would place the United States in the best position for contributing to peace between the Allies and the Central Powers.

House, meanwhile, continued his search for an elusive peace in discussions with the German ambassador. Bernstorff, clearly recognizing the opportunity, urged his government to accept Wilson's offer to arrange negotiations between the Allies and the Central Powers. Bethmann-Hollweg and Zimmermann, lacking Bernstorff's perception of the opportunity or the risks, refused to reconsider the German decision to resort to unrestricted submarine warfare, which already had been made. On January 9, acting on advice from Generals Paul von Hindenburg and Erich Ludendorff, Kaiser Wilhelm II had authorized submarines to attack neutral as

well as enemy ships in the war zones. These Germans hoped
to defeat the Allies before the United States could give them
decisive military assistance on the high seas or the western
front. Learning of this decision, Bernstorff warned that it
would result in war with the United States. Unlike the
military and political leaders in Germany, he did not discount
the military potential of the United States. He urged them
not to sacrifice Wilson's help in ending the war, which would
serve Germany's interests far better than its submarines
ever could. But he argued in vain. Bernstorff's instructions
from Berlin required him to inform Secretary Lansing, which
he did on January 31, that Germany would start unrestricted
submarine warfare in February. As he anticipated, the announcement of this new strategy abruptly terminated the
discussions with House.

Germany's decision to resort to unrestricted submarine
warfare shattered the earlier hopes of both House and Wilson
for peace in the near future. Rather than receiving the cooperation that they had expected, they now faced a crisis with
Berlin. House recorded in his diary that the president "felt as
if the world had suddenly reversed itself; that after going
from east to west, it had begun to go from west to east and
that he could not get his balance." For the past three months
he had nourished the hope that the war might end soon and
that the belligerents might even collaborate with the United
States in creating a league of nations for maintaining permanent peace. But now, as the American peace initiative
ended in obvious failure, Wilson faced the imminent prospect
that Germany's submarines would force the United States
into the war.[29]

IV

Secretary Lansing, in contrast to Wilson and House, accepted the German announcement of unrestricted submarine
warfare without chagrin. He had never expected the American peace initiative to succeed. By early December 1916 he
had concluded that the policy of neutrality placed the United
States in an intolerable position. At the first indications that
Germany might resort to more extensive use of its submarines,
he had advised the president to break diplomatic relations.

Before the Germans announced their decision, Lansing favored war. By this time the State Department had learned unofficially that the Berlin government had decided to expand the use of submarines. He hoped that this decision would force the United States into the war and thereby guarantee the victory of democracy over absolutism. After Bernstorff informed him of the decision to begin unrestricted submarine warfare, Lansing immediately apprised the president and urged him to break diplomatic relations.[30]

At the White House on February 1, 1917, Wilson listened to House's arguments, as well as Lansing's, for sending Bernstorff home. Yet he hesitated to take this action as he still hoped to avoid war. Lansing and House thought that the interests and honor of the United States required an immediate severance of diplomatic relations with Germany, probably followed by a declaration of war. Wilson, in contrast, became increasingly apprehensive that American entry into the war would result in the destruction of western civilization. Having no fear for the immediate security of the United States, he seemed willing to sacrifice even national honor, if necessary, to preserve America's strength for restoring Europe after the war.[31]

Wilson's conception of western civilization, including his belief in white supremacy, made him reluctant to enter the war. Like many others in the United States and Europe, he feared the yellow peril of Japan. He told Lansing that "he had been more and more impressed with the idea that 'white civilization' and its dominion over the world rested largely on our ability to keep this country intact, as we would have to build up the nations ravaged by the war." He had voiced the same concern for avoiding American participation in the war in early January. The president had emphasized to House that "there will be no war. This country does not intend to become involved in this war. We are the only one of the great White nations that is free from war today, and it would be a crime against civilization for us to go in." At the cabinet meeting on February 2, which he convened to consider the submarine crisis, Wilson reiterated the same theme. After raising the question of a possible diplomatic break, he immediately expressed his willingness to consider sacrificing the national honor, if necessary, to thwart what he perceived as a Japanese threat to western civilization.[32]

This racist justification for inaction apparently convinced none of Wilson's associates, and the president moved toward war. The cabinet overwhelmingly shared Lansing's opinion that the only honorable course was to break diplomatic relations with Germany at once. Accepting this advice, Wilson went to Congress on February 3 to explain his decision. He observed that Germany's new submarine strategy, as outlined in its announcement on January 31, directly violated the *Sussex* pledge of May 4, 1916. During the *Sussex* crisis, the United States had warned the German government that its failure to abide by the rules of cruiser warfare would rupture diplomatic relations. Since the German leaders, ignoring this warning, had declared their intention to violate international law, Wilson concluded that the only alternative for the United States was to recall Gerard and order Bernstorff out of the country. He stated that this nation, however, would take no further action until Germany's new strategy resulted in overt incidents.[33]

Wilson refused to seek rapprochement with Germany, preparing instead for national defense. Neither Bernstorff's final exchanges with House nor Switzerland's effort to resolve the German-American crisis produced any positive results. The president declined to negotiate with the Germans until they reversed their decision regarding submarine warfare. He still thought of American interests in terms of neutral rights. Although he was aware of the German government's intention—as part of its price for peace—to retain control over Belgium, annex a slice of France, and collect indemnities, he continued to view these aims as insufficient justification to join the Allies in the war. Still hoping to preserve both peace and honor, Wilson refused to consider belligerency against Imperial Germany except in retaliation for violations of American rights on the high seas by its submarines. He reiterated this view on February 26, when he called upon Congress to authorize the arming of merchant ships.[34]

The Zimmermann telegram dramatically posed another German challenge to American interests. Two days before Wilson advocated an armed merchant marine, Ambassador Page had sent to him and Lansing a copy of this telegram, which the British had acquired. Bernstorff had relayed it from Berlin to the German minister in Mexico City on January 19. In it Zimmermann had proposed an alliance between Mexico and Germany in the event that submarine warfare provoked U.S. entry into the war. He sought to entice the Mexicans by offering German assistance in reconquering Texas, New Mexico, and Arizona. He wanted Mexico to embroil the United States in a border war, but he never anticipated that Germany would make any substantial contribution toward a Mexican victory. The foreign secretary also requested the Mexican government to invite Japan to join this alliance. Although the Zimmermann telegram totally failed to achieve its intended purpose, it provided useful propaganda for the United States. Both House and Lansing welcomed the opportunity it offered. After Lansing leaked it to the press, American newspapers on March 1 published this evidence of a German plot. According to his subsequent assessment, the telegram produced a notable impact on Congress. House also had anticipated this effect. Especially after Zimmermann unexpectedly admitted its authenticity, the disclosure helped mold American public opinion against Germany.[35]

Imperial Germany's indiscriminate use of submarines pushed the United States to the brink of war. News arrived in Washington on March 18 that German submarines had sunk three American merchant ships. In view of these overt acts of aggression, Lansing rejoiced that "war is inevitable." For the first time, he felt free to advise a declaration of war against Germany. He urged Wilson to join the battle in defense of civilization. He explained that "the Entente Allies represent the principle of Democracy, and the Central Powers, the principle of Autocracy, and that it is for the welfare of mankind and for the establishment of peace in the world that Democracy should succeed."[36]

The president, however, still hoped to avoid war. On March 19, in separate conversations with Secretaries Lansing and Daniels, he expressed his desire to protect American shipping without abandoning neutrality. Lansing, apprehensive that the president might fail to act, turned to House for assistance. Sharing this concern, House immediately wrote to Wilson to advocate a declaration of war. He stated that "we can no longer shut our eyes to the fact that we are already in the war and that if we will indicate our purpose to throw all our resources against Germany it is bound to break their morale and bring the war to an earlier close." Not only Lansing and House but also the entire cabinet concluded that war was now inevitable. On March 20 the cabinet unanimously agreed that the president should convene Congress and recommend a declaration of war. They thought that Germany, by resorting to submarine attacks against neutral as well as belligerent shipping, left the United States no alternative. In view of this unanimous advice, Wilson made the inescapable decision.[37]

Calling Congress into session on April 2, the president recommended a declaration of war against Germany and summarized the rationale for his emerging European policy. Throughout the period of neutrality he had hoped to preserve both peace and honor for the United States. Germany's new submarine strategy now forced a choice, which British maritime practices had never done. He explained that "property can be paid for; the lives of peaceful and innocent people cannot be. The present German submarine warfare against commerce is a warfare against mankind." Refusing to sacrifice national honor under these circumstances, he preferred war. Adhering to the same conception of the American mission, Wilson abandoned the passive role of neutrality in favor of the active role of belligerency. He still favored a "peace without victory" and a postwar system of collective security. Referring to his earlier position, he affirmed: "Our object now, as then, is to vindicate the principles of peace and justice in the life of the world as against selfish and autocratic power and to set up amongst the really free and self-governed peoples of the world such a concert of purpose and of action as will henceforth insure the observance of those principles." For the first time, the president now interpreted the European war as a struggle between democracy and absolutism. He endorsed the interpretation, which Lansing had previously emphasized, that democracies desired peace while autocracies originated wars. "A steadfast concert for peace can never be maintained except by a partnership of democratic nations," he asserted. "No autocratic government could be trusted to keep faith with it or observe its covenants."

Wilson's foreign policy, which presupposed a direct relationship between democracy and peace, contained revolutionary implications. He expressed these in welcoming the recent revolution in Russia, which appeared to open that country to orderly progress. It seemed to be moving toward liberal democracy. He proclaimed the provisional Russian government as "a fit partner for a League of Honor." He also hoped for democracy in Germany, distinguishing between the people and their autocratic government. Developing his goal of national self-determination, he proclaimed his willingness "to fight thus for the ultimate peace of the world and for the liberation of its peoples, the German peoples included: for the rights of nations great and small and the privilege of men everywhere to choose their way of life and of obedience. The world must be made safe for democracy. Its peace must be planted upon the tested foundations of political liberty." To justify participation in the European war, Wilson called for the redemption of the Old World. Without changing his fundamental perspective, he projected American ideals onto Europe. His new crusade for democracy replaced his earlier policy of neutrality, but the president adhered to essentially the same mission. Previously, the reconstruction of Europe had seemed to require the United States to stay out of the war, even at the possible risk of sacrificing national honor. Now, in contrast, American belligerency appeared to Wilson as the necessary prelude to a postwar league of nations and a new era of peace.[38]

Four days later, on April 6, 1917, Congress voted overwhelmingly to declare war against Imperial Germany. This action seemed to unite most Americans. As Wilson was preparing his war message, Joseph Tumulty had examined the editorial opinion of the country's leading newspapers. "The consensus," he concluded, "seems to be that the end of the war will be accomplished sooner if we go resolutely about it, in dead earnest, using all the energy we can immediately put forth in preparing ourselves swiftly to put all of our force into the struggle." Even Bryan Democrats, who earlier had favored impartial neutrality, accepted the war as the inescapable consequence of Germany's submarine warfare. Wilson's advocacy of "peace without victory" had captured Bryan's imagination. "The basis of peace which you propose," he told the president, "is a new philosophy—that is, new to governments but as old as the Christian religion, and it is the only foundation upon which a permanent peace can be built." For such a purpose Bryan approved American intervention, joining the broad bipartisan coalition that now favored war.[39]

As he led the nation into war, Wilson justified the abandonment of neutrality by anticipating a postwar league of nations. Although he had not yet formulated his idea of collective security beyond some general principles, it provided the central feature of his new foreign policy. Encouraged by House, the president hoped to achieve "a scientific peace."

Yet he refrained from endorsing any specific plan for realizing this purpose. Herbert Croly and Lippmann, whose views on the foundations of peace he shared, applauded Wilson's emerging vision of liberal internationalism. The promise of international social control attracted not only these progressive journalists but also leaders of the League to Enforce Peace. Taft, too, concluded that "the lesson of the present situation is the necessity for the political organization of the world to stop the spread of a local war into a general conflagration."[40] Drawing upon his knowledge of progressive history and social science, Wilson thus provided a rationale for intervention that captured the imagination of other Americans who shared the same political culture. He promised a new system of collective security to replace the Old World's discredited balance of power and alliances.

Wilson's decision to lead the United States into the European war lacked the qualities of realism. He had not yet defined a national policy toward the specific conflicts in continental Europe. Except for the request in his peace note in December 1916, he had shown little interest in the belligerents' war aims. His vision of postwar collective security transcended those realities. Instead of intervening in the war to restore the European balance of power, he rejected that traditional system for preserving peace among the Great Powers. Only after German submarines had attacked American ships did he call on Congress to declare war. German warfare on the high seas compelled Wilson to act. Indifferent toward the potential for victory by the Central Powers over the Allies, he had neglected to prepare American armed forces for fighting in Europe. Even his plans for military preparedness anticipated the use of military and naval forces only for defense in the Western Hemisphere or on the high seas, not in the Old World itself. Wilson's ideals for a future peace exceeded the power of the United States in 1917. This nation could not fulfill them even by intervening in the European war. Although this weakness was obscured by the president's rationale for intervention, political goals and military strategy were not well coordinated. In short, his idea of future collective security provided an inadequate basis for a realistic foreign policy during the world war.[41]

Notes

1. Viscount Grey of Fallodon, *Twenty-five Years, 1892-1916*, 2 vols. (London: Hodder & Stoughton, 1925), 2:126-29. For Allied war aims see the outstanding studies by Rothwell, *British War Aims*, and Stevenson, *French War Aims*.

2. House to Grey, March 10, 1916, Grey to House, March 24, 1916, House Papers, Drawer 9, File 8; House to Wilson, April 8, 1916, House Papers, Drawer 49, File 6. See also John Milton Cooper, Jr., "The British Response to the House-Grey Memorandum: New Evidence and New Questions," *Journal of American History* 59 (March 1973): 958-71.

3. House Diary, March 29-30, 1916; House to Wilson, April 3, 1916, House Papers, Drawer 49, File 6; Lansing to Wilson, March 27, 1916, Wilson to Lansing, March 30, 1916, *Foreign Relations: Lansing Papers* 1:537-39; Lansing to Wilson, March 27, 1916, Diary of Colonel House, March 29-30, 1916, House to Wilson, April 3, 1916, in Link, *Papers* 36:371-73, 377-81, 387-91, 405.

4. House Diary, April 6, 1916; House to Grey, April 7, 1916, House Papers, Drawer 9, File 8; House to Grey, [April 6, 1916], Diary of Colonel House, April 6, 1916, in Link, *Papers* 36:421-26.

5. Grey to House, April 7, 8, 1916, House Papers, Drawer 9, File 8; House to Wilson, April 19, 1916, House Papers, Drawer 49, File 6; Page to Wilson, March 26, 30, 1916, in Link, *Papers* 36:369, 384-87.

6. Lansing to Gerard, April 18, 1916, *Foreign Relations, 1916*, Sup., pp. 232-34; House Diary, April 5-6, 1916; Lansing to Wilson, April 10, 12, 15, May 5, 6, 1916, Wilson to Lansing, April 17, 1916, *Foreign Relations: Lansing Papers* 1:542-65; Gerard to Lansing, May 5, 1916, *Foreign Relations, 1916*, Sup., pp. 257-60; Lansing to Wilson, April 10, 12, 1916, Draft of *Sussex* Note, [April 10, 1916], Diary of Colonel House, April 11, 1916, House to Wilson, April 15, 22, 24, 27, 1916, Bernstorff to House, April 14, 26, 1916, Wilson to Lansing, April 17, 1916, Wilson to House, May 5, 1916, in Link, *Papers* 36:447-56, 459-63, 466-71, 486-87, 490-96, 526-27, 541-42, 558-59; Bernstorff to House, April 14, 26, 1916, House to Bernstorff, April 15, 1916, House Papers, Drawer 2, File 45; House to Wilson, April 22, 1916, House Papers, Drawer 49, File 6; Wilson to House, May 5, 1916, House Papers, Drawer 49, File 17; Link, *Wilson* 4:222-79.

7. Hamilton Holt (editor of *The Independent*) to Wilson, May 11, 1916, Wilson Papers, Ser. 4, File 333; Tumulty to Wilson, May 16, 1916, Wilson to Tumulty, May 17, 1916, Tumulty Papers, Box 4; House to Wilson, May 7, 9, 14, 1916, House to Grey, May 7, 1916, House Papers, Drawer 49, File 9; Wilson to House, May 8, 9, 12, 1916, House Papers, Drawer 49, File 17; House to Grey, May 10, 1916, Grey to House, May 12, 1916, House Papers, Drawer 9, File 8; William Howard Taft to House, May 9, 1916, House to Taft, May 11, 1916, House Papers, Drawer 18, File 32; Taft to Wilson, April 11, 1916, Wilson to Taft, April 14, 1916, House to Wilson, May 7, 1916, Wilson to House, May 8, 1916, House to Grey, May 7, 1916, in Link, *Papers* 36:458-59, 481, 631-32, 652-53; Wilson to House, May 9, 1916, Taft to Wilson, May 9, 1916, House to Wilson, May 9, 1916,

House to Grey, May 10, 1916, Wilson to Taft, May 18, 1916, Tumulty to Wilson, May 19, [1916], Holt to Wilson, May 11, 1916, Wilson to Tumulty, c. May 19, 1916, in Link, *Papers* 37:3, 6-7, 75-76.

8. Memorandum by Ray Stannard Baker, [May 12, 1916], Wilson to House, May 18, 1916, House to Wilson, May 21, 1916, Memorandum, [May 24, 1916], Diary of Colonel House, May 24, 1916, Lansing to Wilson, May 25, 1916, in Link, *Papers* 37:36-37, 68-69, 88-91, 102-9; Wilson to House, May 16, 18, 1916, House Papers, Drawer 49, File 17; House to Wilson, May 19, 1916, House's suggestion for Wilson's speech of May 27, 1916, May 21, 1916, House Papers, Drawer 49, File 6.

9. Baker and Dodd, *Public Papers* 4:184-88; Address in Washington to the League to Enforce Peace, [May 27, 1916], in Link, *Papers* 37:113-16.

10. Holt to Wilson, May 29, 1916, Walter Lippmann to Henry F. Hollis (U.S. senator), May 29, 1916, in Link, *Papers* 37:120, 166; Walter Lippmann, *The Stakes of Diplomacy* (New York: Henry Holt, 1915), pp. 107, 125, 155, 187, passim. During World War II, Lippmann abandoned Wilson's liberal internationalism and advocated realpolitik in *U.S. Foreign Policy*. Although some elements of his later viewpoint were evident during World War I, he still epitomized the Wilsonian combination of idealism and practicality rather than the realism of his mature political philosophy. For an excellent account of the changes in Lippmann's thinking from World War I to World War II see Ronald Steel, *Walter Lippmann and the American Century* (Boston: Little, Brown, 1980), pp. 88-170, 404-17.

11. House to Grey, May 11, 23, 1916, House Papers, Drawer 9, File 8; House to Grey, May 23, 1916, House to Wilson, May 28, 1916, Wilson to House, May 29, 1916, in Link, *Papers* 37:100, 117-18.

12. House to Grey, May 27, June 8, July 15, 1916, Grey to House, May 29, June 28, August 28, 1916, House Papers, Drawer 9, File 8; House to Wilson, May 23, 31, 1916, House Papers, Drawer 49, File 7; Wilson to House, June 22, 1916, House Papers, Drawer 49, File 17; Page to Wilson, June 1, 1916, House to Wilson, June 9, 14, 25, 27, July 12, 14, 1916, House to Grey, June 8, July 15, 1916, Page to House, May 30, June 2, 1916, Plunkett to House, June 7, 1916, James Bryce (former British ambassador to the United States) to House, June 12, 1916, Alfred G. Gardiner (British author) to House, June 15, 1916, Franklin K. Lane (U.S. secretary of the interior) to Wilson, July 6, 1916, Noel Buxton (British MP) to Lane, July 5, [1916], Memorandum by Noel Buxton, [July 5, 1916], Grey to House, June 28, 1916, in Link, *Papers* 37:143-47, 177-80, 225-27, 294-96, 311-13, 370-72, 411-13, 422-24; Buxton to House, August 19, 1916, Bryce to House, August 26, 1916, Grey to House, August 28, 1916, in Link, *Papers* 38:54-55, 85-86, 89-92.

13. Wilson to House, July 23, 1916, House Papers, Drawer 49, File 17; Frank L. Polk (State Department counselor) to Page, July 26, 1916, *Foreign Relations, 1916*, Sup., pp. 421-22.

14. Baker and Dodd, *Public Papers* 4:275-91; House to Wilson, May 29, June 18, 1916, Wilson to House, July 2, 1916, in Link, *Papers* 37:121, 265-66, 345-46; Colloquy with Members of the American Neutral Conference, August 30, 1916, in Link, *Papers* 38:108-17.

15. For the Republican leaders see Merlo J. Pusey, *Charles Evans Hughes*, 2 vols. (New York: Macmillan, 1951), 1:315-59; Philip C. Jessup, *Elihu Root*, 2 vols. (New York: Dodd, Mead, 1938), 2:332-52; William

Henry Harbaugh, *The Life and Times of Theodore Roosevelt* (New York: Collier Books, 1963), pp. 439-68; John A. Garraty, *Henry Cabot Lodge: A Biography* (New York: Alfred A. Knopf, 1968), pp. 315-35; and William C. Widenor, *Henry Cabot Lodge and the Search for an American Foreign Policy* (Berkeley and Los Angeles: University of California Press, 1979), pp. 221-65.

16. Baker and Dodd, *Public Papers* 4:324-36, 344-49, 356-63, 376-82, 384-94; Address in Omaha, [October 5, 1916], Address in Indianapolis, [October 12, 1916], Campaign Address at Shadow Lawn, October 14, 1916, in Link, *Papers* 38:343-49, 412-19, 430-38.

17. Wilson to House, November 21, 24, 25, 1916, House Papers, Drawer 49, File 17; House to Wilson, October 20, November 20, 1916, House Papers, Drawer 49, File 7; Bernstorff to House, October 18, 1916, House to Bernstorff, October 19, 1916, House Papers, Drawer 2, File 45; Memorandum of Colonel E. M. House of a Conversation with the German Ambassador (Bernstorff), November 20, 1916, *Foreign Relations: Lansing Papers* 1:573; Memorandum by Walter Hines Page, [September 23, 1916], Memorandum by Walter Hines Page, [c. September 23, 1916], Diary of Colonel House, September 24, 1916, House to Wilson, October 20, 1916, Bernstorff to House, October 18, 1916, in Link, *Papers* 38:241-59, 494-96; House to Wilson, November 20, 1916, Wilson to House, November 21, 24, 25, 1916, Page to Wilson, November 24, 1916, Draft of a Peace Note, [c. November 25, 1916], in Link, *Papers* 40:4-6, 20-24, 62-67, 70-74.

18. House to Wilson, July 30, November 6, 30, December 3, 1916, House Papers, Drawer 49, File 7; Bernstorff to House, November 10, 1916, House to Bernstorff, November 12, 1916, House Papers, Drawer 2, File 45; House to Wilson, November 6, 1916, in Link, *Papers* 38:619; House to Wilson, December 3, 1916, in Link, *Papers* 40:132-35.

19. Wilson to House, December 3, 8, 1916, House Papers, Drawer 49, File 17; Wilson to Lansing, December 9, 1916, Draft of a Note to Entente Powers, [December 13, 1916], Draft of a Note to Central Powers, [December 13, 1916], in Link, *Papers* 40:197-200, 222-29.

20. Wilson to Lansing, December 17, 1916, Ray Stannard Baker Papers, Ser. I, Box 8, Library of Congress, Washington, DC; Wilson to Lansing, December 17, 18, 1916, Lansing to Wilson, December 17, 1916, Appeal for a Statement of War Aims, [December 18, 1916], in Link, *Papers* 40:256-62, 272-76; Lansing to Page et al., December 18, 1916, *Foreign Relations, 1916*, Sup., pp. 97-99; Lansing to Bernstorff, December 20, 1916, Botschaft Washington, 4A34 (Friedensverhandlungen), Heft 9a, Bd. 1, Politisches Archiv des Auswärtigen Amts (Political Archives of the Foreign Office), Bonn, Germany.

21. Joseph C. Grew (U.S. chargé in Berlin) to Lansing, December 12, 12, 1916, Lansing to Page et al., December 16, 1916, *Foreign Relations, 1916*, Sup., pp. 87-90, 94-95; Lansing to Wilson, December 14, 1916, Grew to Lansing, December 12, 12, 1916, Diary of Colonel House, December 14, 1916, Wilson to Lansing, December 15, 1916, [Lansing] to Page, December 16, 1916, Wilson to House, December 19, 1916, in Link, *Papers* 40:230-33, 237-43, 250, 276; Wilson to Lansing, December 15, 1916, R. S. Baker Papers, Ser. I, Box 8; House Diary, December 14, 1916; Wilson to House, December 19, 1916, House Papers, Drawer 49, File 17;

Bernstorff to House, December 16, 1916, House Papers, Drawer 2, File 45, and Botschaft Washington, 4A34 (Friedensverhandlungen), Heft 9a, Bd. 1, Politisches Archiv des Auswärtigen Amts.

22. House to Wilson, December 17, 18, 1916, House Papers, Drawer 49, File 7; House Diary, December 17-18, 1916; House to Wilson, December 17, 1916, in Link, *Papers* 40:262; Page to Lansing, December 19, 1916, Sharp to Lansing, December 29, 1916, *Foreign Relations, 1916*, Sup., pp. 101-2, 123-25.

23. Gerard to Lansing, December 26, 1916, *Foreign Relations, 1916*, Sup., pp. 117-18; Count [Johann von] Bernstorff, *My Three Years in America* (New York: Charles Scribner's Sons, 1920), p. 321; Bernstorff to *New Yorker Staats-Zeitung*, December 24, 1916, Zimmermann to Bernstorff, January 4, 1917, Botschaft Washington, 4A34 (Friedensverhandlungen), Heft 9a, Bd. 1, Politisches Archiv des Auswärtigen Amts; Gerard to Lansing, January 2, 1917, in Link, *Papers* 40:383-84.

24. House Diary, December 27, 1916; House to Wilson, December 27, 28, 1916, House Papers, Drawer 49, File 7; Wilson to House, December 28, 1916, House Papers, Drawer 49, File 17; House to Wilson, December 27, 1916, in Link, *Papers* 40:337.

25. Bernstorff, *My Three Years*, pp. 270-325; Bernstorff to German Foreign Office, December 29, 1916, in Link, *Papers* 40:362-65. For an excellent account of Bernstorff's efforts to prevent war between the United States and Germany see Reinhard R. Doerries, *Washington-Berlin, 1908/1917* (Düsseldorf: Schwann, 1975), pp. 106-19, 149-64, 218-57; and idem, *Imperial Challenge: Ambassador Count Bernstorff and German-American Relations, 1908-1917* (Chapel Hill: University of North Carolina Press, 1989), pp. 85-97, 127-40, 191-231.

26. Bernstorff to House, January 9, 1917, House to Bernstorff, January 17, 1917, House Papers, Drawer 2, File 46; House to Bernstorff, January 17, 1917, Botschaft Washington, 4A34 (Friedensverhandlungen), Heft 9a, Bd. 1, Politisches Archiv des Auswärtigen Amts; House to Wilson, January 15, 16, 17, 18, 1917, House Papers, Drawer 49, File 8; Wilson to House, January 16, 17, 19, 1917, House Papers, Drawer 49, File 18; House Diary, January 15, 1917; Bernstorff, *My Three Years*, pp. 325-58; House to Wilson, January 15, 16, 17, 18, 1917, Bernstorff to Bethmann-Hollweg, January 16, 1917, Wilson to House, January 17, 1917, in Link, *Papers* 40:477-78, 493-94, 504-8, 516-17. For Germany's policy toward the United States see especially Karl E. Birnbaum, *Peace Moves and U-Boat Warfare: A Study of Imperial Germany's Policy towards the United States, April 18, 1916-January 9, 1917* (Stockholm: Almqvist & Wiksell, 1958); and also May, *The World War and American Isolation*, pp. 197-301, 387-415.

27. House Diary, January 3, 11, 1917; Wilson to House, January 19, 1917, House Papers, Drawer 49, File 18; House to Wilson, January 19, 1917, House Papers, Drawer 49, File 8; Bernstorff to House, January 18, 1917, House Papers, Drawer 2, File 46, and Botschaft Washington, 4A34 (Friedensverhandlungen), Heft 9a, Bd. 1, Politisches Archiv des Auswärtigen Amts; Diary of Colonel House, January 3, 11, 1917, Lansing to Wilson, January 10, 1917, Grew to Lansing, December 21, 1916,

William G. Sharp (U.S. ambassador to France) to Lansing, January 10, 1917, Wilson to Lansing, January 11, 1917, Wilson to House, January 19, 1917, House to Wilson, January 19, 1917, Bernstorff to House, January 18, 1917, in Link, *Papers* 40:402-5, 428-36, 438-42, 445-47, 524-26.

28. Baker and Dodd, *Public Papers* 4:407-14; Address to the Senate, January 22, 1917, in Link, *Papers* 40:533-39.

29. Wilson to House, January 24, 1917, House Papers, Drawer 49, File 18; House to Wilson, January 20, 25, 26, 30-31, 1917, House Papers, Drawer 49, File 8; House Diary, January 31, February 1, 1917; House to Bernstorff, January 19, 1917, Bernstorff to House, January 20, 1917, House Papers, Drawer 2, File 46; House to Bernstorff, January 19, 1917, Bernstorff to House, January 20, 1917, Bernstorff to German Foreign Office, January 26, 1917, Botschaft Washington, 4A34 (Friedensverhandlungen), Heft 9a, Bd. 1, Politisches Archiv des Auswärtigen Amts; House to Wilson, January 20, 1917, Bernstorff to House, January 20, 1917, in Link, *Papers* 40:526-29; Wilson to House, January 24, 1917, House to Wilson, January 25, 26, 26, 1917, Lansing to Wilson, January 25, 1917, House to Lansing, January 24, 1917, Bernstorff to Bethmann-Hollweg, January 27, 1917, Bethmann-Hollweg to Bernstorff, January 29, 1917, Diary of Colonel House, February 1, 1917, in Link, *Papers* 41:3-4, 17-19, 24-27, 49-52, 59-63, 86-89.

30. Lansing Diary, I, December 3, 1916, II, January 24, 1917; Memorandum by the Secretary of State, December 1, 1916, Lansing to Wilson, December 8, 1916, January 31, 1917, *Foreign Relations: Lansing Papers* 1:227-37, 575-76, 582-84; Lansing to U.S. Ambassadors, December 21, 1916, *Foreign Relations, 1916*, Sup., pp. 106-7; Lansing to Wilson, January 12, 17, 23, 1917, Bernstorff to Lansing, January 10, 1917, Gerard to Lansing, January 21, 1917, in Link, *Papers* 40:447-53, 509, 552-53; Lansing to Wilson, January 31, 1917, Bernstorff to Lansing, January 31, 1917, in Link, *Papers* 41:71-79; Zimmermann to Bernstorff, January 27, 1917, Bernstorff to Lansing, January 31, 1917, Botschaft Washington, 4A34 (Friedensverhandlungen), Heft 9a, Bd. 1, Politisches Archiv des Auswärtigen Amts.

31. House Diary, February 1, 1917; Bernstorff to House, January 31, 1917, Diary of Colonel House, February 1, 1917, Lansing to Wilson, February 2, 2, 1917, in Link, *Papers* 41:80-82, 86-89, 96-100; Bernstorff to House, January 31, 1917, House Papers, Drawer 2, File 46, and Botschaft Washington, 4A34 (Friedensverhandlungen), Heft 9a, Bd. 1, Politisches Archiv des Auswärtigen Amts; Lansing to Wilson, February 2, 2, 1917, *Foreign Relations: Lansing Papers* 1:591-92.

32. Lansing Diary, II, February 4, 1917; House Diary, February 4, 1917; David F. Houston, *Eight Years with Wilson's Cabinet: 1913 to 1920*, 2 vols. (Garden City: Doubleday, Page, 1926), 1:229.

33. Lansing Diary, II, February 4, 1917; Houston, *Eight Years* 1:227-31; Baker and Dodd, *Public Papers* 4:422-26; Address to a Joint Session of Congress, February 3, 1917, Memorandum by Robert Lansing, February 4, 1917, F. K. Lane to George Whitfield Lane (lawyer), February 9, 1917, in Link, *Papers* 41:108-12, 118-25, 183-84; Lansing to Bernstorff, February 3, 1917, Botschaft Washington, 4A34 (Friedensverhandlungen), Heft 9a, Bd. 1, Politisches Archiv des Auswärtigen Amts.

34. Bernstorff to House, February 3, 1917, House to Bernstorff, February 4, 1917, House Papers, Drawer 2, File 46; House to Bernstorff, February 2, 4, 1917, Bernstorff to House, February 3, 1917, Botschaft Washington, 4A34 (Friedensverhandlungen), Heft 9a, Bd. 1, Politisches Archiv des Auswärtigen Amts; House to Wilson, February 2, 4, 1917, House Papers, Drawer 49, File 8; Gerard to Lansing, February 4, 1917, House Papers, Drawer 49, File 18; House to Wilson, February 2, 4, 1917, House to Bernstorff, February 2, 1917, Bernstorff to House, February 3, 1917, Wilson to House, February 7, 12, 1917, Gerard to [Lansing], February 4, 1917, Wilson to Lansing, February 9, 12, 1917, Lansing to Wilson, February 12, 23, 1917, Polk to Lansing, February 10, 1917, in Link, *Papers* 41:95-96, 117-18, 137-38, 173-75, 201-5, 273-77; Baker and Dodd, *Public Papers* 4:431.

35. Page to Wilson, February 24, 1917, House to Wilson, February 27, 1917, Memorandum by Robert Lansing, March 4, 1917, in Link, *Papers* 41:280-82, 296-97, 321-27; Frederick Katz, *The Secret War in Mexico: Europe, the United States, and the Mexican Revolution* (Chicago: University of Chicago Press, 1981), pp. 350-66; Barbara W. Tuchman, *The Zimmermann Telegram* (New York: Ballantine Books, 1958).

36. Lansing to Wilson, March 19, 1917, *Foreign Relations: Lansing Papers* 1:626-28.

37. Lansing to House, March 19, 1917, House Papers, Drawer 12, File 12; House to Wilson, March 19, 1917, House Papers, Drawer 49, File 8; Lansing to House, March 19, 1917, House to Lansing, March 20, 1917, *Foreign Relations: Lansing Papers* 1:628-30; Lansing Diary, II, March 19-20, 1917; House Diary, March 19, 22, 1917; E. David Cronon, ed., *The Cabinet Diaries of Josephus Daniels, 1913-1921* (Lincoln: University of Nebraska Press, 1963), pp. 116-18; Houston, *Eight Years* 1:241-45; Lansing to House, March 19, 1917, Diary of Josephus Daniels, March 19-20, 1917, Memorandum by Robert Lansing, March 20, 1917, in Link, *Papers* 41:429-30, 436-45.

38. Baker and Dodd, *Public Papers* 5:6-16; Diary of Colonel House, March 28, 1917, Address to a Joint Session of Congress, April 2, 1917, in Link, *Papers* 41:496-98, 519-27; House Diary, April 2, 1917.

39. Tumulty to Wilson, March 24, 1917, in Link, *Papers* 41:462-64, and Tumulty Papers, Box 5; Bryan to Wilson, January 26, April 6, 1917, Wilson to Bryan, February 2, 1917, Wilson Papers, Ser. 4, File 2400; Link, *Wilson* 5:390-431.

40. Report of a News Conference by Charles Merz (journalist), January 8, [1917], Remarks at a Press Conference, [January 15, 1917], House to Wilson, January 22, 1917, Croly to Wilson, January 23, 1917, in Link, *Papers* 40:421-23, 470-77, 539, 559; Lippmann to Wilson, January 31, 1917, Memorandum by Louis Paul Lochner (American Peace Society director), February 1, 1917, Newton D. Baker (U.S. secretary of war) to Wilson, February 7, 1917, Taft to Baker, February 6, 1917, House to Wilson, February 19, March 9, 1917, Jusserand to French Foreign Ministry, March 7, 1917, Lippmann to Wilson, March 11, 1917, in Link, *Papers* 41:83, 89-92, 153-55, 250-51, 354-57, 373-76, 388-90.

41. Richard W. Leopold, "The Problem of American Intervention, 1917: An Historical Retrospect," *World Politics* 2 (April 1950): 405-25, reviewed the historical literature, especially of the interwar revisionists, and called for "a more rounded and more realistic understanding of the

problem of American intervention in 1917." Reacting to the original realist critique, as well as to the interwar revisionism, scholars in the 1950s and 1960s praised the president's statecraft; see, for example, Daniel M. Smith, "National Interest and American Intervention, 1917: An Historiographical Appraisal," *Journal of American History* 52 (June 1965): 5-24; and Buehrig, *Woodrow Wilson and the Balance of Power*, p. 144. Most recent scholarship on Wilson's foreign policy has continued this theme; see, for example, Cooper, *The Warrior and the Priest*, pp. 303-23; and Calhoun, *Power and Principle*, p. 140. Patrick Devlin, *Too Proud to Fight: Woodrow Wilson's Neutrality* (New York: Oxford University Press, 1975), p. 676, substantially circumvents this historiographical question.

CHAPTER 4

War and Revolution

As the United States made the transition from neutrality to belligerency, President Wilson developed a new policy toward Europe. Before the declaration of war against Germany, he had not approved a strategy for the armed forces or a comprehensive peace program. Still unclear was the link between military methods and political goals in his conduct of foreign relations. The idea of a league of nations, initially fostered in the context of neutrality, became a general war aim. Wilson eventually gave more substance to this vague idea, but for now the abstract concept served in lieu of a more precise definition.

Wilson wanted to retain American independence in fighting the war and defining the peace. During the war the United States became an Associated rather than an Allied power. His belief in the country's innocence and uniqueness shaped the role of the United States. He projected American ideals onto the world as the universal basis for permanent peace, thereby internationalizing his conception of nationalism. He hoped to eradicate the causes of war, not merely to achieve some limited objectives in the current war. Instead of seeking to preserve the balance of power in a plural world, the United States engaged in a holy war to redeem the Old World.

Joseph Tumulty, while favoring intervention, advised the president to preserve national independence. On the eve of the American declaration of war he had brought to Wilson's attention an editorial from the New York *Evening Post*, which urged the nation to determine its own role in cooperation with the Allies. "The United States," it affirmed, "may temporarily join hands with the Allies, for the sake of better securing our aims, but this country must not at any time lose a free hand. If we are driven into war by the course of Germany, we must remain masters of our own destiny."[1]

Wilson's liberal internationalism incorporated the traditional American desire for isolation from Europe. In his second inaugural address on March 5, 1917, he had summarized his view of the world war. "We have been deeply wronged upon the seas, but we have not wished to wrong or injure in return," he had affirmed. Americans, he continued, "have retained throughout the consciousness of standing in some sort apart, intent upon an interest that transcended the immediate issues of the war itself." Believing this, he thought that it was more important to maintain his unilateral discretion for the eventual definition of peace conditions than to define a specific policy. After American entry into the war he issued an appeal to the nation. "There is not a single selfish element, so far as I can see, in the cause we are fighting for," he emphasized. "We are fighting for what we believe and wish to be the rights of mankind and for the future peace and security of the world."[2] In his view the United States was pursuing this altruistic purpose to transcend the old European rivalries and reform the international system.

The president expected Divine Providence to assist the United States in fulfilling its redemptive purpose, however vaguely defined. "There are times when words seem empty and only action seems great," he proclaimed on Memorial Day. "Such a time has come, and in the providence of God America will once more have an opportunity to show the world that she was born to serve mankind."[3] Religion and patriotism were joined in Wilson's appeal to the American people to take up arms.

Following the declaration of war by Congress, the British and French governments sent special missions to Washington to coordinate their political and military actions with the United States. The Allies revealed to the Wilson administration the desperate situation of their forces on the western front and pleaded for American troops as reinforcements. Foreign Secretary Arthur J. Balfour, head of the British mission, disclosed the Allies' secret treaties, but U.S. officials did not wish to discuss them. They wanted to avoid what Colonel Edward House called "secret entanglement with Europe." Wilson's friend hoped to postpone consideration of specific war aims while guarding against even the appearance of an alliance. He and Balfour discussed only the general outline of a future peace. "I said to him," House noted in his diary, "what I once said to Grey, that if we are to justify our being in the war, we should free ourselves entirely from petty, selfish thoughts and look at the thing broadly and from a world viewpoint. Balfour agreed to this with enthusiasm." This agreement would allow the Allies and the United States to fight against their common enemy regardless of whether they shared the same war aims.[4]

Responding to the Allies' requests for help, Wilson made the unprecedented decision to send American troops to Europe for combat. But neither he nor the War Department had adequately prepared for this action. The General Staff, which was responsible for developing war plans, had anticipated only a defensive war against Imperial Germany outside Europe. It had planned to defend the United States and the Western Hemisphere against a German attack but not to send an American army abroad. Before it could significantly influence the outcome of the war, the United States needed to raise, train, and transport troops to the western front. The War Department delayed this difficult task until after Wilson had delivered his war message to Congress. As a consequence of this delay, preparations were inadequate for the U.S. military role that the Allies anticipated.[5]

Wilson designated General John J. Pershing as commander in chief of the still nonexistent American Expeditionary Forces in Europe. On May 26, 1917, Secretary of War Newton D. Baker and Acting Chief of Staff Tasker H. Bliss ordered Pershing to France, where he would plan and eventually conduct military operations against Germany. Baker instructed him to cooperate with the Allies, "but in so doing, the underlying idea must be kept in view that the forces of the United States are a separate and distinct component of the combined forces, the identity of which must be preserved." This aloofness remained more important for American leaders than the need for coordination.

Pershing recognized the magnitude of his responsibilities and the lack of American preparations. Reporting to Baker on the situation in France during the summer of 1917, he warned that "we shall not be in a position to render any material assistance before next spring." Three years after the beginning of the European war, U.S. armed forces still were not ready for anything more than symbolic involvement. It would take one more year before they could start making a substantial military contribution on the western front. This lack of preparedness presented a grave, although indirect, threat to the United States. The Russian Revolution, with its ominous implications for the eastern front, opened the possibility of a German victory over the Allies before the Americans could enter the war decisively on the western front. In his approach to war Wilson had overlooked the significance of the European balance of power. His failure to identify a strategic equilibrium among the Great Powers as a vital American interest left the United States unprepared for the dangerous prospect that Germany might defeat the Allies.[6]

II

Wilson's response to the Russian Revolution stressed the ideological importance of the eastern front. After Czar Nicholas II's abdication, the provisional government welcomed American entry into the war in the name of "Russian democracy." Wilson promptly sent a special mission to this new republic for the purpose of assuring its government of American friendship and encouraging it to remain in the war against Germany. Elihu Root, who led this mission, delivered the president's message to the Russian people on May 26. "We are fighting for the liberty, the self-government, and the undictated development of all peoples," Wilson wrote, "and every feature of the settlement that concludes this war must be conceived and executed for that purpose." Vaguely referring to a future league of nations, he proclaimed that "the free peoples of the world must draw together in some common covenant, some genuine and practical cooperation that will in effect combine their force to secure peace and justice in the dealings of nations with one another." In this message he appealed to the ideal of a community of nations to preserve a just peace but not to the realistic goal of maintaining the balance of power for the sake of national survival. The difference between his idea of collective security and traditional power politics might not have appeared substantial at this time, but it was extremely important for the future course of American foreign relations.[7]

House encouraged Wilson to appeal to German liberals with a message similar to the one that Root delivered in Russia. After discussing it with Sir Eric Drummond, Balfour's private secretary, he urged the president to distinguish between the German people and the military autocracy that controlled their government. House advised him that "it is not fair to the peoples of Russia, of Great Britain, of France, of Italy and of the United States to be asked to treat with a military caste that is in no way representative of the German people themselves." Yet, with Drummond's concurrence, he cautioned against a personal attack on the kaiser in order to keep open the possibility of liberal democracy under a constitutional monarchy. "The situation in Russia," House warned, "will accentuate the feeling that it is better not to make a too violent change from an autocracy to a republic." Favoring a moderate revolution, he recommended an appeal to the German people against their government, for "Imperial Germany should be broken down within as well as from without."[8]

Concurring in this assessment, Wilson decided to deliver an assault on the Imperial German government in an address on Flag Day. He wanted to criticize "the present military masters of Germany" without alienating the Allies by making a liberal statement of peace conditions. House saw the possibility of fulfillilng this potentially contradictory assignment by condemning the evils of the enemy, emphasizing the Prussian ambitions for conquest and the American and Allied refusal to negotiate with Germany's military oligarchy. It seemed more prudent for the president to denounce the enemy than to clarify American war aims. House urged him to develop the theme of his war message, noting that "you have come to be the spokesman for Democracy as indeed the Kaiser is the spokesman for Autocracy."[9]

Wilson received similar suggestions for his Flag Day speech from Tumulty, who summarized Germany's ambitions as "world dominion." Depicting the war as "a struggle between democracy and feudalism," he wanted the United States and the Allies to protect their "common civilization" against the menace of "barbaric rule." Tumulty thought that a German triumph would represent "a victory for autocracy over the free forces of democracy." Like House, he encouraged Wilson to seek "the overthrow of the military power which has brought so much of suffering upon the world." Rejecting negotiations, he advocated total victory for the Allied and Associated Powers. To justify this purpose, Tumulty placed the frontier motif in a universal context: "It is time for Americans to realize that the frontiers of freedom are their frontiers. Where the battle is joined the flag must go. America has outgrown the day when she could live apart from the rest of the world. If America is to remain free, the world must be free." In short, the nation's liberty depended on universal freedom, not on a stable balance of power in a plural world. The worldwide projection of American ideals and practices was, in Tumulty's imagination, the only alternative to isolation from the Old World.[10]

In his Flag Day address on June 14, Wilson proclaimed a democratic war against autocratic rulers. He developed the themes that House and Tumulty had suggested. He asserted that the military masters of Germany had started the war against the Allies in Europe and then expanded it throughout the world. They had forced the United States to abandon neutrality and were seeking to extend "German military power and political control across the very center of Europe and beyond the Mediterranean into the heart of Asia." Rejecting peace initiatives from Berlin, the president distinguished between the Imperial German government and the German people: "We know now as clearly as we knew before we were ourselves engaged that we are not the enemies of the German people and they are not our enemies. They did not originate or desire this hideous war or wish that we should be drawn into it; and we are vaguely conscious that we are fighting their cause, as they will some day see it, as well as our own." Depicting the United States in a universal struggle for freedom, Wilson announced "a People's War, a war for freedom and justice and self-government amongst all the nations of the world, a war to make the world safe for the peoples who live upon it and have made it their own, the German people themselves included."[11] The president thus defined his purpose as a crusade for democracy.

Randolph S. Bourne, a radical critic of this kind of "war-liberalism," recognized that the Flag Day address marked the collapse of the administration's strategy. Wilson previously had pursued a negotiated "peace without victory," but now he supported the Allies in their desire to defeat the Central Powers. This change in the official American purpose, Bourne apprehended, would shift the initiative for peace from the president to the Council of Workers' and Soldiers' Deputies in Russia. The president's address, he explained in an August 1917 article, committed the United States to all-out war, noting that it "implies that America is ready to pour out endless blood and treasure, not to the end of a negotiated peace, but to the utter crushing of the Central Powers, to their dismemberment and political annihilation. The war is pictured in that address as a struggle to the death against the military empire of Mittel-Europa." Whether the president recognized it or not, the United States was now fighting for the Allies' goal of military victory. "The American role changes from that of mediator in the interest of international organization to that of formidable support to the breaking of this menace to the peace and liberty of Europe."

Bourne appreciated the irony of this change in policy. He understood that if the Central Powers posed a threat to the United States so great as to require an all-out American response at this time, then Wilson should have recognized and responded to this danger long before. Bourne noted that "the menace of Mittel-Europa has existed ever since the entrance of Bulgaria in 1915. If it now challenges us and justifies our change of strategy, it challenged us and justified our assault a full two years ago." Yet this kind of strategic analysis never troubled the president, whose reaction to the European war reflected his ideological orientation. Bourne also appreciated the inherent difficulty of liberating the German people from their government: "If the German people cannot effect their own political reorganization, nobody can do it for them. They would continue to prefer the native Hohenzollerns to the most liberal government imposed by their conquering enemies." As he recognized, the United States lacked the power to reshape the world according to its own image.[12]

Bourne was one of the few intellectuals to challenge the prevailing attitudes of American political culture during the world war. This young radical journalist questioned the premises of liberal internationalism. Unlike Herbert Croly and Walter Lippmann, he refused to justify involvement in the war with the promise of a future league. He observed that the pragmatism or so-called realism of these liberals masked their irrational enthusiasm for war. "If these realists had had time in the hurry and scuffle of events to turn their philosophy on themselves," he complained, "they might have seen how thinly disguised a rationalization this was of their emotional undertow." Bourne understood that the war generated a momentum beyond the rational control of statesmen: "It is a little unbridled for the realist's rather nice sense of purposive social control." Unfortunately, American progressives suffered from the illusion that they could shape the world in accordance with their ideals. Rejecting this hope for mastery over international relations, Bourne warned that neither Wilson nor anyone else could achieve "any liberal control of events."[13]

Never recognizing American dependence on the Allies, Wilson overestimated his capacity to transform international relations. With a false sense of national security, he exaggerated the power of the United States to control foreign affairs. Despite his change in policy in 1917, he continued to assert independence and aloofness from the Allies. He voiced this attitude in an interview in mid-July with Sir William Wiseman, chief of British intelligence in the United States. The president, Wiseman reported to London, "pointed out that while the U.S. was now ready to take her place as a world-power, the strong feeling throughout the country was to play a 'lone hand,' and not commit herself to any alliance with any foreign power." With a unilateral approach to wartime diplomacy, Wilson still wanted to avoid the complications of the Allied secret treaties.[14]

Wiseman recognized potential benefits as well as complications for British diplomacy. In August he prepared a perceptive memorandum on Anglo-American relations. The president, he observed, "has the greatest confidence in the future of the Anglo-Saxon race, and believes that the security of the World can best be maintained by an understanding between the democracies of Great Britain and the United States." Wilson's liberal crusade seemed to enjoy strong support at home, yet Americans wanted to avoid an alliance. Their attitude toward the Old World expressed an absence of fear about the war's consequences. "It is important to realise," Wiseman noted, "that the American people do not consider themselves in any danger from the Central Powers." Aware of the difficulties arising from this ignorance of European affairs, the British intelligence officer also saw the opportunity. He concluded that "America is for the first time keenly interested in European problems. Americans consider that

Washington has become the diplomatic centre of the world. The American people, however, have no great knowledge of European problems, or any fixed ideas as to their settlement." Such ignorance with regard to the specific issues in the Old World would afford Great Britain the chance to guide the United States in its new role as a world power. "It is no exaggeration to say that the foreign policy of America for many years to come is now in process of formation, and very much depends on the full sympathetic and confidential exchange of views between the leaders of the British and American people."[15]

Wilson's rejection of negotiations with the Imperial German government placed the United States in a difficult position in August 1917, when Pope Benedict XV appealed for peace. Calling for peace on the basis of the status quo ante bellum, the pope urged both the Central Powers and the Allied and Associated Powers to compromise. Colonel House, fearful that a failure to respond might cause internal problems in the Allied countries and even in the United States, encouraged the president to answer this papal appeal. He advised him to promise peace in "a spirit of liberalism and justice" while exploiting mass discontent in Germany and Austria-Hungary by refusing to negotiate with the military autocrats. "A statement from you regarding the aims of this country," House suggested, "would bring about almost revolution in Germany in the event the existing government dared to oppose them." Although welcoming the overthrow of the German government, he wanted to prevent a more radical revolution in Russia. "You can make a statement," House assured Wilson, "that will not only be the undoing of autocratic Germany, but one that will strengthen the hands of the Russian liberals in their purpose to mold their country into a mighty republic." This advice naively assumed that words from Washington could exert a decisive influence over European events.[16]

Despite his initial reluctance, the president answered the pope by blaming the Imperial German government for obstructing peace. He refused to deal with "the ruthless master of the German people." Adhering to his new policy, he called instead for revolution in Germany as a precondition for "the possibility of a covenanted peace." He sought to accomplish this goal through effective propaganda. To mold public opinion at home and abroad he had established the Committee on

Public Information under the chairmanship of George Creel, a progressive journalist. Among others, Lippmann and Croly had recommended this kind of executive management of wartime publicity. The Creel committee thus delivered Wilson's democratic message to the European and American people. Various reformers participated in this endeavor to advertise Americanism and denounce the German menace. Among those working for the Creel committee were progressive scholars such as historian Frederick Jackson Turner.[17]

Wilson's propagandistic reply to the pope still left the United States without a definite foreign policy. Nevertheless, House applauded it as "a declaration of human liberty." He thought that it would promote the redemptive American mission in Europe, for it contained "the fundamentals of a new and greater international morality." House reminded the president that "America will not and ought not to fight for the maintenance of the old, narrow and selfish order of things. You are blazing a new path, and the world must follow, or be lost again in the meshes of unrighteous intrigue." This encouragement delighted Wilson, and so did the popular response to his reply. Yet he recognized that the United States lacked a clear definition of peace terms. He realized that ideals eventually would need to be translated into more precise guidelines. Consequently, he asked House to prepare for the future peace conference by organizing the collection of data. Welcoming this assignment, House began to assemble a group of experts, known as the Inquiry, to undertake this work. Lippmann served as the Inquiry's influential secretary, before going to Europe in 1918 as a War Department propagandist to proclaim Wilson's ideals behind enemy lines in Germany.[18]

For most of 1917 the lack of definite war aims caused no alarm in the Wilson administration. Nor did the president's failure to coordinate ends and means bother Pershing. Concentrating on his military duties, the general pledged to continue "with all my strength, in the full assurance that, with the aid of Divine Providence, we shall succeed in our righteous cause of saving democracy to the world." Like Wilson, he expected this result to follow naturally from military victory. He, too, ignored the need for a closer linkage between the military and political facets of American foreign policy.[19]

III

The Bolshevik Revolution in Russia finally stimulated Wilson into defining American war aims in greater detail. Once the Bolsheviks seized control of Petrograd on November 7, 1917, they sought peace with Imperial Germany on the eastern front. The president now sensed the implications for the Allies and the United States of a separate Russo-German peace. Charles Edward Russell, who recently had returned from Russia as a member of the Root mission, advised him to initiate a publicity campaign to convince the Russian people that their revolution's success depended upon their continuance in the war. As this suggestion corroborated his own inference, Wilson submitted it to Creel for appropriate action by his committee. He was still fighting the war with words.[20]

Speaking to the American Federation of Labor convention a few days later, the president urged Russia to remain in the war. Unresponsive to the Russian people's yearning for peace, he sought to convince them by blaming Germany for the war. He questioned how "any group of persons should be so ill-informed as to suppose, as some groups in Russia apparently suppose, that any reforms planned in the interest of the people can live in the presence of a Germany powerful enough to undermine or overthrow them by intrigue or force? Any body of free men that compounds with the present German Government is compounding for its own destruction." He failed to grasp that the Russian people might understand their condition from a different perspective and, consequently, that the Bolshevik appeal for peace might exploit a popular sentiment. Publicity emanating from the White House or the Creel committee was irrelevant in war-weary Russia.[21]

The sense of urgency that Wilson expressed in his plea to the Russian people now gripped other American leaders. General Pershing outlined for Secretary Baker the potential consequences of a separate peace on the eastern front. He noted that the Allies currently enjoyed an advantage in troop strength on the western front, but that "the shifting of German divisions from the east to that front would overcome this superiority and give the Central Powers the superiority and would justify an offensive by them." Secretary Lansing worried that the removal of Russia as a military factor on the eastern front might prevent the Allied and Associated Powers from defeating Germany. He feared that the German army might even overwhelm the Allies on the western front and march into Paris before American troops could make a significant contribution during the summer of 1918. Tumulty paid less attention to the Bolshevik Revolution's military implications as he continued to view the war in ideological terms. Submitting suggestions for the president's annual message to Congress, he stressed the American role in "the crusade for greater democracy" and for "the extermination of the menace of German militarism." Until the United States and the Allies achieved such a victory, Tumulty thought that the reaffirmation of principles that Wilson had outlined in his "peace without victory" address would suffice as a statement of war aims.[22]

In his annual message on December 4, Wilson responded to the Russian Revolution by elaborating his idea of collective security. Although acknowledging the yearning for peace in Russia and throughout the world, he reaffirmed his determination to achieve victory. He denied that the Allied and Associated Powers had any aggressive ambitions. Vaguely defining their aims, the president heralded a future league of nations. He intended to exclude the Imperial German government from this new community of peaceful nations. "The worst that can happen to the detriment of the German people is this," he explained, "that if they should still, after the war is over, continue to be obliged to live under ambitious and intriguing masters interested to disturb the peace of the world, men or classes of men whom the other peoples of the world could not trust, it might be impossible to admit them to the partnership of nations which must henceforth guarantee the world's peace. That partnership must be a partnership of peoples, not a mere partnership of governments." In short, the preservation of peace would depend upon the triumph of democracy in Germany and in other nations that might join the league.

Failure of the Russian people to understand the American and Allied aims, Wilson thought, accounted for their desire for peace without victory. If the Russians had understood the western nations' real purpose, the provisional government might not have fallen to the Bolsheviks. In his opinion, a German-Bolshevik conspiracy explained this confusion. He asserted that "the Russian people have been poisoned by the very same falsehoods that have kept the German people in the dark, and the poison has been administered by the very same hands." Rejecting the Bolshevik proposal for peace negotiations, he preferred "to push this great war of freedom and justice to its righteous conclusion." Toward that end Wilson called upon Congress to declare war against the Austro-Hungarian Empire, which it did on December 7, 1917.

Wilson entertained no doubt about the virtue of the United States or the venality of the Central Powers. This contrast between good and evil justified the war. "The cause being just and holy," he proclaimed, "the settlement must be of like motive and quality. For this we can fight, but for nothing less noble or less worthy of our traditions." In this holy war he identified American ideals with God's redemptive purpose: "A supreme moment of history has come. The eyes of the people have been opened and they see. The hand of God is laid upon the nations. He will show them favor, I devoutly believe, only if they rise to the clear heights of His own justice and mercy."[23]

Wilson delivered this righteous message, and decided to prepare a more detailed explanation of his design for a new world order, after House had failed to gain the Inter-Allied Conference's endorsement of American war aims. At David Lloyd George's instigation, House had gone to Europe in November as the president's representative to coordinate wartime policies with the Allies. He and the British prime minister had hoped somehow to end the stalemate on the western front. The Bolshevik Revolution, coinciding with the conference, had lent greater urgency to the coordination of military plans and the definition of war aims. House and the Allied premiers had established the Supreme War Council to unify military strategy, but they failed to agree on terms for an acceptable peace. Upon his return to the United States, House reported the Inter-Allied Conference's decisions to Wilson, who then decided to formulate a unilateral pronouncement of war aims. Lansing encouraged him to seize this opportunity to increase the German people's dissatisfaction with their government's policies. Using data which House had obtained from the Inquiry, the president began to prepare his famous Fourteen Points address.[24]

As Wilson completed his preparations, Lloyd George outlined the British war aims in an address before the Trade Union Conference in London on January 5, 1918. Overcoming his government's reluctance to state publicly its minimum objectives, he expressed many of the themes that Wilson had previously articulated. "We are not fighting a war of aggression against the German people," the prime minister affirmed. "Their leaders have persuaded them that they are fighting a war of self-defense against a league of rival nations, bent on the destruction of Germany. That is not so. The destruction or disruption of Germany or the German people has never been a war aim with us from the first day of this war to this day." After giving a similar assurance to Austria-Hungary and, with more qualification, to Turkey, he proceeded with a critical analysis of the Central Powers' peace terms. "It is impossible," he concluded, "to believe that any edifice of permanent peace could be erected on such a foundation as this. Mere lip-service to the formula of no annexations and no indemnities or the right of self-determination is useless." Lloyd George asserted, on the contrary, that "a just and a lasting peace" would require the restoration of sanctity of treaties, the settlement of territorial disputes on the basis of self-determination, and "the creation of some international organization, to limit the burden of armaments and diminish the probability of war." With this last vague reference the British prime minister committed his government to a league of nations as an essential condition for peace.[25]

When Wilson learned that Lloyd George planned to give this speech, he feared it might overshadow his own forthcoming address. Through House he urged the prime minister not to announce any British war aims that conflicted with the principles that he had outlined in his annual message to Congress. After reading Lloyd George's speech and recognizing the similarity between British and American objectives, the president momentarily hesitated. But then he finished his own statement for delivery to a joint session of Congress.[26]

In his Fourteen Points address on January 8, Wilson responded to the challenge of separate peace negotiations at Brest-Litovsk between the Central Powers and the new Soviet government in Russia. Outlining his peace program, he called for "open covenants of peace, openly arrived at," to replace the old diplomacy of secret treaties. He advocated freedom of the seas, equality of trade, and reduction of armaments "to the lowest point consistent with domestic safety." He recommended an "absolutely impartial adjustment" of colonial claims, but without specifying how to achieve this goal. For the first time in the American diplomatic tradition, the president suggested guidelines for the settlement of territorial questions in Europe and the Middle East. Despite its previous diplomatic, commercial, and cultural relations with European countries, the United States had never before involved itself to this extent in the political and territorial issues of the Old World. In his final point, Wilson reaffirmed his commitment to a postwar league, proclaiming that "a general association of nations must be formed under specific covenants for the purpose of affording mutual guarantees of political independence and territorial integrity to great and small states alike." He offered the prospect of membership for a reformed Germany in this international organization. "We do not wish to fight her either with arms or with hostile arrangements of trade, if she is willing to associate herself with us and the other peace-loving nations of the world in covenants of justice and law and fair dealing." Anticipating the acceptance of these conditions, Wilson heralded a postwar era of peace.[27]

Wilson's Fourteen Points address evoked generally favorable responses in Allied countries. The American ambassadors in London, Paris, and Rome reported overall approval by the Allied governments and genuine enthusiasm in the press. Lloyd George conveyed his gratitude that British and American peace policies were "so entirely in harmony." In the French Chamber of Deputies, Foreign Minister Stéphen Pichon endorsed the principles that both Lloyd George and Wilson had proclaimed. He said that the three essential conditions for "a just and durable peace" were respect for the "sacred character" of treaties, adjustment of territorial disputes on the basis of self-determination, and limitation of armaments. This French program coincided closely with the British prime minister's, except for placing less emphasis on a league of nations. "As for the society of nations," Pichon stated, "victory alone can bring it to realization." That was something the Allied and Associated Powers could create after they had defeated the Central Powers. In general, the Italians, as well as the British and the French, seemed to accept the Fourteen Points.[28]

Although the apparent unity of purpose between the United States and the Allies delighted Wilson, Americans were still detached from the realities of war in Europe. "I believe the country, press, and the Administration," Wiseman reported to London, following an interview with the president, "are really more concerned in the preparations that America is making to take her part in the war rather than the actual state of affairs in Europe."[29] The American people were still largely unaware of the implications for their own national security of a German victory over the Allies. Failing to recognize the importance of the European balance of power for the United States, the president had neglected to educate the nation about this connection. Instead, Wilson projected American ideals overseas and hoped that propaganda and eventual military victory somehow would facilitate this reformation of the Old World.

Agreement in principle between the United States and the Allies provided no assurance that they could implement their war aims in practice. Secretary Lansing anticipated difficulty. He expected complications from the goal of self-determination in European and colonial territorial settlements. "The principle of 'self-determination,' " he confided to his diary, "cannot be applied to the populations of these German colonies, since they consist chiefly of savages too low in the scale of civilization to be able to reach an intelligent decision." These were problems that would arise after an American and Allied victory, itself not yet conceded by the Central Powers.

Lansing's private reservations were mild in comparison with the criticism from Berlin and Vienna. On January 24, German Chancellor Georg von Hertling and Austro-Hungarian Foreign Minister Ottokar Czernin von Chudenitz rejected Wilson's Fourteen Points as conditions for peace. Referring to the Russo-German negotiations at Brest-Litovsk as an indication of their genuine desire for peace, they contrasted their position with the American and Allied demand for victory. Hertling and Czernin emphasized the impracticality of most of the Fourteen Points but suggested that some of these principles might serve as a basis for negotiations. Avoiding any commitment, they voiced minimal interest in a league of nations. "We have sympathy," said Hertling, "with the idea of a league of nations. If proposals are based on the spirit of humanity we shall be ready to study the question." Czernin adopted a neutral stance, announcing only that from Austria-Hungary the president would not encounter "any opposition to his proposal regarding the idea of a league of nations."[30]

Wilson welcomed the replies of Hertling and Czernin as indications of growing weakness in the Central Powers. He thought that his words were beginning to force them onto the defensive. Encouraged by House, he wanted to exploit the differences between the German people and their government and between Germany and Austria-Hungary. In accordance with his conception of open diplomacy, Wilson decided to deliver another address to Congress. The president did not, however, want Congress to request information from him as the occasion for this address or, as House noted, "to think they could control him in any way or take part in handling foreign affairs." Before addressing a joint session of Congress on February 11, Wilson shared his intentions with Wiseman, who immediately informed Balfour. Although the president acted unilaterally, he maintained a fairly good liaison with the British.[31]

Sensing weakness in the Central Powers, Wilson used his ideals for the practical purpose of dividing the enemy. He attempted to split Austria-Hungary from Germany by contrasting Czernin's "very friendly tone" with Hertling's "very vague and very confusing" reply. Yet he denounced the Berlin goverment's practice of separate negotiations with Soviet Russia. Criticizing Germany for seeking through bilateral negotiations with the various Allies to establish a new balance of power, Wilson rejected that kind of international organization. The president viewed this German method for balancing power among nations as part of the discredited old diplomacy that he associated with the Congress of Vienna. Instead of restoring that system, he favored "a new international order based upon broad and universal principles of right and justice." Such a universal peace, in Wilson's view, would not entangle his country in the political and territorial conflicts of the Old World. Indeed, he asserted, "the United States has no desire to interfere in European affairs or to act as arbiter in European territorial disputes. She would disdain to take advantage of any internal weakness or disorder to impose her own will upon another people."

Wilson's vision of collective security presupposed that other nations wanted the same kind of world that the United States did. His paradoxical vision of peace was at once universal and unilateral. "We are indomitable in our power of independent action," he concluded, "and can in no circumstances consent to live in a world governed by intrigue and force. We believe that our own desire for a new international order under which reason and justice and the common interests of mankind shall prevail is the desire of enlightened men everywhere." Convinced of that happy coincidence, he neglected to wrestle with the hard choices that would otherwise arise.[32]

IV

Although Wilson's address received some praise from the Allies, it failed to accomplish his purpose of disrupting the Central Powers. Their position improved substantially during the spring of 1918 with the conclusion of a separate peace with Russia. The Treaty of Brest-Litovsk, which the Soviet delegation signed under German duress on March 3, ended the war on the eastern front. The movement of German troops for a western offensive created a military crisis for the United States and the Allies. Reporting to Balfour, Wiseman shrewdly characterized the Wilson administration's attitude at this time. He observed that "they are so unfamiliar with European—in fact, with international—affairs that the Foreign Ambassador must be very patient indeed. The Administration also seem inclined to be slow to face unpleasant truths; particularly, they still cling to the hope that they may 'talk' the Germans into a just peace. But this attitude must not be mistaken for any weakening in their determination to win. After they have done their talking, you will find they will go on fighting whatever the sacrifices may be." Germany's offensive on the western front, coinciding with ratification of the Treaty of Brest-Litovsk, forced Wilson to reassess the political and military situation. He now began to doubt that American propaganda could disrupt the Central Powers by turning the German people against their government or by separating Austria-Hungary from Germany. He recognized the need for greater American military effort to support the Allies and prevent a German victory.[33]

Republican leaders doubted both the president's resolve and his ability to do what was necessary to win the war. Theodore Roosevelt expressed his despair over Wilson's leadership in a letter to an English friend. Assigning himself the role of "trying to wake up the American people to their shortcomings, and to spur Wilson into action," he explained: "Wilson is at heart a pacifist; he is not pro-German, but neither is he pro-Ally or pro-American—he is purely pro-Wilson. . . . Moreover, he is a rhetorician pure and simple, and an utterly inefficient administrator. He is a very adroit demagogue, skilled beyond any man we have ever seen in appealing to the yellow streak in people. But he has not the slightest understanding of the need of efficiency in a desperate crisis like this." To prod Wilson into action, Roosevelt decided to deliver a hard-hitting address to the Republican state convention in Maine.[34]

Other Republicans, including Root, Henry Cabot Lodge, and William H. Taft, shared Roosevelt's sense of urgency. Believing that TR's " 'rampaging' up and down the country" had been a key factor in forcing Wilson to send American troops to Europe in the first place, Taft wanted to maintain this kind of political pressure on him. He advised Roosevelt to denounce the president's willingness to enter into a public debate with Hertling, which might lead to a peace treaty with "the Potsdam gang." Now was the time for all-out military effort, not for premature peace negotiations. Taft urged Roosevelt to remind the American people of the Democratic administration's long-standing negligence in military preparedness but to avoid too personal an attack on Wilson. Root similarly encouraged TR to use the occasion to stress the Republicans' loyal support for vital war measures and to chide the Democrats for their poor leadership.[35]

Because Pershing's troops were just beginning to contribute militarily on the western front, the British and French armies bore the brunt of Germany's spring offensive. During the first week, British losses amounted to 120,000 men. Lloyd George urgently appealed to Wilson for more troops before Germany could achieve victory. One year after the United States had entered the world war, the American Expeditionary Forces numbered only 367,000 soldiers. The president promised to transport to France 120,000 infantry per month from April through July. Although thankful for this commitment, Lloyd George instructed Lord Reading, the British ambassador to the United States, to monitor its fulfillment. He emphasized that success or failure in the current battle would depend upon American reinforcements. "We have so often had large promises in past which have invariably been falsified in result," explained the prime minister, "that this last undertaking may not be carried out in actual practice." As Reading consulted Baker about the implementation of Wilson's pledge, Wiseman sought to impress upon House the gravity of the military situation. Despite Allied fears, the War Department would surpass the U.S. commitment to deliver troops. By the end of June the American Expeditionary Forces exceeded one million men.[36]

Although the Wilson administration failed to convince skeptics either at home or abroad that the United States would appropriately assist the Allies, it remained optimistic about the future. House was quite sanguine. "I do not feel at all depressed over the news which comes from the Western Front," he confidently wrote to Pershing. If the United States could transport enough troops to Europe to replace Allied casualties during the spring and summer, he anticipated, "Germany will see the end of her ambitions." But Senator Lodge doubted that the War Department actually would deliver the promised troops. He lamented that the administration had not sent these men to France six months earlier, before Germany began its offensive. "The fact is," he concluded, "I do not think that Baker and the President—who considers Baker the ablest public official he has ever known—meant to do any fighting." Under these conditions, as he viewed them, Lodge refused to acquiesce silently in Wilson's leadership. He confided that "I get a little weary of the people who abuse Congress and call upon us to stand blindly by the President as if the President was the country, which he is not."[37]

Wilson sought to encourage the Allies by a strong denunciation of German militarism and yet leave open the prospect of peace. On the anniversary of the American declaration of war, he delivered a short address in Baltimore. He wanted to assure Germany that the United States intended no injustice or aggression but firmly opposed the German military leaders' ambitions. He characterized their purpose as the creation of an empire from the Baltic through eastern Europe to the Middle East, and on to India and the Far East. "In such a program," the president said, "our ideals, the ideals of justice and humanity and liberty, the principle of free self-determination of nations upon which all the modern world insists, can play no part. They are rejected for the ideals of power, for the principle that the strong must rule the weak, that trade must follow the flag, whether those to whom it is taken welcome it or not, that the peoples of the world are to be made subject to the patronage and overlordship of those who have the power to enforce it." This strong criticism of German military leaders pleased the British government. Balfour conveyed his delight that the president had chosen "a particularly opportune moment to remind Germany and Austria of the inexhaustible resources of America and of her determination to carry on the war until German militarism is defeated."[38]

Despite this strong denunciation of German militarism, Wilson proclaimed a policy of peace. In off-the-record comments to foreign correspondents he explained the assumptions underlying his address to give "the real key to the present foreign policy of the United States." He expressed his willingness to negotiate with the existing Imperial German government on the basis of his principles. He wanted to achieve permanent peace through the realization of justice for all belligerents, including the Central Powers as well as the Allies. His concept of justice still remained vague. Seeking mutual accommodation, he hoped to avoid the need for enforcing the peace settlement. This result would enable the United States to escape from postwar entanglement in the Old World.

Wilson's current willingness to negotiate reflected a major shift in his thinking. Previously, he had contrasted the German people and their government, but now he recognized their essential unity. From this insight he concluded that the United States must either deal with the existing German government or impose a new government onto the country. He rejected this latter alternative, which would prolong the war, explaining that "I am not fighting for democracy except for the peoples that want democracy."[39]

V

Political realities in Europe challenged the intellectual foundations of Wilson's foreign policy. He had presupposed that the entire pattern of world history pointed toward the expansion of democracy. Other nations should move progressively toward the realization of the same ideals and practices that already characterized the United States. Believing that all peoples shared these aspirations and followed this pattern of progressive history, he underestimated the difficulty of developing democratic institutions in the Old World. The

president thought that the United States could foster democratic revolutions in other countries by employing the methods of international social control. Effective propaganda could
shape public opinion and turn these peoples against their
autocratic governments. While military intervention also
might be required, it alone could not accomplish this redemptive purpose. But, in combination with the universal
trend toward democracy in world history and with the appli-
cation of social science to international relations, the United
States might use the European war to fulfill this mission.

Developments in Germany and Russia during 1918 revealed the intellectual bankruptcy of liberal internationalism.
The German people, as the president himself now recognized,
were unwilling to revolt against the kaiser's government.
Instead, they continued to fight for military victory against
the Allies. Words from Washington were not sufficient to
bring Germany to accept either peace or democracy. Moreover,
the war-weary people of Russia failed to establish democratic
institutions. They opted instead for a separate peace with
Germany. As the Bolsheviks consolidated their power, their
radical revolution challenged Wilson's understanding of progressive history. They, too, believed in progress but did not
look to the United States as the world's model. Their promise
of socialism differed substantially from his vision of liberal
democracy and capitalism. The Bolsheviks offered a very
different vision of orderly progress.[40]

As the president's liberal internationalism encountered
the challenge of bolshevism, he eventually acquiesced in the
persistent Allied request for armed intervention in Siberia
and northern Russia. He agreed to send American troops
primarily because of his desire to satisfy the Allies during the
critical period of the war in the summer of 1918. Although
the action was inherently anti-Bolshevik, Wilson never intended to use military power to topple the Soviet government.
Justifying intervention as a wartime necessity, he limited its
objectives. He sought to prevent supplies at Archangel,
Murmansk, and Vladivostok from falling into German hands
and to facilitate the evacuation of the stranded Czecho-
Slovak Legion from Russia. He also hoped to curb Japanese
ambitions in Siberia. American troops went into Russia without any clear direction relative to the internal consequences
for that country. Because the relationship between this mili-

tary operation and the war against the Central Powers was also poorly defined, the purpose of intervention was not clear. American foreign policy suffered from this confusion.[41]

Wilson's response to the Russian Revolution revealed the limits of American power to reform the Old World. As a practical politician, he recognized these limits. In mid-October 1918 he explained to Wiseman why he was not willing to collaborate with the Allies in using military intervention to determine the political outcome of the Russian civil war. "My policy regarding Russia," he told the British agent, "is very similar to my Mexican policy. I believe in letting them work out their own salvation, even though they wallow in anarchy for a while. I visualize it like this: A lot of impossible folk, fighting among themselves. You cannot do business with them, so you shut them all up in a room and lock the door and tell them that when they have settled matters among themselves you will unlock the door and do business."[42] In other words, the United States and the Allies could not control the situation in Russia, and here he was not willing to attempt the impossible.

Implicitly, if not consciously, the president acknowledged the inability of his administration to implement his new foreign policy in Europe. Neither Germany nor Russia cooperated with the United States in creating the new order of liberal internationalism. The German people, rather than responding to Wilson's call for a democratic revolution, persevered in the war. They still accepted the imperial government's political and military leadership. Moreover, German military success had forced the new Soviet regime to sign the Treaty of Brest-Litovsk. Instead of remaining a faithful ally and developing a democratic government, Russia had abandoned the war on the eastern front. This combination of events in the Old World revealed the inadequacies of Wilson's new foreign policy, but he did not reconsider the fundamental premises of liberal internationalism.

Although neither Germany nor Russia moved toward the kind of democracy and peace that he had expected, Wilson still hoped that American ideals and practices would prevail in the Old World. He retained his progressive philosophy of history and his vision of international social control, despite contradictions with European realities. He devoted his energy in 1918 to the immediate task of winning the war. Beyond a vague hope, there was no clear connection between the armed intervention either against Germany or in Russia and the achievement of a new world order. Poor coordination between military strategy and political goals characterized the president's statecraft. But, at that time and even later, few Americans recognized this lack of realism.

Notes

1. Tumulty to Wilson, March 24, 1917, Tumulty Papers, Box 5.
2. Baker and Dodd, *Public Papers* 5:2, 22.
3. Ibid. 5:53.
4. House Diary, April 14, 22, 26, 28-30, May 9, 13, 1917; House to Wilson, April 22, 1917, House Papers, Drawer 49, File 8; House to Wilson, April 22, 1917, Diary of Colonel House, April 26, 28-30, 1917, in Link, *Papers* 42:120, 142-43, 155-58, 160-62, 168-73.
5. U.S. Department of the Army, Historical Division, *United States Army in the World War, 1917-1919: Policy-Forming Documents, American Expeditionary Forces,* 17 vols. (Washington, DC: Government Printing Office, 1948), 2:2-10; Daniel R. Beaver, *Newton D. Baker and the American War Effort, 1917-1919* (Lincoln: University of Nebraska Press, 1966), pp. 39-41; Edward M. Coffman, *The War to End All Wars: The American Military Experience in World War I* (New York: Oxford University Press, 1968), pp. 42-43; Richard D. Challener, *Admirals, Generals, and American Foreign Policy, 1898-1914* (Princeton: Princeton University Press, 1973), p. 24.
6. N. D. Baker to John J. Pershing, May 26, 1917, Tasker H. Bliss to Pershing, May 26, 1917, in John J. Pershing, *My Experiences in the World War,* 2 vols. (New York: Frederick A. Stokes, 1931), 1:1-40; Frederick Palmer, *Newton D. Baker: America at War,* 2 vols. (New York: Dodd, Mead, 1931), 1:170-72.
7. Paul Mulioukov (Russian Provisional Government foreign minister) to Wilson, April 10, 1917, Lansing to Wilson, April 12, 1917, Wilson Papers, Ser. 4, File 64; Baker and Dodd, *Public Papers* 5:50-51.
8. House to Wilson, May 20, 30, 1917, House Papers, Drawer 49, File 8; House Diary, May 19-20, 1917; House to Wilson, May 20, 30, 1917, in Link, *Papers* 42:354-55, 425.
9. Wilson to House, June 1, 1917, House Papers, Drawer 49, File 18; House to Wilson, June 5, 1917, House Papers, Drawer 49, File 8; Wilson to House, June 1, 1917, House to Wilson, June 5, 1917, in Link, *Papers* 42:433, 456.
10. Tumulty to Wilson, n.d., Suggestions: Flag Day Speech of the President, June 14, 1917, Tumulty Papers, Box 5.
11. Baker and Dodd, *Public Papers* 5:60-67; House Diary, June 13-15, 1917; Flag Day Address, June 14, 1917, in Link, *Papers* 42:498-504.
12. Randolph S. Bourne, "The Collapse of American Strategy," *The Seven Arts* 2 (August 1917): 409-24, in Carl Resek, ed., *War and the Intellectuals: Essays by Randolph S. Bourne, 1915-1919* (New York: Harper & Row, 1964), pp. 22-35.

13. Bourne, "A War Diary," *The Seven Arts* 2 (September 1917): 5-47, in Resek, *War and the Intellectuals*, pp. 36-47.

14. W. B. Fowler, *British-American Relations, 1917-1918: The Role of Sir William Wiseman* (Princeton: Princeton University Press, 1969), pp. 243-46; House to David Lloyd George, July 15, 1917, House Papers, Drawer 12, File 32.

15. Fowler, *British-American Relations*, pp. 246-54; Memorandum on Anglo-American Relations, August 1917, William Wiseman Papers, Drawer 90, File 4, Yale University Library, New Haven, Connecticut.

16. House to Wilson, August 15, 17, 1917, House Papers, Drawer 49, File 9; Wilson to House, August 16, 1917, House Papers, Drawer 49, File 18; House Diary, August 18-19, 23, 1917; House to Wilson, August 15, 17, 19, 1917, Diary of Colonel House, August 18, 1917, in Link, *Papers* 43:471-72, 508-9, 521-23. See also Dragan Zivojinović, "Robert Lansing's Comments on the Pontifical Peace Note of August 1, 1917," *Journal of American History* 56 (December 1969): 556-71.

17. Wilson to House, August 22, 1917, Draft of the President's answer to the Pope's peace proposal, House Papers, Drawer 49, File 18; House Diary, August 23, 1917; Wilson to House, August 23, 1917, Lansing to Page, August 27, 1917, in Link, *Papers* 44:33-36, 57-59; Baker and Dodd, *Public Papers* 5:93-96; Stephen Vaughn, *Holding Fast the Inner Lines: Democracy, Nationalism, and the Committee on Public Information* (Chapel Hill: University of North Carolina Press, 1980); Robert C. Hilderbrand, *Power and the People: Executive Management of Public Opinion in Foreign Affairs, 1897-1921* (Chapel Hill: University of North Carolina Press, 1981), pp. 142-64; Billington, *Frederick Jackson Turner*, pp. 347-49.

18. House to Wilson, August 24, September 4, 1917, House Papers, Drawer 49, File 9; Wilson to House, September 2, 1917, House Papers, Drawer 49, File 18; House Diary, August 29, September 4-5, 7, 10, 13, 20, 22, 25, October 5-6, 13, 1917; House to Wilson, August 24, September 4, 1917, Wilson to House, September 2, 1917, Diary of Colonel House, September 5, 10, October 13, 1917, in Link, *Papers* 44:40-41, 120-21, 149-50, 157, 184-86, 378-82; Lawrence E. Gelfand, *The Inquiry: American Preparations for Peace, 1917-1919* (New Haven: Yale University Press, 1963); Steel, *Walter Lippmann*, pp. 128-54.

19. Pershing to Wilson, October 8, 1917, John J. Pershing Papers, Box 213, Library of Congress, Washington, DC. For Pershing's perspective on the war see Donald Smythe, *Pershing: General of the Armies* (Bloomington: Indiana University Press, 1986), pp. 1-237.

20. Charles Edward Russell, Memorandum, November 7, 1917, Wilson to Russell, November 10, 1917, Wilson to George Creel, November 10, 1917, Wilson Papers, Ser. 4, Box 64; Wilson to Creel, November 10, 1917, Russell to Wilson, November 7, 1917, Wilson to Russell, November 10, 1917, in Link, *Papers* 44:557-58.

21. Baker and Dodd, *Public Papers* 5:93-96; Address in Buffalo to the American Federation of Labor, [November 12, 1917], in Link, *Papers* 45:11-17.

22. Pershing to N. D. Baker, November 15, 1917, Pershing Papers, Box 19; Lansing Diary, II, October 24, December 31, 1917; Tumulty to Wilson, November 30, 1917, President's Message Suggestion, Tumulty Papers, Box 5; Tumulty to Wilson, November 30, 1917, President's Message Suggestion, in Link, *Papers* 45:163-65.

23. Baker and Dodd, *Public Papers* 5:128-39; Annual Message on the State of the Union, December 4, 1917, in Link, *Papers* 45:194-202.

24. David Lloyd George to House, September 4, 1917, House to Lloyd George, September 24, 1917, House Papers, Drawer 49, File 9; House Diary, September 16, 26, 29, October 13, 21, 24, 29, November 3, 10, 13-14, 16-17, 20-22, 24-25, 27, December 1, 5, 17-18, 22, 31, 1917, January 3-4, 9, 1918; Lansing to Wilson, December 25, 1917, Present Situation: The War Aims and Peace Terms It Suggests, Wilson Papers, Ser. 5A, Box 2; Diary of Colonel House, September 16, October 13, 24, 1917, Memorandum by Sidney Edward Mezes, David Hunter Miller, and Walter Lippmann (of the Inquiry), in Link, *Papers* 44:200-203, 378-82, 437-39; Diary of Colonel House, December 17-18, 1917, January 4, 9, 1918, in Link, *Papers* 45:317-18, 323-27, 458-74, 550-59. See also Trask, *The United States and the Supreme War Council*, for the origins and operation of this council's attempt to coordinate political and military affairs.

25. Arthur J. Balfour to Robert Cecil (British assistant secretary of state), December 29, 1917, Arthur J. Balfour Papers, 49738/183-90, British Museum, London, England; House Diary, January 19, 1918; House to Wilson, January 20, 1918, House Papers, Drawer 49, File 10; Page to Lansing, January 6, 1918, Address of the British Prime Minister (Lloyd George) before the Trade Union Conference at London, January 5, 1918, *Foreign Relations, 1918: World War*, Sup. 1, 1:4-12. See also Rothwell, *British War Aims*, pp. 143-84.

26. Lansing to Wilson, January 2, 1918, David R. Francis (U.S. ambassador to Russia) to Lansing, December 31, 1917, Lansing, Memorandum on Non-Recognition of a Russian Government, January 6, 1918, Wilson Papers, Ser. 5A, Box 2; Francis to Lansing, December 31, 1917, Lansing to Wilson, January 2, 1918, in Link, *Papers* 45:411-14, 427-30.

27. Baker and Dodd, *Public Papers* 5:155-62; *Foreign Relations, 1918: World War*, Sup. 1, 1:12-17; Address to a Joint Session of Congress, January 8, 1918, in Link, *Papers* 45:534-39.

28. Colville Barclay (British embassy counselor in Washington, DC) to Wilson, January 13, 1918, Wilson to Barclay, January 16, 1918, Wilson Papers, Ser. 4, Box 63; W. H. Page to Lansing, January 10, 1918, Nelson Page (U.S. ambassador to Italy) to Lansing, January 10, 1918, Sharp to Lansing, January 10, 14, 1918, *Foreign Relations, 1918: World War*, Sup. 1, 1:17-21, 28-31; Barclay to Wilson, January 13, 1918, in Link, *Papers* 45:578-79; Wilson to Barclay, January 16, 1918, in Link, *Papers* 46:4. For differences between French and American war aims see Stevenson, *French War Aims*, pp. 94-114; and David Stevenson, "French War Aims and the American Challenge, 1914-1918," *Historical Journal* 22, No. 4 (1979): 877-94.

29. William Wiseman, Notes on Interview with the President, January 23, 1918, Wiseman to Drummond, January 25, 25, 1918, Balfour Papers, 49741/2-13; Fowler, *British-American Relations*, pp. 254-58; Memorandum by Sir William Wiseman, January 23, 1918, in Link, *Papers* 46:85-88.

30. Lansing Diary, III, January 10, 1918; John W. Garrett (U.S. minister to the Netherlands) to Lansing, January 24, 1918, Wilson to Lansing, January 30, 1918, *Foreign Relations, 1918: World War*, Sup. 1, 1:38-42, 54-59.

31. House Diary, January 27, 29, February 7-11, 1918; House to Wilson, January 31, February 1, 3, 5, 1918, House Papers, Drawer 49, File 10; Wiseman to Balfour, February 4, 1918, Balfour Papers, 49741/19-23; Fowler, *British-American Relations*, pp. 259-62; Diary of Colonel House, January 27, February 8-10, 1918, House to Wilson, January 31, February 1, 3, 5, 1918, Gordon Auchincloss (House's son-in-law) to Wilson, February 3, 1918, in Link, *Papers* 46:114-17, 181, 207, 221-29, 250-51, 290-91, 313-14, 316-18.

32. Baker and Dodd, *Public Papers* 5:177-84; *Foreign Relations, 1918: World War*, Sup. 1, 1:108-13; Address to a Joint Session of Congress, February 11, 1918, in Link, *Papers* 46:318-24.

33. House to Wilson, February 15, 1918, House Papers, Drawer 49, File 10, and Link, *Papers* 46:350-51; Wiseman to Balfour, March 14, 1918, Balfour Papers, 49741/56-60; Lord Reading to Balfour, March 27, 1918, Wiseman Papers, Drawer 90, File 3; Fowler, *British-American Relations*, pp. 266-67.

34. Roosevelt to Arthur Hamilton Lee (British MP), February 21, 1918, Roosevelt to Taft, March 4, 1918, Roosevelt to Henry L. Stimson (former U.S. secretary of war), March 12, 1918, Roosevelt to Taft, March 16, 1918, in Elting E. Morison, ed., *The Letters of Theodore Roosevelt*, 8 vols. (Cambridge: Harvard University Press, 1951-1954), 8:1286-91, 1294, 1298-99, 1301.

35. Taft to Elihu Root, March 11, 1918, Elihu Root Papers, Box 166, Library of Congress, Washington, DC; Taft to Roosevelt, March 11, 1918, Roosevelt to Root, March 4, 1918, Root Papers, Box 163.

36. Balfour to Reading, April 1, 2, 1918, Reading to Balfour, April 10, 18, 21, 1918, Wiseman to House, April 24, 1918, Wiseman Papers, Drawer 90, File 3; House to Wilson, April 9, 1918, House Papers, Drawer 49, File 10; William Wiseman, Notes on Interview with the President, April 1, 1918, Balfour Papers, 49741/73-76; Fowler, *British-American Relations*, pp. 267-71; Lloyd George to Reading, March 28, 1918, Reading to Lansing, April 2, 1918, *Foreign Relations, 1918: World War*, Sup. 1, 1:180-82, 188; N. D. Baker to Bliss, April 29, May 7, 1918, Tasker Howard Bliss Papers, Box 75, Library of Congress, Washington, DC; Lloyd George to Reading, March 28, 1918, Reading to Lloyd George, March 28, 1918, Wiseman to Balfour, c. March 28, 1918, House to Wilson, April 9, 1918, in Link, *Papers* 47:181-85, 302-4; Baker to Wilson, July 1, 1918, Newton D. Baker Papers, Box 8, Library of Congress, Washington, DC, and Link, *Papers* 48:476-77.

37. House to Pershing, April 27, 1918, House Papers, Drawer 49, File 10; Lodge to John T. Morse, Jr. (historian), May 16, 1918, Henry Cabot Lodge Papers, File 1918 (H-Q), Massachusetts Historical Society, Boston.

38. House Diary, March 28, April 9, 1918; Baker and Dodd, *Public Papers* 5:198-202; *Foreign Relations, 1918: World War*, Sup. 1, 1:200-203; Reading to Wilson, April 13, 1918, Wilson Papers, Ser. 4, File 63; Diary of Colonel House, March 28, April 9, 1918, An Address, April 6, 1918, Reading to Wilson, April 13, 1918, in Link, *Papers* 47:185-86, 267-70, 307-10, 334-35.

39. President to Foreign Correspondents, April 8, 1918, Tumulty Papers, Box 5; Remarks to Foreign Correspondents, April 8, 1918, in Link, *Papers* 47:284-89.

40. For the Soviet-American ideological confrontation see Mayer, *Political Origins of the New Diplomacy*; Levin, *Woodrow Wilson and World Politics*, pp. 1-119; and Gardner, *Safe for Democracy*, pp. 124-75. For my critique of New Left historiography, especially of Mayer and Levin, see Lloyd E. Ambrosius, "The Orthodoxy of Revisionism: Woodrow Wilson and the New Left," *Diplomatic History* 1 (Summer 1977): 199-214.

41. George F. Kennan, *Russia Leaves the War* (Princeton: Princeton University Press, 1956); idem, *The Decision to Intervene* (Princeton: Princeton University Press, 1958); Betty Miller Unterberger, *The United States, Revolutionary Russia, and the Rise of Czechoslovakia* (Chapel Hill: University of North Carolina Press, 1989); idem, "Woodrow Wilson and the Russian Revolution," in Link, *Woodrow Wilson and a Revolutionary World*, pp. 49-104. See also Linda Killen, *The Russian Bureau: A Case Study in Wilsonian Diplomacy* (Lexington: University Press of Kentucky, 1983); Eugene P. Trani, "Woodrow Wilson and the Decision to Intervene in Russia: A Reconsideration," *Journal of Modern History* 48 (September 1976): 440-61; and Calhoun, *Power and Principle*, pp. 185-218.

42. Fowler, *British-American Relations*, p. 288.

CHAPTER 5

American Ideals and European Realities

Realities of the Old World created a dilemma for President Wilson as he anticipated the future peace. Neither Imperial Germany nor Soviet Russia accommodated to his vision of collective security. This conflict between American ideals and European realities produced ambivalence in his approach to negotiations with the Imperial German government. He hoped that a reformed Germany would join the future league of nations. But if the German people remained faithful to the kaiser's government, then the question of membership for Imperial Germany in the league would confront him. The Allies rejected this possibility. But if the president accepted this solution, he would sacrifice his ideal of a universal world community. Continuation of the wartime divisions, by maintaining a balance of power, would perpetuate the very international order that he hoped to change. Alternatively, he might seek to impose a democratic government onto Germany. But this, too, would entangle the United States in the Old World.

Wilson hoped to escape from entanglement in Europe by creating a league that would give the United States the controlling influence in world affairs. Refusal of the Europeans to fit into his pattern of liberal internationalism, especially the very existence of the Imperial German and Soviet governments, confronted him with an exceedingly difficult task as he sought to clarify his war aims in greater detail than the Fourteen Points. This problem delayed his attempt to plan for the future peace.

II

If the president were to succeed in redeeming the Old World by creating a new order of international relations, he needed to translate his ideals into specific policies. Colonel Edward House advised Wilson to formulate a practical plan for a new league of nations. Warning that further delay might allow others to seize the initiative, he claimed that "the whole world" regarded him as "the champion of the idea" and expected him to develop it. In Great Britain and France as well as the United States, people were increasingly concerned about his reluctance to proceed with the idea of collective security. House urged action.[1]

Wilson, however, concentrating on military victory against the Central Powers, enunciated only general principles. During the critical period in the summer of 1918 he postponed the hard questions concerning a new league. At Mount Vernon on July 4 he called for total victory in the war, announcing that "the settlement must be final." Like Secretary of State Robert Lansing, he demanded "the destruction of every arbitrary power anywhere that can separately, secretly, and of its single choice disturb the peace of the world; or, if it cannot be presently destroyed, at the least its reduction to virtual impotence." The peace settlement, he said, should conform to the ideal of national self-determination. As House had advised, he asserted that all nations should accept "the same principles of honor and respect for the common law of civilized society that govern the individual citizens of all modern states." Proposing a new order of collective security, he called for "an organization of peace" to enable "free nations" to mobilize public opinion against any threat to peace and justice. Such a league would provide an alternative to the discredited balance of power. "What we seek," Wilson concluded, "is the reign of law, based upon the consent of the governed and sustained by the organized opinion of mankind."[2]

As prospects for military victory improved, the president finally moved beyond ideals to a more precise definition of collective security. General John J. Pershing, who had so reported to the new chief of staff, Peyton C. March, in June 1918, now felt confident that the American and Allied armies could stop the Germans on the western front. That month

American and French forces had taken the offensive against the German army. Pershing informed Wilson that this was "the first serious attack against the Germans."[3]

With this shift in the military balance the president became more optimistic about reforming the Old World. His Christian crusade for democracy might yet culminate in a new international order. George Herron persuaded him that Allied public opinion would welcome his call for "the creation of a new earth." Expecting Germany to launch a new peace initiative, Herron also thought that such a call would protect the Allies from this danger. Appealing to Wilson's fundamental beliefs, the Social Gospel theologian told him that he was uniquely qualified to herald "this world-revolution." He alone could summon the world to enter a new era in which "men shall be no longer creatures but creators, . . . directing the course of evolution, and writing hence the history of the future rather than of the past." Because he possessed "the requisite universal confidence of mankind" and "an indisputable spiritual authority over the world," he could overcome "the present chaos." Herron's appeal deeply moved Wilson, who then asked House to prepare a specific plan for a postwar league.[4]

Germany's possible membership in the league continued to plague the United States. House agreed with Lord Grey, who favored Germany's eventual inclusion. He hoped to overcome French resistance in order to create a universal community of nations. The future league's purpose, he advised the president, should be "the maintenance throughout the world of peace, security, progress and orderly government." As its "keystone," House wanted individual honor and morality to serve as the standards for international behavior. He sought to abolish espionage, naively hoping that this reform would encourage the Allies to permit Germany to join the league. He continued to prefer binding arbitration, backed by economic sanctions, as the principal method for resolving conflicts.

House wanted all great powers, but not small nations, in the league. Expecting every nation to conform to the league's standards, he viewed it as a global organization for peace, despite the exclusion of weak states. He advocated a mutual guarantee of territorial integrity and political independence, but he balanced this obligation with a provision for territorial changes in accordance with national self-determination. House affirmed that "the peace of the world is superior in importance and interest to questions of boundary." In accordance with Wilson's understanding of international social control, such a league would facilitate both enforcement and revision of the peace treaty. House also expected the league to formulate a plan for reducing national armaments. He did not regard it as a permanent military alliance against Germany.[5]

Wilson revised House's recommendations as he began to prepare his draft of a covenant. In mid-August he finally sought to transform general principles into a specific plan. He, too, proposed binding arbitration to create a powerful league. Still, except for sanctions to force potential belligerents to resolve their disputes through arbitration, he wanted to avoid American entanglement in the Old World. He omitted the idea of a world court. Moreover, like House, he balanced the mutual guarantee of political independence and territorial integrity with the possibility of territorial changes. On the critical question of Germany's membership in the league, Wilson remained ambivalent. "If we formed the league while we were still fighting," he explained, "it would inevitably be regarded as a sort of Holy Alliance aimed at Germany. This would not be the purpose of the American people. Germany should be invited to join the family of nations, providing she will behave according to the rules of the Society." He still wished to delay the league's creation until the peace conference in order to keep open the possibility of membership for a reformed Germany in the new system of collective security.[6]

House expected the U.S. Senate and the Allies to resist a Wilsonian peace. Fearful that the president's influence at home and abroad might decrease with victory, he encouraged him to proclaim the future league in a public address. Wilson, too, wanted to retain the initiative. Moreover, the rising prospect of military victory against the Central Powers helped him to ignore the fundamental dilemma that had earlier plagued him. Despite the persistent refusal of the Old World—especially Imperial Germany and Soviet Russia—to conform to his pattern for the future, he decided to elaborate the ideals of liberal internationalism.[7]

Wilson explained his conception of collective security in New York on September 27, 1918. Regarding the new league as the prerequisite for permanent peace, he called for its creation at the peace conference. He repudiated the French view of an anti-German alliance and instead anticipated eventual membership for a reformed Germany. To provide security for all belligerents, including former enemies, he still hoped to transform international relations. He noted, however, that "Germany will have to redeem her character, not by what happens at the peace table, but by what follows." Affirming the ideal of "impartial justice," he asserted that "there can be no leagues or alliances or special covenants and understandings within the general common family of the League of Nations." The president reconciled his universal principles with the unilateralism of traditional American isolation from the Old World. "We still read Washington's immortal warning against 'entangling alliances' with full comprehension and an answering purpose," he emphasized. A new world order, based on "common understandings" and "common rights," might yet emerge after military victory over the Central Powers.[8]

Henry Cabot Lodge remained skeptical about Wilson's vision of collective security. Lacking the progressive faith of liberal internationalists, the senator doubted the feasibility of reforming international relations. More pessimistic and realistic in his outlook, he saw the war as a genuine tragedy. He refused to escape into the dream of redeeming the Old World. Like Henry Adams, whose autobiography he edited for posthumous publication, Lodge did not think that the United States could predict and control the future by applying the methods of social science. In his study of history Adams had searched in vain for some unifying principle to bring order out of the current chaos. He contrasted twentieth-century multiplicity with thirteenth-century unity under God's sovereignty. Unlike Wilson, whose faith in God provided the foundation for his belief in the universality of the world, Adams could not find this principle in religion. Nor could he discover it in science. Despite his attempts to apply the laws of science to the study of history, Adams had failed to find any principle that could unite the disparate events of human affairs by adequately explaining cause and effect. Without such a law, the historian could either impose his own idea onto the past or admit his failure. In *The Education of Henry Adams*, he brilliantly elucidated his own failure.[9] As a conservative, like Adams, Lodge understood power politics. Unlike Wilson, he wanted to defeat Germany in order to create a new balance of power in Europe. He shared that goal with the Allies.[10]

To Lodge, Wilson's vision of collective security was irrelevant to realistic peacemaking. The Republican leader understood this fundamental problem with liberal internationalism. No universal league could substitute for a balance of power as the basis for a durable peace. Prevention of another war, in the senator's judgment, would require not only Germany's "unconditional surrender" but also close collaboration between the United States and the Allies after the war. These western powers should therefore exclude Germany from any postwar league.[11]

Germany and Austria-Hungary appealed to Wilson for peace negotiations on the basis of his Fourteen Points. The president welcomed this prospect but also wanted to commit the Allies to his principles. He sent House to Europe to consult them about an armistice. For Wilson, the first three and last of his Fourteen Points were "the essentially American terms." He wanted not only the abolition of secret treaties, freedom of the seas, and commercial equality but also, above all, the creation of a league of nations. He repudiated any settlement that would provide "only European arrangements of peace." House attempted at first to persuade, and then to coerce, the Allies into accepting the Fourteen Points without reservations. But then he compromised to gain at least the Allies' general acceptance of the president's peace program. He experienced the limits of American power in European affairs but obscured this fact by calling the compromise "a great diplomatic victory." When Wilson endorsed this compromise, he, too, implicitly acknowledged the inability of the United States to control postwar international relations. All of the belligerents now committed themselves to his conditions for peace, but with reservations. The Old World did not welcome American redemption.[12]

Disregarding this reality, Wilson heralded the opportunity to establish liberal internationalism. "America is the leader of the liberal thought of the world," he assured Senator Key Pittman of Nevada, "and nobody from any quarter should be allowed to interfere with or impair that leadership without giving an account of himself, which can be made very difficult." Collapse of the Austro-Hungarian Empire substantially improved the military situation for the Allied and Associated Powers. The American Expeditionary Forces now numbered over two million men. Victory over the Central Powers was finally certain for the United States and the

Allies. On their behalf, Secretary Lansing offered on November 5 to conclude peace with the Imperial German government on the basis of Wilson's principles.[13]

Events within Germany appeared to prove the validity of Wilson's progressive interpretation of history. Contrary to his doubts a few months earlier, prospects for democratic revolution improved as the Germans experienced military defeat. After Kaiser Wilhelm II was forced to abdicate, a new republican government quickly accepted the conditions that Lansing had presented. The simultaneous advent of peace and democracy seemed to fulfill the promise of American ideals. Once the German delegation signed the armistice on November 11, 1918, House rejoiced that "autocracy is dead." Wilson, too, welcomed the apparent triumph of democracy in Germany. Reporting the armistice to a joint session of Congress, he announced that "the arbitrary power of the military caste of Germany which once could secretly and of its own single choice disturb the peace of the world is discredited and destroyed." He naively proclaimed that "everything for which America fought has been accomplished." An optimistic president, momentarily ignoring bolshevism in Russia and antidemocratic elements in Germany, anticipated "the establishment of just democracy throughout the world." Seeking democratic revolution in the Old World, he reaffirmed the American mission to foster this historic development.[14]

Liberal internationalism combined idealism and practicality. In a shrewd analysis of the diplomatic style that Wilson epitomized, Sir William Wiseman had observed that "the American is undoubtedly an idealist. He was never afraid of Germany, or jealous of her. American troops go to Europe with a rather vague idea that they are going to democratize Europe, and put the Kaiser in particular, and all autocrats generally, out of business; an ingenuous notion that they want to make the rest of the world as democratic as they believe their own country to be." Americans seemed unable to recognize any self-interest in their crusade to make the world safe for democracy. But they demonstrated a practicality along with this missionary impulse. "For all their idealism," Wiseman recognized, "the Americans are a people with shrewd common sense; and when the difficulties have become more apparent they will no doubt quite cheerfully accept a very much modified Utopia."

Wilson evidenced the dualism of the American character. "He is by turns a great idealist and a shrewd politician," observed Wiseman, "and he will not hesitate to attempt to put into practice his greatest ideals, though he will probably always under-estimate the difficulties and the opposition confronting him." He was not a realistic statesman in pursuit of a new balance of power. Instead, he approached peace-making as a practical idealist. He wanted to reform the Old World. "The President," Wiseman noted, "regards the war— or rather the peace which will follow it—as a great opportunity for remodelling the whole structure of international affairs. He is not so much interested in the adjustment of this claim or that—the limitation of one power, and the strengthening of another—but his mind visualizes a new world in which there shall be no tyranny and no war."[15]

Wilson's liberal idealism expressed his Christian faith. Patriotism and religion coincided in his understanding of American nationalism. In his Thanksgiving proclamation after the armistice, he rejoiced that "God has in His good pleasure given us peace. It has not come as a mere cessation of arms, a mere relief from the strain and tragedy of war. It has come as a great triumph of right. Complete victory has brought us, not peace alone, but the confident promise of a new day as well in which justice shall replace force and jealous intrigue among the nations." Military success, he now anticipated, opened the possibility of fulfilling American ideals. When he later arrived in Paris for the peace conference, the president praised the American soldiers and sailors, who epitomized the "true spirit" of their country, for their contribution to "this war of redemption." He still expected the triumph of liberal internationalism.[16]

III

Wilson's foreign policy culminated in the creation of the League of Nations. At the Paris Peace Conference of 1919, in collaboration with the British, he succeeded in drafting the Covenant for this new international organization. He regarded it as the key feature of the Versailles treaty, although Germany would be excluded from the League during the initial postwar years. Combining the idealism and practicality of his diplomatic style, it promised both order and change in international relations. Article 10 offered a mutual guarantee of territorial integrity and political independence for nations in the new League, yet Article 19 anticipated future adjustments in the peace settlement. Providing for both enforcement and revision, the Covenant thus embodied the methods of international social control. Although the president, with British assistance, wrote his own conception of collective security into the Covenant, he emphasized its universal character. He expected all nations to conform to the standards of Anglo-American liberalism.[17]

Upon completing the initial draft of the Covenant, Wilson presented it to a plenary session of the peace conference on February 14. He expected the League to preserve peace by organizing public opinion, stressing that "throughout this instrument we are depending primarily and chiefly upon one great force, and that is the moral force of the public opinion of the world." Yet he realized the potential inadequacy of "the overwhelming light of the universal expression of the condemnation of the world." If public opinion failed to preserve peace, he anticipated the use of military power, asserting that "if the moral force of the world will not suffice, the physical force of the world shall." But the president did not intend to commit the United States to a new international status quo. Emphasizing the League's flexibility, he called it "a vehicle of power, but a vehicle in which power may be varied at the discretion of those who exercise it and in accordance with the changing circumstances of the time." He announced that "a living thing is born." Wilson viewed the League as a practical way to reform the Old World on a continuing basis. "It is practical, and yet it is intended to purify, to rectify, to elevate."[18]

Wilson reaffirmed these themes when he presented the Versailles treaty, including the slightly revised Covenant, to the U.S. Senate on July 10, 1919. Collective security was the central feature of his new foreign policy. The United States, he emphasized, had intervened in the European war to redeem the Old World. "We entered the war as the disinterested champions of right, and we interested ourselves in the terms of the peace in no other capacity." The American Expeditionary Forces had fought as "crusaders" to bring "salvation" to Europe. Military victory over the Central Powers had opened the opportunity for the United States and the Allies to establish peace on the basis of his Fourteen Points. Despite the difficulties, he thought that the peace treaty embodied these principles. "It was not easy to graft the new order of ideas on the old," he admitted, "and some of the fruits of the grafting may, I fear, for a time be bitter."

Wilson defended the Covenant as the most essential part of the peace treaty with Germany. In accordance with his conception of collective security, he viewed "the League of Nations as an indispensable instrumentality for the maintenance of the new order." By replacing the old order of a balance of power and alliances, it provided the only hope for future peace. "The united power of free nations must put a stop to aggression," he explained, "and the world must be given peace. If there was not the will or the intelligence to accomplish that now, there must be another and a final war and the world must be swept clean of every power that could renew the terror. The League of Nations was not merely an instrument to adjust and remedy old wrongs under a new treaty of peace. It was the only hope for mankind." In other words, Wilson viewed the League as an end in itself, not just as a means to implement the treaty. It epitomized the new order of international relations.

Through the League, Wilson expected the United States to provide "moral leadership" for the world. No longer isolated as it had been before the Spanish-American War, this nation would assume its responsibilities as a new world power. He viewed this new American position as a God-given destiny. "The stage is set, the destiny disclosed," the president told the Senate. "It has come about by no plan of our conceiving, but by the hand of God who led us into this way. We cannot turn back. We can only go forward, with lifted eyes and freshened spirit, to follow the vision. It was of this that we dreamed at our birth. America shall in truth show the way. The light streams upon the path ahead, and nowhere else."[19]

In reality, however, Wilson had failed to make the world safe for democracy. Neither the Weimar Republic nor Soviet Russia, which were both excluded from membership in the League, embraced his vision of a new international order. Nor did the Allies entrust their future to this form of collective security. Although generally denying the implications of this failure, on one occasion in August 1919 he admitted to Lansing his growing despair over the Old World's refusal to conform to his ideals. He even considered keeping the United States out of the League for this reason. "When I see such conduct as this [by the Romanians in Hungary], when I learn of the secret treaty of Great Britain with Persia, when I find Italy and Greece arranging between themselves as to the division of western Asia Minor, and when I think of the greed and utter selfishness of it all," the president explained, "I am almost inclined to refuse to permit this country to be a member of the League of Nations when it is composed of such intriguers and robbers. I am disposed to throw up the whole business and get out."[20] The president, as he privately acknowledged, was painfully aware that his crusade for democracy had not transformed the Old World.

IV

Ironically, while Wilson was concentrating on creating the League, the American Expeditionary Forces jeopardized the traditional civil-military relationship in one crucial case. Although largely unknown at the time, the breakdown of civilian control over the military in this instance evidenced another weakness in his statecraft. Poor coordination between political ends and military means had begun to erode presidential authority during the war. "In the actual conduct of operations," General Pershing later recalled, "I was given entire freedom and in this respect was to enjoy an experience unique in our history."[21] This pattern culminated in a serious episode of inadequate civilian control and military professionalism after the war.

Without the president's authorization, or even his knowledge, military intelligence officers from Pershing's headquarters initiated contacts with prominent German leaders and maintained them throughout the peace conference. These secret German-American negotiations posed fundamental questions about the practice of democratic government in the United States. While Wilson was seeking to foster democracy throughout the world, the tradition of civilian control over military affairs was eroding in his own country.

After the armistice, Pershing established an advance headquarters at Trier in Germany, transferring some officers there from his general headquarters at Chaumont in France. Colonel Arthur L. Conger, chief of the intelligence section at Trier, and other members of Pershing's general staff, soon established direct contact with the top military and civilian leaders in the new German republic. Wilson was only partially informed about their activities. The American Commission to Negotiate Peace, including the president and other delegates to the peace conference, received only abridged military intelligence reports, which did not reveal the full scope of these negotiations. The reports failed to disclose that the American officers were seeking to shape the future peace. Although largely unsuccessful, this military diplomacy would encourage the German leaders to expect a treaty more in accordance with their interpretation of the Fourteen Points than with Wilson's. Thus was fostered the Germans' conviction that the president betrayed them to the Allies by eventually approving conditions of peace that violated his Fourteen Points. By attempting to influence the proceedings of the Allied and Associated Powers and by misleading the Germans, Conger and his military colleagues would interfere with the official diplomacy of the peace conference.[22]

Colonel Conger initiated the secret negotiations in December 1918 with Walter Loeb, who was affiliated with the intelligence department of the Workers' and Soldiers' Council in Frankfurt, one of many such councils in the new German republic. At Conger's invitation, Loeb went to Pershing's headquarters in Trier, where the ranking officer, Brigadier General Preston Brown, joined the discussion. The American officers began to encourage false expectations of a rift between the United States and the Allies. Stressing the American commitment to Wilson's Fourteen Points, they made a fundamental distinction between these conditions for peace and the harsher terms of the armistice. Critical of France, they expressed the desire for reconciliation with Germany. Both Brown and Conger emphasized the importance of convening a national assembly and establishing a legitimate democratic government in Berlin, suggesting that these political developments would facilitate an American supply of food for Germany.[23]

Loeb reported these meetings to the supreme command of the German army. General Wilhelm Groener, who had replaced Erich Ludendorff as quartermaster general, seized the opportunity to pursue the direct contact with the United States. He sent Baron Paul von Eltz Rübenach to Trier to deliver a statement to Conger, explaining that the army's commanders had formed an "alliance" with Friedrich Ebert, the foremost Social Democratic leader in Germany's new republican government, to prevent a radical revolution. He proposed in particular an alliance between Berlin and Washington to "fight against Bolshevists" and, for this purpose, urged the inclusion of Germany in the future league of nations. This proposal called for collaboration between Germany and the United States to stabilize the former's democratic revolution against the threat of bolshevism.[24]

American military officers continued to intervene in German politics. In Trier in late January, Conger once more impressed upon Loeb the advantages to Germany of adopting a republican constitution like that of the United States. Loeb reported this conversation to the German foreign minister, Count Ulrich von Brockdorff-Rantzau, informing him that Ebert was fully aware of the connection with Conger. President Wilson, unfortunately, was not equally well informed by Pershing's staff.[25]

These American officers generally pursued the goals of liberal internationalism but not as part of a coordinated foreign policy. With its unauthorized military diplomacy, Pershing's headquarters fostered false German expectations. The new government of the Weimar Republic pursued secret negotiations with the United States. Loeb notified Brockdorff-Rantzau and Matthias Erzberger, the prominent leader of the Center party who had signed the armistice and who continued to deal with its implementation for the German government, about an encouraging discussion with Conger. They, in turn, informed Ebert, the republic's first president, and Philipp Scheidemann, its Social Democratic chancellor. After consideration by the entire cabinet, Erzberger and Brockdorff-Rantzau gave instructions to Loeb, who was scheduled to meet Conger in Trier. On March 30, Loeb submitted to Conger an unofficial statement of "Peace Conditions Acceptable to Germany." Although the document was unofficial, the Germans promised to approve a peace settlement that fulfilled this interpretation of the Fourteen Points.[26]

The secret German-American negotiations eventually failed because President Wilson never authorized them. Conger and his colleagues in Pershing's general staff were misrepresenting the official American position during the peace conference. Wilson joined the Allies at Versailles in refusing the concessions that Brockdorff-Rantzau demanded. By encouraging the German leaders to expect a lenient treaty, conforming to their interpretation of the Fourteen Points

rather than Wilson's, the military diplomacy provided a substantial basis for their emerging conviction that the president
betrayed Germany for the Allies' sake. The Germans did not
know that the American officers had operated without instructions from responsible civilians. Indeed, American delegates to the peace conference, including Wilson himself,
received only carefully edited reports, which revealed nothing
about the intelligence officers' persistent endeavors to influence the peacemaking. Nor did General Pershing communicate
with the president through the War Department. Although
Conger possibly exceeded his instructions, he probably did
not depart very far from them. Too many officers from
Pershing's headquarters were personally involved in the secret negotiations for their activities to have escaped the
general's attention. Because their frequent reports offered
ample opportunity for him to curtail this unauthorized military diplomacy, Pershing was directly responsible for it.[27]
    The president also contributed to this unfortunate epi-
sode by neglecting to coordinate political and military policies.
While pursuing his vision of collective security, he permitted
Pershing too much autonomy. Wilson's diplomatic style thus
fostered the conditions for this breakdown of civilian control.
Poor civil-military coordination characterized his statecraft.
He might have used American military officers to encourage
the Germans to establish a democratic government. But, in
fact, he did not employ such a method. To the extent that the
officers pursued this goal, they operated on their own initiative. Instead of being designed by Wilson to promote democracy in the Weimar Republic, the secret German-American
negotiations evidenced a further weakness in his attempt to
foster liberal internationalism.

V

The limits of American control over foreign affairs had
thwarted Wilson's attempt to redeem Europe. Not only Russia and Germany but also the Allies had resisted his mission
to inaugurate a new era of international relations. As a
consequence, Wilson yearned for American isolation from the
Old World in order to avoid entanglement in its traditional
rivalries. Clinging to his ideals, however, he still endeavored
to win the Senate's approval of the peace treaty. Despite the

disparity between his liberal internationalism and European realities, the president wanted the United States to join the League without reservations. But he was never able to achieve this goal.[28]

Other liberals expressed their disillusionment by denouncing the Versailles treaty, and especially the League of Nations. The philosopher-educator John Dewey, along with Herbert Croly and Walter Lippmann, enthusiastically had endorsed American belligerency as a crusade for democracy. To reconcile liberal idealism with their pragmatism, they had escalated their future expectations in order to vindicate the war by its ostensible outcome. They had justified the war's terrible costs by anticipating the triumph of democracy and peace in the postwar world. Expecting the United States to play the redemptive role of transforming international relations, they inevitably experienced disappointment. The Paris Peace Conference of 1919 failed to realize their ideals. Consequently, Dewey, Croly, and Lippmann denounced the peace treaty with Germany and opposed American participation in the League to enforce it. Their unrealistic belief that the United States could control the modern world produced this postwar liberal disillusionment. But that degree of influence over international relations was beyond the capacity of any nation. The reality of competing national interests had forced the president to compromise with the Allies, and even with Germany. Despite his best efforts, the United States lacked the power to redeem the Old World.[29]

In Lippmann's view, American liberalism had failed both at home and abroad. This failure prompted him to begin reassessing the intellectual foundations of American progressivism. Eventually, this process of disillusionment would culminate in his realistic critique of U.S. foreign policy during and after World War II. But he had not yet developed the conservative philosophy of his later years. Critical of the peace treaty in 1919, he wanted the United States to accept no obligation in the League to enforce it. Moreover, he noted the irony that Wilson, who had promised to make the world safe for democracy, threatened civil liberties at home. During the treaty fight, wartime hysteria reached a climax in the Red Scare of 1919-20. This form of social control was not what Lippmann had anticipated. "You know what hopes were put in this administration," he complained to Secretary Newton D. Baker, "how loudly and insistently it proclaimed its loyalty to the cause of freedom. Well, it was possible to fail in those hopes. It was credible that the wisdom and the strength to realize them would be lacking. But it is forever incredible that an administration announcing the most spacious ideals in our history should have done more to endanger fundamental American liberties than any group of men for a hundred years." Lippmann blamed the president and others in the executive branch for this tragic and ironic outcome: "They have instituted a reign of terror in which honest thought is impossible, in which moderation is discountenanced, in which panic supplants reason."[30]

Some proponents of the League of Nations did not experience the liberal disillusionment that characterized Lippmann, Croly, and Dewey. John Bates Clark and Franklin Giddings, Wilson's longtime friends, persevered in their support of the president on this question. More realistic in their expectations, they had not anticipated the redemption of the Old World. They were therefore less prone to suffer from disappointment. After the war, Clark continued to advocate a workable league. He wanted the United States to cooperate with the Allies to preserve the favorable balance of power that they had established through victory over Germany. Against the threat of a resurgent Germany he thought that this kind of postwar league could maintain peace. Expecting international rivalry to persist, he advocated a responsible role for the United States in the existing international system. In Clark's view, the League of Nations could not fulfill the dream of a new world order. Giddings likewise adopted a practical attitude toward international organization. Acknowledging the League's imperfections, he nevertheless praised it as an instrument for peace. He rejoiced that the English-speaking people, who were the most democratic in the world, would exert the preponderant power in the League. Both Clark and Giddings continued to support Wilson throughout the treaty fight.[31]

In the end, however, Wilsonian statecraft failed to fulfill its promise. Despite his best efforts, the president could not make the world safe for democracy. The German government, under duress, had reluctantly authorized its delegation to sign the peace treaty at Versailles. But, like the Russians, the Germans did not welcome their assigned place in the postwar international order. The United States had not redeemed the Old World by creating the League. Eventually rejecting the Versailles treaty, it declined even to participate in this experiment in collective security.

Moreover, while seeking to promote American ideals and practices in other countries, President Wilson had sacrificed liberal values at home. The breakdown of civilian control over the military evidenced a serious weakness in the nation's democracy. Wartime hysteria, which culminated in the Red Scare, also revealed the darker side of American progressivism. These internal developments, as well as the persistence of power politics in foreign affairs, constituted the ultimate failure of Wilson's liberal crusade. It was not so easy to promote democracy abroad or even to preserve it at home. Instead of a new world community in which democracy flourished, providing a foundation for collective security and peace, these were the consequences of his leadership during the First World War. Postwar realities did not conform to his promise of liberal internationalism.

VI

A sharp contrast between war and peace characterized Wilson's thinking about international relations. Although he had developed his conception of collective security during the world war, he postponed the creation of the League of Nations until the peace conference. Initially, he had seen no reason for the United States to abandon its neutrality, although he was beginning to anticipate a postwar league. Offering American mediation to end the European war, the president emphasized that he was not interested in the belligerents' war aims. Both Allied and German statesmen had encouraged this distinction between war and peace in order to prevent American interference with their plans. Subsequently, Wilson used the idea of collective security to justify intervention, but he still refused to define his principles in detail. Even when he finally outlined his Fourteen Points, in response to the Russian Revolution, these provided the basis for future peace rather than for wartime strategy. The president hesitated to clarify his vision of a postwar league until the imminent defeat of the Central Powers. Paradoxically, the very existence of the Imperial German government had delayed his attempt to draft a covenant. Because he wanted to transcend the old order of a balance of power and alliances, he waited until the war's end before seeking to implement his idea of collective security.

A remarkable consequence of Wilson's sharp distinction between war and peace was his failure to coordinate political and military policies. During the period of American neutrality, he had neglected military preparedness, except for the direct defense of the United States and the Western Hemisphere against an attack. Although he was developing his vision of collective security at that time, he did not anticipate the use of his country's armed forces in the Old World. Even after intervention in 1917, the United States had lacked a coordinated foreign policy. The president sent American troops to Europe to fight against Germany, but he did not use military strategy to achieve his political goals in any particular way. Wilson simply expected victory to bring the opportunity to implement his Fourteen Points. In marked contrast to the Allies, especially France, he neglected military strategy as a means to political ends. He regarded that kind of strategic thinking as part of the discredited old order. One serious consequence of this neglect was the breakdown of civilian control over the military. Rather than integrating military and diplomatic affairs, he concentrated instead on the separate aspects of winning the war and defining the peace. In that sense, ironically, the idea of collective security was irrelevant to his wartime strategy.

Wilson's approach to war and peace had demonstrated both idealism and practicality. On one level, drawing upon his understanding of the American past, he articulated a vision of the future. Projecting the ideals of his own political culture onto the world, he heralded a new era of peace. American nationalism provided the model for his liberal internationalism, while progressive history and social science furnished the intellectual foundations for his foreign policy. He hoped to create a viable league of nations to replace the balance of power and alliances. On another level, while pursuing a new world order, he operated prudently in the arena of international diplomacy. He sought to mediate the European war without abandoning American neutrality. When Imperial Germany's submarine warfare eventually forced the United States to intervene, he used the idea of collective security to rally public opinion behind the American war effort. Beyond the expectations of his critics at home and abroad, he provided the essential reinforcements to the Allies to defeat the Central Powers. Simultaneously, he developed his vision of a postwar league into a specific covenant. The president demonstrated considerable skill in the practical aspects of both diplomatic and military affairs, but the limitations of his leadership arose from the inadequate linkage between ideals and practice. Failure to coordinate short-term means with long-term ends characterized his diplomatic style, thus constituting a form of statecraft that expressed the traditional dualism of the American character.

Wilson's liberal internationalism suffered from a serious lack of realism. He never recognized that American security depended upon the European balance of power. For this reason he had sought at first to remain neutral without regard for the potential danger of a German victory over the Allies. By offering mediation he hoped to end the war before it involved the United States, regardless of the consequences for European belligerents. He led the nation into the war only after Germany resorted to unrestricted submarine warfare. His emerging conception of collective security promised peace at a low price. The new League of Nations, he anticipated, would enable the United States to control foreign affairs without entangling itself in the Old World. It would epitomize the new era of international relations. But postwar Europe, including the Allies as well as Soviet Russia and Weimar Germany, refused to conform to Wilson's liberal ideals. The world did not fit his pattern of progressive history or accept the United States as its model. Nor did it acquiesce in the League's postwar attempt at international social control.

In the final analysis, Wilsonian statecraft did not merit the accolades of "sublime realism" or "higher realism." Recent scholarship has confused Wilson's prudence or practicality with classic realism. Some historians have contended that he sought to preserve the European balance of power; but he specifically repudiated that international system. They have argued that he served the national interest with consummate skill; but he reiterated his indifference toward the belligerents' war aims and ignored the connection between the European peace settlement and American security. They have claimed that he coordinated the ends and means of U.S. foreign policy; but he led a militarily unprepared nation into war for purposes that were still undefined except as general principles. Recent scholars often have used the original realists' terminology without either accepting or repudiating their fundamental critique of Wilson's statecraft.

American political culture shaped Wilson's liberal internationalism and limited his understanding of world affairs. He overestimated the ability of the United States to convince other nations to adopt its ideals and practices. Pluralism still characterized the modern world, despite its growing interdependence. Wilson was neither conservative nor radical enough to escape the limitations of Anglo-American liberalism in the international arena. Contrary to the prevalent interpretation in recent scholarship, the president's combination of idealism and practicality failed to produce a realistic foreign policy for the United States. Instead of realism, the political culture of American progressivism manifested itself in Wilsonian statecraft during World War I.

Notes

1. House to Wilson, June 25, 1918, House Papers, Drawer 49, File 10, and Link, *Papers* 48:424-25.

2. Baker and Dodd, *Public Papers* 5:231-35; *Foreign Relations, 1918: World War*, Sup. 1, 1:268-71; Address at Mount Vernon, [July 4, 1918], in Link, *Papers* 48:514-17; Wiseman to Eric Drummond (Balfour's private secretary), June 15, 1918, Balfour Papers, 49741/89.

3. Raymond Poincaré (French president) to Wilson, June 12, 1918, Wilson to Poincaré, June 13, 1918, Wilson Papers, Ser. 4, File 185; Pershing to March, June 19, 1918, Pershing Papers, Box 123, and Peyton C. March Papers, Box 22, Library of Congress, Washington, DC; Pershing to Wilson, June 28, 1918, Wilson to Pershing, July 24, 1918, Wilson Papers, Ser. 4, File 4944; Pershing to Wilson, June 27, 1918, Pershing Papers, Box 213; House to Georges Clemenceau (French premier), July 1, 1918, House Papers, Drawer 5, File 4; N. D. Baker to Bliss, May 31, 1918, Bliss Papers, Box 75; Pershing to House, June 19, 1918, House to Pershing, July 4, 1918, House Papers, Drawer 15, File 45; Wilson to Poincaré, June 13, 1918, in Link, *Papers* 48:301; Wilson to Pershing, July 24, 1918, in Link, *Papers* 49:74.

4. George D. Herron to Wilson, May 31, July 6, 1918, Wilson to Lansing, July 1, 1918, Wilson to House, July 8, 1918, in Link, *Papers* 48:210-17, 473-74, 538-40, 549-50; Wilson to House, July 8, 1918, House Papers, Letterbook IV.

5. House to Wilson, July 11, 14, 16, 1918, House Papers, Drawer 49, File 11A, and Link, *Papers* 48:592-93, 608, 630-37; Arthur C. Murray (British MP) to Wiseman, July 5, 1918, Wiseman to Murray (House to Grey), July 9, 1918, House Papers, Drawer 9, File 9; House Diary, July 9, 13-15, 1918; Viscount Grey, *The League of Nations* (New York: George H. Doran, 1918), Wilson Papers, Ser. 5A, Box 3; Suggestion for a Covenant of a League of Nations, July 16, 1918, Doc. 2, David Hunter Miller, *The Drafting of the Covenant*, 2 vols. (New York: G. P. Putnam's Sons, 1928),

2:7-11; U.S. Department of State, *Papers Relating to the Foreign Relations of the United States, 1919: The Paris Peace Conference*, 13 vols. (Washington, DC: Government Printing Office, 1942-1947), 1:497-501; Wiseman to Cecil, July 18, 1918, in Link, *Papers* 49:11-20. See also Klaus Schwabe, "Woodrow Wilson and Germany's Membership in the League of Nations, 1918-19," *Central European History* 8 (March 1975): 3-22.

6. House Diary, August 15, 1918; Wiseman to Reading, August 18, 1918, Balfour Papers, 49741/215-17, and David Lloyd George Papers, F/43/1/14, House of Lords Record Office (formerly in the Beaverbrook Library), London, England; Fowler, *British-American Relations*, pp. 278-83; Wilson to House, September 7, 1918, House Papers, Drawer 49, File 19; Wilson's First Draft, Doc. 3, Miller, *Drafting of the Covenant* 2:12-15; Reading to Balfour, July 24, 1918, Diary of Colonel House, August 15, 1918, Wiseman to Reading, August 16, 1918, Wiseman to Murray, August 30, 1918, Wilson to House, September 7, 1918, in Link, *Papers* 49:83, 265-68, 273-75, 397-99, 466-71.

7. Cecil to Wiseman, August 19, 1918, House Papers, Drawer 20, File 47; House to Wilson, September 3, 1918, House Papers, Drawer 49, File 11A; House Diary, August 22, 25, September 9, 24, 1918; House to Wilson, September 3, 1918, Diary of Colonel House, September 9, 1918, in Link, *Papers* 49:428-29, 508-9.

8. Baker and Dodd, *Public Papers* 5:253-61; *Foreign Relations, 1918: World War*, Sup. 1, 1:316-21.

9. Henry Adams, *The Education of Henry Adams: An Autobiography* (Boston: Houghton Mifflin, 1918), pp. 12, 401.

10. Lodge to Root, July 18, 1918, Lodge Papers, File 1918 (R-Z); Lodge to Bryce, August 2, 1918, Bryce to Lodge, September 4, 1918, Lodge Papers, File 1918 (General Correspondence, A-G).

11. U.S. Senate, 65th Cong., 2d sess., *Congressional Record*, vol. 56, pt. 11, pp. 11170-72 (October 10, 1918); Lodge to Wm. R. Thayer (historian), October 14, 17, 1918, Lodge Papers, File 1918 (R-Z); Lodge to Bryce, September 28, 1918, Lodge to W. S. Bigelow (physician, author), October 12, 1918, Lodge to John Jay Chapman (author), October 15, 1918, Lodge Papers, File 1918 (General Correspondence, A-G).

12. House Diary, October 9, 13, 15, 28-31, 1918; Frederick Oederlin (Swiss chargé in Washington, DC) to Wilson, October 6, 1918, W. A. F. Ekengren (Swedish minister to the United States) to Lansing, October 7, 1918, Lansing to Oederlin, October 8, 1918, Oederlin to Lansing, October 14, 1918, House to Wilson, October 30 (#8), 30 (#9), 30 (#12), 30 (#13), November 3 (#38), 3 (#41), 4 (#42), 1918, Wilson to House, October 30 (#4), October 31 (#6), 1918, *Foreign Relations, 1918: World War*, Sup. 1, 1:337-38, 341, 343, 357-58, 421-27, 448, 455-57, 460-62; Wilson to House, ca. October 29 (#3), 1918, House to Wilson, October 30 (#4), 31 (#5), 1918, Wilson Papers, Ser. 2, Box 186; Lloyd George to House, November 3, 1918, House Papers, Drawer 12, File 32; Wilson to House, November 4 (#8), 4 (#9), 1918, House to Wilson, November 5 (#6), 1918, Wilson Papers, Ser. 2, Box 187; Auchincloss Diary, October 11, 29-November 4, 1918, Gordon Auchincloss Papers, Drawer 55, Files 83-84, Yale University Library, New Haven, Connecticut; Eric Geddes (British first lord of the admiralty) to Lloyd George, October 13, 1918, Lloyd George Papers, F/18/2/23.

13. Lansing to Hans Sulzer (Swiss minister to the United States), November 5, 1918, House to Lansing, November 11, 1918, *Foreign Relations, 1918: World War*, Sup. 1, 1:468-69, 494-98; N. D. Baker to Wilson, October 22, 1918, N. D. Baker Papers, Box 8; Wilson to Key Pittman, November 7, 1918, Wilson Papers, Ser. 2, Box 187. Historians who have maintained the Wilsonian faith agree that the United States might have redeemed the Old World after World War I. For example, Arthur Walworth, *America's Moment, 1918: American Diplomacy at the End of World War I* (New York: W. W. Norton, 1977); idem, *Wilson and His Peacemakers: American Diplomacy at the Paris Peace Conference, 1919* (New York: W. W. Norton, 1986), view this as the opportune time for "the American prophet of peace" to fulfill his vision in "a world to be saved by democracy"; and Robert H. Ferrell, *Woodrow Wilson and World War I, 1917-1921* (New York: Harper & Row, 1985), p. 157, argues that "in 1919 the United States was strong enough to have made the world safe for democracy" and that "one must not underestimate the possibilities of reformation and redemption, national as well as personal."

14. House to Wilson, November 10 (#9), 11 (#13), 1918, House Papers, Drawer 49, File 11B, and Wilson Papers, Ser. 2, Box 187; Baker and Dodd, *Public Papers* 5:294-302; Announcement by President Wilson, November 11, 1918, House to Wilson, November 11 (#13), 1918, *Foreign Relations, 1919: Paris Peace Conference* 1:1.

15. William Wiseman, Notes on an Interview with the President at the White House, October 16, 1918, Attitude of the United States and of President Wilson Towards the Peace Conference, c. October 20, 1918, Fowler, *British-American Relations*, pp. 283-96.

16. Baker and Dodd, *Public Papers* 5:303-4, 324-25.

17. Edward H. Buehrig, "Woodrow Wilson and Collective Security," in idem, ed., *Wilson's Foreign Policy in Perspective* (Bloomington: Indiana University Press, 1957), pp. 34-60; Lloyd E. Ambrosius, "Wilson's League of Nations," *Maryland Historical Magazine* 65 (Winter 1970): 369-93; George W. Egerton, "The Lloyd George Government and the Creation of the League of Nations," *American Historical Review* 79 (April 1974): 419-44.

18. *Foreign Relations, 1919: Paris Peace Conference* 3:209-15; Baker and Dodd, *Public Papers* 5:413-29.

19. U.S. Senate, 66th Cong., 1st sess., *Congressional Record*, vol. 58, pt. 3, pp. 2336-39 (July 10, 1919); Baker and Dodd, *Public Papers* 5:537-52.

20. Lansing Diary, V, August 20, 1919.

21. Pershing, *My Experiences* 1:37. This point is especially emphasized in Smythe, *Pershing*, pp. 6, 11, 89, 93-94, 118, 163, 168, 221-22.

22. For the controversy over this episode in military diplomacy see Lloyd E. Ambrosius, "Secret German-American Negotiations during the Paris Peace Conference," *Amerikastudien/American Studies* 24, no. 2 (1979): 288-309, and the critique of this article in Klaus Schwabe, *Woodrow Wilson, Revolutionary Germany, and Peacemaking, 1918-1919: Missionary Diplomacy and the Realities of Power* (Chapel Hill: University of North Carolina Press, 1985), pp. 299-394. Unfortunately, Smythe, *Pershing*, pp. 245-63, overlooks this episode. See also the earlier accounts in Fritz T. Epstein, "Zwischen Compiègne und Versailles: Geheime amerikanische Militärdiplomatie in der Periode des Waffenstillstandes 1918/19: Die

Rolle des Obersten Arthur L. Conger," *Vierteljahrshefte für Zeitgeschichte* 3 (October 1955): 412-45; and Klaus Schwabe, *Deutsche Revolution und Wilson-Frieden: Die amerikanische und deutsche Friedensstrategie zwischen Ideologie und Machtpolitik 1918/19* (Düsseldorf: Droste Verlag, 1971).

23. Walter Loeb, Bericht über die Unterredung mit Oberst Conger, December 4, 1918, Walter Loeb, Bericht über unsere Fahrt in das amerikanische Hauptquartier an die Reichs-Regierung, December 13, 1918, Kassette III, Mappe 14, Carl Giebel Papers, Friedrich-Ebert-Stiftung, Bonn-Bad Godesberg, Germany, and A.A. Weimar, III, Politisches Archiv des Auswärtigen Amts, Bonn, Germany.

24. Statement of Paul Freiherr von Eltz Rübenach to A. L. Conger, December 30, 1918, General Headquarters, G-2, File 091, Record Group 120, Series 7, Box 5164, Records of the American Expeditionary Forces, National Archives, Washington, DC; Wilhelm Groener, *Lebenserinnerungen* (Göttingen: Vandenhoeck & Ruprecht, 1957), pp. 484-87.

25. Loeb to Ulrich von Brockdorff-Rantzau, January 27, 1919, Walter Loeb, Bericht über den Aufenthalt im amerikanischen Hauptquartier am 25. & 26. Januar 1919, und die Unterredung mit Herrn Oberst Conger, January 17, 1919, Weltkrieg 30, Bd. 17, Politisches Archiv des Auswärtigen Amts, Bonn, Germany.

26. Loeb to Auswärtiges Amt, March 28, 1919, Loeb to Bernstorff, March 24, April 1, 1919, W. E. L[oeb]., memorandum, March 30, 1919, Walter Loeb, Peace Conditions Acceptable to Germany, Weltkrieg 30 Geh., Bd. 1, Politisches Archiv des Auswärtigen Amts, Bonn, Germany; Reichsminister to Friedrich Ebert, March 28, 1919, Telegramm aus Frankfurt, March 28, 1919, Loeb to Philipp Scheidemann, March 4, 24, 1919, R43I/1, 164, Akten der Reichskanzlei, Bundesarchiv, Koblenz, Germany; Epstein, "Zwischen Compiègne und Versailles," pp. 419-22; Hagen Schulze, ed., *Akten der Reichskanzlei, Weimarer Republik: Das Kabinett Scheidemann, 13. Februar bis 20. Juni 1919* (Boppard: Harold Boldt Verlag, 1971), pp. 109-116; Loeb to Brockdorff-Rantzau, March 24, 1919, Brockdorff-Rantzau Papers, Politisches Archiv des Auswärtigen Amts, Bonn, Germany.

27. Loeb to Ebert, August 5, 1919, Weltkrieg 30 Geh., Bd. 1, Politisches Archiv des Auswärtigen Amts; General Pershing's Diary, December 20, 1918, January 16-17, February 10-13, 22-23, March 22-23, April 17-18, 23, May 22, 1919, Pershing Papers, Box 4-5.

28. For my critique of Wilson's diplomacy during the Paris Peace Conference and his relations with the Senate in 1919-20 see Ambrosius, *Woodrow Wilson and the American Diplomatic Tradition*.

29. John C. Farrell, "John Dewey and World War I: Armageddon Tests a Liberal's Faith," *Perspectives in American History* 9 (1975): 299-340.

30. Lippmann to N. D. Baker, January 17, 1920, N. D. Baker Papers, Box 12.

31. John Bates Clark, "A Workable League," *New York Times*, November 11, 1918; idem, "If This League Fails: The Alternative Is a League for War Dominated by Germany," ibid, June 1, 1919; Franklin H. Giddings, "The United States among Nations," *The Independent* 98 (June 14, 1919): 399-400; idem, "What the War Was Worth," ibid. 99 (July 5, 1919):

16-17; idem, "What Did It?" ibid. 104 (November 20, 1920): 262-64; Statement prepared by Dr. Hamilton Holt and the Committee, [October 27, 1920], List of persons who called on the President, [October 27, 1920], Albert Sidney Burleson Papers, vol. 26, Library of Congress, Washington, DC.

Bibliography

Manuscript Collections

British Museum, London, England
    Arthur J. Balfour Papers
Friedrich-Ebert-Stiftung, Bonn-Bad Godesberg, Germany
    Carl Giebel Papers
House of Lords Record Office (formerly in the Beaverbrook Library),
London, England
    David Lloyd George Papers
Library of Congress, Washington, DC
    Newton D. Baker Papers
    Ray Stannard Baker Papers
    Tasker Howard Bliss Papers
    Albert Sidney Burleson Papers
    Diary of Robert Lansing
    Peyton C. March Papers
    John J. Pershing Papers
    Elihu Root Papers
    Joseph P. Tumulty Papers
    Woodrow Wilson Papers
Massachusetts Historical Society, Boston, Massachusetts
    Henry Cabot Lodge Papers
Politisches Archiv des Auswärtigen Amts (Political Archives of the
Foreign Office), Bonn, Germany
    Brockdorff-Rantzau Papers
Yale University Library, New Haven, Connecticut
    Gordon Auchincloss Papers
    Diary of Edward M. House
    Edward M. House Papers
    William Wiseman Papers

Unpublished Government Documents

Bundesarchiv (Federal Archives), Koblenz, Germany
    Akten der Reichskanzlei
National Archives, Washington, DC
    Records of the American Expeditionary Forces
Politisches Archiv des Auswärtigen Amts (Political Archives of the
Foreign Office), Bonn, Germany
    A.A. Weimar, III
    Botschaft Washington, 4A34 (Friedensverhandlungen)
    Weltkrieg 30
    Weltkrieg 30 Geh.

Government Publications

U.S. Department of the Army, Historical Division. *United States
    Army in the World War, 1917-1919: Policy-Forming Documents,
    American Expeditionary Forces*. Vol. 2. Washington, DC: Gov-
    ernment Printing Office, 1948.
U.S. Department of State. *Papers Relating to the Foreign Relations
    of the United States: The Lansing Papers, 1914-1920*. Vols. 1-2.
    Washington, DC: Government Printing Office, 1939-1940.
_____. *Papers Relating to the Foreign Relations of the United
    States, 1915*, Supplement: *The World War*. Washington, DC:
    Government Printing Office, 1928.
_____. *Papers Relating to the Foreign Relations of the United
    States, 1916*, Supplement: *The World War*. Washington, DC:
    Government Printing Office, 1929.
_____. *Papers Relating to the Foreign Relations of the United
    States, 1918*, Supplement 1: *The World War*. Vol. 1. Washing-
    ton, DC: Government Printing Office, 1933.
_____. *Papers Relating to the Foreign Relations of the United
    States, 1919: The Paris Peace Conference*. Vols. 1, 3. Washing-
    ton, DC: Government Printing Office, 1942-43.
U.S. Senate. *Congressional Record*, 56th Cong., 1st sess., vol. 33,
    pt. 1 (1900); 65th Cong., 2d sess., vol. 56, pt. 11 (1918); 66th
    Cong., 1st sess., vol. 58, pt. 3 (1919).

Published Documents

Baker, Ray Stannard, and Dodd, William E., eds. *The Public Papers of Woodrow Wilson: College and State.* Vol. 2. New York: Harper & Brothers, 1925.

———. *The Public Papers of Woodrow Wilson: The New Democracy.* Vols. 3-4. New York: Harper & Brothers, 1926.

———. *The Public Papers of Woodrow Wilson: War and Peace.* Vol. 5. New York: Harper & Brothers, 1927.

Cronon, E. David, ed. *The Cabinet Diaries of Josephus Daniels, 1913-1921.* Lincoln: University of Nebraska Press, 1963.

Jacobs, Wilbur R. *The Historical World of Frederick Jackson Turner: With Selections from His Correspondence.* New Haven: Yale University Press, 1968.

———, ed. *Frederick Jackson Turner's Legacy: Unpublished Writings in American History.* San Marino: Henry E. Huntington Library, 1965.

Link, Arthur S., ed. *The Papers of Woodrow Wilson.* Vols. 5-8, 12, 27-38, 40-49. Princeton: Princeton University Press, 1968-1990.

Morison, Elting E., ed. *The Letters of Theodore Roosevelt.* Vol. 8. Cambridge: Harvard University Press, 1954.

Schulze, Hagen, ed. *Akten der Reichskanzlei, Weimarer Republik: Das Kabinett Scheidemann, 13. Februar bis 20. Juni 1919.* Boppard: Harold Boldt Verlag, 1971.

Memoirs and Books

Adams, Henry. *The Education of Henry Adams: An Autobiography.* Boston: Houghton Mifflin, 1918.

Adams, Henry M. *Prussian-American Relations, 1775-1871.* Cleveland: Press of Western Reserve University, 1960.

Ambrosius, Lloyd E. *Woodrow Wilson and the American Diplomatic Tradition: The Treaty Fight in Perspective.* Cambridge: Cambridge University Press, 1987.

Barraclough, Geoffrey. *An Introduction to Contemporary History.* New York: Penguin Books, 1964.

Bartlett, Ruhl J. *The League to Enforce Peace.* Chapel Hill: University of North Carolina Press, 1944.

Beaver, Daniel R. *Newton D. Baker and the American War Effort, 1917-1919*. Lincoln: University of Nebraska Press, 1966.

Bernstorff, Count [Johann von]. *My Three Years in America*. New York: Charles Scribner's Sons, 1920.

Billington, Ray Allen. *Frederick Jackson Turner: Historian, Scholar, Teacher*. New York: Oxford University Press, 1973.

Birnbaum, Karl E. *Peace Moves and U-Boat Warfare: A Study of Imperial Germany's Policy towards the United States, April 18, 1916-January 9, 1917*. Stockholm: Almqvist & Wiksell, 1958.

Blum, John M. *Joe Tumulty and the Wilson Era*. Boston: Houghton Mifflin, 1951.

Blumenthal, Henry. *A Reappraisal of Franco-American Relations, 1830-1871*. Chapel Hill: University of North Carolina Press, 1959.

Bond, F. Fraser. *Mr. Miller of "The Times"*. New York: Charles Scribner's Sons, 1931.

Bourne, Randolph S., ed. *Towards an Enduring Peace: A Symposium of Peace Proposals and Programs, 1914-1916*. New York: American Association for International Conciliation, [1916].

Bragdon, Henry Wilkinson. *Woodrow Wilson: The Academic Years*. Cambridge: Harvard University Press, 1967.

Briggs, Mitchell Pirie. *George D. Herron and the European Settlement*. Stanford: Stanford University Press, 1932.

Brooks, Van Wyck. *Three Essays on America*. New York: E. P. Dutton, 1970.

Bryce, James. *The American Commonwealth*. Vol. 2. London: Macmillan, 1889.

Buehrig, Edward H. *Woodrow Wilson and the Balance of Power*. Bloomington: Indiana University Press, 1955.

————, ed. *Wilson's Foreign Policy in Perspective*. Bloomington: Indiana University Press, 1957.

Calhoun, Frederick S. *Power and Principle: Armed Intervention in Wilsonian Foreign Policy*. Kent: Kent State University Press, 1986.

Challener, Richard D. *Admirals, Generals, and American Foreign Policy, 1898-1914*. Princeton: Princeton University Press, 1973.

Clark, John Bates. *The Control of Trusts: An Argument in Favor of Curbing the Power of Monopoly by a Natural Method*. New York: Macmillan, 1901.

Claude, Inis L. *Power and International Relations*. New York: Random House, 1962.

Clements, Kendrick A. *William Jennings Bryan: Missionary Isolationist*. Knoxville: University of Tennessee Press, 1982.

————. *Woodrow Wilson: World Statesman*. Boston: Twayne, 1987.

Cline, Myrtle A. *American Attitude toward the Greek War of Independence, 1821-1828*. Atlanta: Higgins-McArthur, 1930.

Coffman, Edward M. *The War to End All Wars: The American Military Experience in World War I*. New York: Oxford University Press, 1968.

Coogan, John W. *The End of Neutrality: The United States, Britain, and Maritime Rights, 1899-1915*. Ithaca: Cornell University Press, 1981.

Cooper, John Milton, Jr. *The Vanity of Power: American Isolationism and World War I, 1914-1917*. Westport: Greenwood, 1969.

_____. *Walter Hines Page: The Southerner as American, 1855-1918*. Chapel Hill: University of North Carolina Press, 1977.

_____. *The Warrior and the Priest: Woodrow Wilson and Theodore Roosevelt*. Cambridge: Harvard University Press, 1983.

Craig, Gordon A., and George, Alexander L. *Force and Statecraft: Diplomatic Problems of Our Time*. New York: Oxford University Press, 1983.

Croly, Herbert. *The Promise of American Life*. New York: Capricorn Books, 1964.

Crunden, Robert M. *Ministers of Reform: The Progressives' Achievement in American Civilization*. Urbana: University of Illinois Press, 1984.

Davis, Calvin DeArmond. *The United States and the Second Hague Peace Conference: American Diplomacy and International Organization, 1899-1914*. Durham: Duke University Press, 1975.

DeBenedetti, Charles. *Origins of the Modern American Peace Movement, 1915-1929*. Millwood: KTO Press, 1978.

DeConde, Alexander. *This Affair of Louisiana*. New York: Charles Scribner's Sons, 1976.

Devlin, Patrick. *Too Proud to Fight: Woodrow Wilson's Neutrality*. New York: Oxford University Press, 1975.

Dodd, William E. *Woodrow Wilson and His Work*. Garden City: Doubleday, Page, 1920.

Doerries, Reinhard R. *Imperial Challenge: Ambassador Count Bernstorff and German-American Relations, 1908-1917*. Chapel Hill: University of North Carolina Press, 1989.

——.*Washington-Berlin, 1908/1917*. Düsseldorf: Pädagogischer Verlag Schwann, 1975.

Dowty, Alan. *The Limits of American Isolation: The United States and the Crimean War*. New York: New York University Press, 1971.

Egerton, George W. *Great Britain and the Creation of the League of Nations*. Chapel Hill: University of North Carolina Press, 1978.

Ferrell, Robert H. *Woodrow Wilson and World War I, 1917-1921*. New York: Harper & Row, 1985.

Field, James A., Jr. *America and the Mediterranean World, 1776-1882*. Princeton: Princeton University Press, 1969.

Fischer, Fritz. *Germany's Aims in the First World War*. New York: W. W. Norton, 1967.

———. *World Power or Decline: The Controversy over Germany's Aims in the First World War*. New York: W. W. Norton, 1974.

Floto, Inga. *Colonel House in Paris: A Study of American Policy at the Paris Peace Conference, 1919*. Princeton: Princeton University Press, 1973.

Forcey, Charles. *The Crossroads of Liberalism: Croly, Weyl, Lippmann, and the Progressive Era, 1900-1925*. New York: Oxford University Press, 1961.

Fowler, W. B. *British-American Relations, 1917-1918: The Role of Sir William Wiseman*. Princeton: Princeton University Press, 1969.

Gardner, Lloyd C. *Safe for Democracy: The Anglo-American Response to Revolution, 1913-1923*. New York: Oxford University Press, 1984.

Garraty, John A. *Henry Cabot Lodge: A Biography*. New York: Alfred A. Knopf, 1968.

Gatzke, Hans W. *Germany's Drive to the West: A Study of Germany's Western War Aims during the First World War*. Baltimore: Johns Hopkins Press, 1966.

Gazley, John Gerlow. *American Opinion of German Unification, 1848-1871*. New York: Columbia University Press, 1926.

Gelfand, Lawrence E. *The Inquiry: American Preparations for Peace, 1917-1919*. New Haven: Yale University Press, 1963.

George, Alexander L., and George, Juliette L. *Woodrow Wilson and Colonel House: A Personality Study*. New York: Dover, 1964.

Giddings, Franklin Henry. *Democracy and Empire: Their Psychological, Economic and Moral Foundations*. New York: Macmillan, 1900.

———. *Studies in the Theory of Human Society*. New York: Macmillan, 1922.

Gilderhus, Mark T. *Pan-American Visions: Woodrow Wilson in the Western Hemisphere, 1913-1921*. Tucson: University of Arizona Press, 1986.

Graebner, Norman A. *Empire on the Pacific: A Study in American Continental Expansion*. New York: Ronald Press, 1955.

Gregory, Ross. *Walter Hines Page: Ambassador to the Court of St. James's*. Lexington: University Press of Kentucky, 1970.

Grey, Viscount, of Fallodon. *Twenty-five Years, 1892-1916*. Vol. 2. London: Hodder & Stoughton, 1925.

Groener, Wilhelm. *Lebenserinnerungen*. Göttingen: Vandenhoeck & Ruprecht, 1957.

Harbaugh, William Henry. *The Life and Times of Theodore Roosevelt*. New York: Collier Books, 1963.

Healy, David. *U.S. Expansionism: The Imperialist Urge in the 1890s*. Madison: University of Wisconsin Press, 1970.

Herman, Sondra R. *Eleven against War: Studies in American Internationalist Thought, 1898-1921*. Stanford: Hoover Institution Press, 1969.

Herron, George D. *Woodrow Wilson and the World's Peace*. New York: Mitchell Kennerley, 1917.

Higham, John. *History: The Development of Historical Studies in the United States*. Englewood Cliffs: Prentice-Hall, 1965.

Hilderbrand, Robert C. *Power and the People: Executive Management of Public Opinion in Foreign Affairs, 1897-1921*. Chapel Hill: University of North Carolina Press, 1981.

Hinsley, F. H., ed. *British Foreign Policy under Sir Edward Grey*. Cambridge: Cambridge University Press, 1977.

_____. *Power and the Pursuit of Peace: Theory and Practice in the History of Relations between States*. Cambridge: Cambridge University Press, 1963.

Hofstadter, Richard. *The Progressive Historians: Turner, Beard, Parrington*. New York: Vintage Books, 1970.

Hopkins, Charles Howard. *The Rise of the Social Gospel in American Protestantism, 1865-1915*. New Haven: Yale University Press, 1940.

Houston, David F. *Eight Years with Wilson's Cabinet: 1913 to 1920*. Vol. 1. Garden City: Doubleday, Page, 1926.

Janowitz, Morris. *The Last Half-Century*. Chicago: University of Chicago Press, 1978.

Jessup, Philip C. *Elihu Root*. Vol. 2. New York: Dodd, Mead, 1938.

Katz, Frederick. *The Secret War in Mexico: Europe, the United States, and the Mexican Revolution*. Chicago: University of Chicago Press, 1981.

Kellogg, Louise P., ed. *The Early Writings of Frederick Jackson Turner*. Madison: University of Wisconsin Press, 1938.

Kennan, George F. *American Diplomacy, 1900-1950*. Chicago: University of Chicago Press, 1951.

_____. *The Decision to Intervene*. Princeton: Princeton University Press, 1958.

_____. *Russia Leaves the War*. Princeton: Princeton University Press, 1956.

Kernek, Sterling J. *Distractions of Peace during War: The Lloyd George Government's Reactions to Woodrow Wilson, December, 1916-November, 1918*. Philadelphia: American Philosophical Society, 1975.

Killen, Linda. *The Russian Bureau: A Case Study in Wilsonian Diplomacy*. Lexington: University Press of Kentucky, 1983.

Kuehl, Warren F. *Seeking World Order: The United States and International Organization to 1920*. Nashville: Vanderbilt University Press, 1969.

LaFeber, Walter. *The New Empire: An Interpretation of American Expansion, 1860-1898*. Ithaca: Cornell University Press, 1963.

Levin, N. Gordon, Jr. *Woodrow Wilson and World Politics: America's Response to War and Revolution*. New York: Oxford University Press, 1968.

Link, Arthur S. *The Higher Realism of Woodrow Wilson and Other Essays*. Nashville: Vanderbilt University Press, 1971.

———. *Wilson: The Struggle for Neutrality, 1914-1915*. Vol. 3. Princeton: Princeton University Press, 1960.

———. *Wilson: Confusions and Crises, 1915-1916*. Vol. 4. Princeton: Princeton University Press, 1964.

———. *Wilson: Campaigns for Progressivism and Peace, 1916-1917*. Vol. 5. Princeton: Princeton University Press, 1965.

———. *Wilson the Diplomatist: A Look at His Major Foreign Policies*. Baltimore: Johns Hopkins Press, 1957.

———. *Woodrow Wilson: Revolution, War, and Peace*. Arlington Heights: AHM, 1979.

———, ed. *Woodrow Wilson and a Revolutionary World, 1913-1921*. Chapel Hill: University of North Carolina Press, 1982.

Lippmann, Walter. *The Cold War: A Study in U.S. Foreign Policy*. New York: Harper & Row, 1947.

———. *Drift and Mastery: An Attempt to Diagnose the Current Unrest*. Englewood Cliffs: Prentice-Hall, 1961.

———. *Men of Destiny*. New York: Macmillan, 1927.

———. *The Stakes of Diplomacy*. New York: Henry Holt, 1915.

———. *U.S. Foreign Policy: Shield of the Republic*. Boston: Little, Brown, 1943.

Marchand, C. Roland. *The American Peace Movement and Social Reform, 1898-1918*. Princeton: Princeton University Press, 1972.

Marraro, Howard R. *American Opinion on the Unification of Italy, 1846-1861*. New York: Columbia University Press, 1932.

Martin, Laurence W. *Peace without Victory: Woodrow Wilson and the British Liberals*. New Haven: Yale University Press, 1958.

May, Ernest R. *Imperial Democracy: The Emergence of America as a Great Power*. New York: Harcourt, Brace & World, 1961.

———. *The World War and American Isolation, 1914-1917*. Cambridge: Harvard University Press, 1959.

Mayer, Arno J. *Political Origins of the New Diplomacy, 1917-1918*. New Haven: Yale University Press, 1959.

———. *Politics and Diplomacy of Peacemaking: Containment and Counterrevolution at Versailles, 1918-1919*. New York: Alfred A. Knopf, 1967.

Merk, Frederick. *Manifest Destiny and Mission in American History: A Reinterpretation*. New York: Vintage Books, 1963.

———. *The Monroe Doctrine and American Expansionism, 1843-1849*. New York: Vintage Books, 1966.

————. *The Oregon Question: Essays in Anglo-American Diplomacy & Politics*. Cambridge: Harvard University Press, 1967.

Miller, David Hunter. *The Drafting of the Covenant*. Vol. 2. New York: G. P. Putnam's Sons, 1928.

Morgenthau, Hans J. *In Defense of the National Interest: A Critical Examination of American Foreign Policy*. New York: Alfred A. Knopf, 1951.

————. *Scientific Man vs. Power Politics*. Chicago: University of Chicago Press, 1946.

Mulder, John M. *Woodrow Wilson: The Years of Preparation*. Princeton: Princeton University Press, 1978.

Noble, David W. *Historians against History: The Frontier Thesis and the National Covenant in American Historical Writing since 1830*. Minneapolis: University of Minnesota Press, 1965.

————. *The Progressive Mind, 1890-1917*. Chicago: Rand McNally, 1970.

Osborn, George C. *Woodrow Wilson: The Early Years*. Baton Rouge: Louisiana State University Press, 1968.

Osgood, Robert Endicott. *Ideals and Self-Interest in America's Foreign Relations: The Great Transformation of the Twentieth Century*. Chicago: University of Chicago Press, 1953.

Palmer, Frederick. *Newton D. Baker: America at War*. Vol. 1. New York: Dodd, Mead, 1931.

Patterson, David S. *Toward a Warless World: The Travail of the American Peace Movement, 1877-1914*. Bloomington: Indiana University Press, 1976.

Pershing, John J. *My Experiences in the World War*. Vol. 1. New York: Frederick A. Stokes, 1931.

Pletcher, David M. *The Diplomacy of Annexation: Texas, Oregon, and the Mexican War*. Columbia: University of Missouri Press, 1973.

Pusey, Merlo J. *Charles Evans Hughes*. Vol. 1. New York: Macmillan, 1951.

Resek, Carl, ed. *War and the Intellectuals: Essays by Randolph S. Bourne, 1915-1919*. New York: Harper & Row, 1964.

Ross, Edward Alsworth. *The Old World in the New: The Significance of Past and Present Immigration to the American People*. New York: Century, 1914.

————. *Seventy Years of It: An Autobiography*. New York: D. Appleton-Century, 1936.

————. *Social Control: A Survey of the Foundations of Order*. New York: Macmillan, 1901.

Rothwell, V. H. *British War Aims and Peace Diplomacy, 1914-1918*. Oxford: Clarendon Press, 1971.

Rystad, Göran. *Ambiguous Imperialism: American Foreign Policy and Domestic Politics at the Turn of the Century*. Lund: Esselte Studium, 1975.

Saveth, Edward N. *American Historians and European Immigrants: 1875-1925*. New York: Columbia University Press, 1948.

Schmitt, Bernadotte E., and Vedeler, Harold C. *The World in the Crucible, 1914-1919*. New York: Harper & Row, 1984.

Schwabe, Klaus. *Deutsche Revolution und Wilson-Frieden: Die amerikanische und deutsche Friedensstrategie zwischen Ideologie und Machtpolitik 1918/19*. Düsseldorf: Droste Verlag, 1971.

_____. *Woodrow Wilson, Revolutionary Germany, and Peacemaking, 1918-1919: Missionary Diplomacy and the Realities of Power*. Chapel Hill: University of North Carolina Press, 1985.

Seymour, Charles. *American Diplomacy during the World War*. Baltimore: Johns Hopkins Press, 1934.

Smith, Daniel M. *Robert Lansing and American Neutrality, 1914-1917*. Berkeley and Los Angeles: University of California Press, 1958.

Smith, Henry Nash. *Virgin Land: The American West as Symbol and Myth*. Cambridge: Harvard University Press, 1950.

Smith, Michael Joseph. *Realist Thought from Weber to Kissinger*. Baton Rouge: Louisiana State University Press, 1986.

Smythe, Donald. *Pershing: General of the Armies*. Bloomington: Indiana University Press, 1986.

Stearns, Harold. *Liberalism in America: Its Origins, Its Temporary Collapse, Its Future*. New York: Boni & Liveright, 1919.

Steel, Ronald. *Walter Lippmann and the American Century*. Boston: Little, Brown, 1980.

Stevenson, David. *The First World War and International Politics*. New York: Oxford University Press, 1988.

_____. *French War Aims against Germany, 1914-1919*. Oxford: Clarendon Press, 1982.

Stromberg, Roland N. *Collective Security and American Foreign Policy: From the League of Nations to NATO*. New York: Frederick A. Praeger, 1963.

Strout, Cushing. *The Pragmatic Revolt in American History: Carl Becker and Charles Beard*. New Haven: Yale University Press, 1958.

Thompson, John A. *Reformers and War: American Progressive Publicists and the First World War*. Cambridge: Cambridge University Press, 1987.

Thorsen, Niels Aage. *The Political Thought of Woodrow Wilson, 1875-1910*. Princeton: Princeton University Press, 1988.

Trask, David F. *Captains & Cabinets: Anglo-American Naval Relations, 1917-1918*. Columbia: University of Missouri Press, 1972.

————. *The United States and the Supreme War Council: American War Aims and Inter-Allied Strategy, 1917-1918.* Middletown: Wesleyan University Press, 1961.

Tuchman, Barbara W. *The Zimmermann Telegram.* New York: Ballantine Books, 1958.

Turner, Frederick Jackson. *The Frontier in American History.* New York: Henry Holt, 1920.

Tuveson, Ernest Lee. *Redeemer Nation: The Idea of America's Millennial Role.* Chicago: University of Chicago Press, 1968.

Unterberger, Betty Miller. *The United States, Revolutionary Russia, and the Rise of Czechoslovakia.* Chapel Hill: University of North Carolina Press, 1989.

Van Alstyne, R. W. *The Rising American Empire.* Oxford: Basil Blackwell, 1960.

Vaughn, Stephen. *Holding Fast the Inner Lines: Democracy, Nationalism, and the Committee on Public Information.* Chapel Hill: University of North Carolina Press, 1980.

Walworth, Arthur. *America's Moment, 1918: American Diplomacy at the End of World War I.* New York: W. W. Norton, 1977.

————. *Wilson and His Peacemakers: American Diplomacy at the Paris Peace Conference, 1919.* New York: W. W. Norton, 1986.

Wehler, Hans-Ulrich. *Der Aufstieg des amerikanischen Imperialismus.* Göttingen: Vandenhoeck & Ruprecht, 1974.

Weinberg, Albert K. *Manifest Destiny: A Study of Nationalist Expansion in American History.* Baltimore: Johns Hopkins Press, 1935.

Widenor, William C. *Henry Cabot Lodge and the Search for an American Foreign Policy.* Berkeley and Los Angeles: University of California Press, 1979.

Williams, William Appleman. *The Roots of the Modern American Empire: A Study of the Growth and Shaping of Social Consciousness in a Marketplace Society.* New York: Vintage Books, 1969.

Wilson, Woodrow. *Congressional Government: A Study in American Politics.* Boston: Houghton Mifflin, 1900.

————. *Constitutional Government in the United States.* New York: Columbia University Press, 1908.

————. *Division and Reunion: 1829-1889.* New York: Longmans, Green, 1893.

————. *A History of the American People.* Vols. 4, 10. New York: Harper & Brothers, 1918.

————. *The State: Elements of Historical and Practical Politics.* Boston: D. C. Heath, 1889.

Winkler, Henry R. *The League of Nations Movement in Great Britain, 1914-1919.* New Brunswick: Rutgers University Press, 1952.

Articles

Ambrosius, Lloyd E. "The Orthodoxy of Revisionism: Woodrow Wilson and the New Left." *Diplomatic History* 1 (Summer 1977): 199-214.

———. "Secret German-American Negotiations during the Paris Peace Conference." *Amerikastudien / American Studies* 24, no. 2 (1979): 288-309.

———. "Wilson's League of Nations." *Maryland Historical Magazine* 65 (Winter 1970): 369-93.

———. "Woodrow Wilson and the Quest for Orderly Progress." In Norman A. Graebner, ed., *Traditions and Values: American Diplomacy, 1865-1945*, pp. 73-100. Lanham: University Press of America, 1985.

Clark, John Bates. "If This League Fails: The Alternative Is a League for War Dominated by Germany." *New York Times*, June 1, 1919.

———. "A Workable League." *New York Times*, November 11, 1918.

Combs, Jerald A. "Norman Graebner and the Realist View of American Diplomatic History." *Diplomatic History* 11 (Summer 1987): 251-64.

Cooper, John Milton, Jr. "The British Response to the House-Grey Memorandum: New Evidence and New Questions." *Journal of American History* 59 (March 1973): 958-71.

———. " 'An Irony of Fate': Woodrow Wilson's Pre-World War I Diplomacy." *Diplomatic History* 3 (Fall 1979): 425-37.

Curti, Merle Eugene. "Austria and the United States." *Smith College Studies in History* 11, no. 3 (April 1926): 141-206.

Egerton, George W. "Collective Security as Political Myth: Liberal Internationalism and the League of Nations in Politics and History." *International History Review* 5 (November 1983): 496-524.

———. "The Lloyd George Government and the Creation of the League of Nations." *American Historical Review* 79 (April 1974): 419-44.

Epstein, Fritz T. "Zwischen Compiègne und Versailles: Geheime amerikanische Militärdiplomatie in der Periode des Waffenstillstandes 1918/19: Die Rolle des Obersten Arthur L. Conger." *Vierteljahrshefte für Zeitgeschichte* 3 (October 1955): 412-45.

Farrell, John C. "John Dewey and World War I: Armageddon Tests a Liberal's Faith." *Perspectives in American History* 9 (1975): 299-340.

Giddings, Franklin H. "The Relation of Social Theory to Public Policy." *International Conciliation* 58 (September 1912): 3-13.

———. "The United States among Nations." *The Independent* 98 (June 14, 1919): 399-400.

———. "What Did It." *The Independent* 104 (November 20, 1920): 262-64.

———. "What the War Was Worth." *The Independent* 99 (July 5, 1919): 16-17.

Gilderhus, Mark T. "Pan-American Initiatives: The Wilson Presidency and 'Regional Integration,' 1914-17." *Diplomatic History* 4 (Fall 1980): 409-23.

———. "Wilson, Carranza, and the Monroe Doctrine: A Question in Regional Organization." *Diplomatic History* 7 (Spring 1983): 103-15.

Keohane, Robert O. "Theory of World Politics: Structural Realism and Beyond." In Ada W. Finifter, ed., *Political Science: The State of the Discipline*, pp. 503-40. Washington, DC: American Political Science Association, 1983.

Kimball, Jeffrey P. "Realism, Diplomatic History, and American Foreign Relations: A Conversation with Norman A. Graebner." Society for Historians of American Foreign Relations *Newsletter* 18 (June 1987): 11-19.

Krakau, Knud. "American Foreign Relations: A National Style?" *Diplomatic History* 8 (Summer 1984): 253-72.

Leopold, Richard W. "The Problem of American Intervention, 1917: An Historical Retrospect." *World Politics* 2 (April 1950): 405-25.

Leuchtenburg, William E. "Progressivism and Imperialism: The Progressive Movement and American Foreign Policy, 1898-1916." *Mississippi Valley Historical Review* 39 (December 1952): 483-504.

Osborn, George C. "Woodrow Wilson and Frederick Jackson Turner." *Proceedings of the New Jersey Historical Society* 74 (July 1956): 208-29.

Schwabe, Klaus. "Woodrow Wilson and Germany's Membership in the League of Nations, 1918-19." *Central European History* 8 (March 1975): 3-22.

Skinner, Constance Lindsay, ed. "Turner's Autobiographical Letter." *Wisconsin Magazine of History* 19 (September 1935): 91-103.

Smith, Daniel M. "National Interest and American Intervention, 1917: An Historiographical Appraisal." *Journal of American History* 52 (June 1965): 5-24.

Stephenson, Wendall H. "The Influence of Woodrow Wilson on Frederick Jackson Turner." *Agricultural History* 19 (October 1945): 249-53.

Stevenson, David. "French War Aims and the American Challenge, 1914-1918." *Historical Journal* 22, no. 4 (1979): 877-94.

Trani, Eugene P. "Woodrow Wilson and the Decision to Intervene in Russia: A Reconsideration." *Journal of Modern History* 48 (September 1976): 440-61.

Trask, David F. "Woodrow Wilson and the Coordination of Force and Diplomacy." Society for Historians of American Foreign Relations *Newsletter* 12 (September 1981): 12-19.

――――. "Woodrow Wilson and the Reconciliation of Force and Diplomacy: 1917-1918." *Naval War College Review* 27 (January-February 1975): 23-31.

Wilson, Woodrow. "The Ideals of America." *Atlantic Monthly* 90 (December 1902): 721-34.

――――. "The Making of the Nation." *Atlantic Monthly* 80 (July 1897): 1-14.

――――. "The Proper Perspective of American History." *The Forum* 19 (June 1895): 544-59.

Woodward, C. Vann. "The Age of Reinterpretation." *American Historical Review* 66 (October 1960): 1-19.

Zivojinović Dragan. "Robert Lansing's Comments on the Pontifical Peace Note of August 1, 1917." *Journal of American History* 56 (December 1969): 556-71.

Index

AMERICA IN THE MODERN WORLD
STUDIES IN INTERNATIONAL HISTORY

Warren F. Kimball
Series Editor
Professor of History, Rutgers University

Volumes Published

Lawrence Spinelli, *Dry Diplomacy: The United States, Great Britain, and Prohibition* (1989). ISBN 0-8420-2298-8

Richard V. Salisbury, *Anti-Imperialism and International Competition in Central America, 1920–1929* (1989). ISBN 0-8420-2304-6

Gerald K. Haines, *The Americanization of Brazil: A Study of U.S. Cold War Diplomacy in the Third World, 1945–1954* (1989). ISBN 0-8420-2339-9

Harry Harding and Yuan Ming, eds., *Sino-American Relations, 1945–1955: A Joint Reassessment of a Critical Decade* (1989). ISBN 0-8420-2333-X

Lawrence S. Kaplan, Denise Artaud, and Mark R. Rubin, eds., *Dien Bien Phu and the Crisis of Franco-American Relations, 1954–1955* (1990). ISBN 0-8420-2341-0

Michael L. Krenn, *U.S. Policy toward Economic Nationalism in Latin America, 1917–1929* (1990). ISBN 0-8420-2346-1

Akira Iriye and Warren Cohen, eds., *American, Chinese, and Japanese Perspectives on Wartime Asia, 1931–1949* (1990). ISBN 0-8420-2347-X

Edward M. Bennett, *Franklin D. Roosevelt and the Search for Victory: American-Soviet Relations, 1939–1945* (1990). Cloth ISBN 0-8420-2364-X Paper ISBN 0-8420-2365-8

James L. Gormly, *From Potsdam to the Cold War: Big Three Diplomacy, 1945–1947* (1990). Cloth ISBN 0-8420-2334-8 Paper ISBN 0-8420-2335-6

Lloyd E. Ambrosius, *Wilsonian Statecraft: Theory and Practice of Liberal Internationalism during World War I* (1991). Cloth ISBN 0-8420-2393-3 Paper ISBN 0-8420-2394-1